The Challenge of Coalition Government

Since the advent of the Second Republic in Italy in the mid-1990s, a new generation of politicians has announced a shift in the system toward greater governmental leadership, policy innovation, government accountability and responsiveness to the citizens. Yet in recent years government has experienced frequent crises and deadlocks, policy blockades and undisciplined parliamentary majorities. Has the attempt to change the nature of the Italian government totally failed?

This book addresses this question by empirically assessing and theoretically evaluating the outcomes of the new system. It asks whether there has really been a shift toward a more majoritarian democracy and examines why alternation in power has failed to produce a more efficient and responsive government. It evaluates the connections between cabinet, parliament, parties and citizens and, in doing so, brings together diverse areas of inquiry such as government, legislative, party and public opinion studies. Drawing from comparative theory but also considering the impact of country-specific determinants, it explains the very nature of the Italian government from the point of view of its achievements and its failures.

This text will be of key interest to scholars and students of government, comparative and Italian politics, and more broadly those with an interest in government, democracy and Italy.

Nicolò Conti is Associate Professor of Political Science at the Unitelma Sapienza University of Rome.

Francesco Marangoni is Research Fellow at the University of Siena.

Routledge Advances in European Politics

The Challenge of Coalition Government

The Italian case

Edited by Nicolò Conti and
Francesco Marangoni

Routledge
Taylor & Francis Group

LONDON AND NEW YORK

First published 2015
by Routledge
2 Park Square, Milton Park, Abingdon, Oxon OX14 4RN

and by Routledge
711 Third Avenue, New York, NY 10017

First issued in paperback 2017

Routledge is an imprint of the Taylor & Francis Group, an informa business

British Library Cataloguing in Publication Data
A catalogue record for this book is available from the British Library

Library of Congress Cataloging in Publication Data
The challenge of coalition government : the Italian case / edited by
Nicolò Conti and Francesco Marangoni.
pages cm
(Routledge advances in European politics)
Includes bibliographical references and index.
1. Italy—Politics and government—1994- 2. Coalition governments—
Italy. I. Conti, Nicolò. II. Marangoni, Francesco.
JN5452.C46 2015
320.945—dc23
2014024379

ISBN 13: 978-1-138-50417-2 (pbk)
ISBN 13: 978-1-138-81510-0 (hbk)

Typeset in Times New Roman
by Swales & Willis Ltd, Exeter, Devon, UK

Contents

Figures

Tables

Contributors

Enrico Borghetto is a Postdoctoral Researcher at CESNOVA, Centre for Sociological Studies of the Universidade Nova de Lisboa. His research has focused on compliance with EU policies, the Europeanisation of national legislation, legislative studies and European decision-making. He has published articles in international journals such as *European Union Politics*, *Journal of European Public Policy*, *South European Society and Politics* and *International Review of Administrative Sciences*.

Marcello Carammia is a Senior Lecturer at the Institute for European Studies of the University of Malta. His research focuses on political institutions and agenda-setting processes, with a special interest in political parties, EU policy-making and migration policy. His research has appeared in such journals as *European Union Politics*, *Italian Political Science Review* and *Policy Studies Journal*.

Nicolò Conti is Associate Professor of Political Science at the Unitelma Sapienza University of Rome. His main research focus is on parties, elites and the EU and on coalition governance. He has recently edited *Party Attitudes towards the EU in the Member States: parties for Europe, parties against Europe* (2014, Routledge). He has published articles in journals such as *Acta Politica*, *South European Society and Politics*, *Perspectives on European Politics and Society*, *Modern Italy*, *Modern Italian Studies* and *Contemporary Italian Politics*.

Francesco Marangoni is a Postdoctoral Researcher at the University of Siena where he collaborates with the Centre for the Study of Political Change (CIRCaP). His main research interests focus on political elites, legislative behaviour and coalition politics in parliamentary democracies. He has published articles in journals such as *Acta Politica*, *Journal of Legislative Studies* and *Contemporary Italian Politics*.

Vincenzo Memoli is Assistant Professor of Political Science at the University of Catania. His main research interests include democracy and public opinion. His articles have been published in *Acta Politica*, *British Journal of Political Science*, *Democratization*, *Governance* and *International Political Science Review*.

Andrea Pedrazzani is a Postdoctoral Fellow at the Department of Political and Social Sciences, University of Bologna. His research interests include parliamentary processes, legislative behaviour, executive-legislative relations and intra-coalitional politics. He has published articles in journals such as *European Journal of Political Research* and *Government and Opposition*.

Michelangelo Vercesi is Postdoctoral Fellow at the Centre for the Study of Democracy of the Leuphana University Lüneburg. His research mainly focuses on coalition governance, political parties, comparative government and political elites. He has published articles in journals, such as *Government and Opposition* and *Contemporary Italian Politics*.

Francesco Visconti is a PhD candidate in Comparative and European Politics at the University of Siena. His main research focus is on legislative change, policy processes and public opinion.

Introduction

Nicolò Conti and Francesco Marangoni

Coalition governments have traditionally been a major object of political analysis and one of the main topics within political science literature. They represent an attractive subject as they provide a particularly apt focus for inquiring into the major problem of who governs (Browne and Dreijmanis 1982). At least in theory, single-party governments are those making the political process more straight-forward and effective. Single-party governments keep the executive (or better, the party controlling the executive) fully accountable to voters: the sole incumbent governing party does not share responsibilities with any partner for its own decisions and cannot blame any other political counterpart for any eventual poor performance. At the same time, single-party governments are relatively homogeneous for the simple reason that no interparty divisions characterise these executives. Everything else being equal, that makes decision-making potentially rapid and smooth (no interparty confrontation or compromises are needed).

Multi-party governments, on the contrary, not only entail shared (and potentially less clear) responsibilities, they also require some forms of interparty compromise not always easy to reach and to maintain, while the necessity to bargain among coalition partners is likely to frustrate at least some of the policy desires of individual coalition parties. Therefore, there is always a possibility inherent to this kind of government that internal divisions hamper the stability of the executive and lengthen government decision-making.

The rationale of the title of this volume lies behind the following consideration: *governing through coalition* represents a challenge and it is potentially full of risks. That notwithstanding, the empirical records of coalition governments in contemporary parliamentary democracies are quite impressive. Parliamentarism – especially under a proportional electoral law that tends to multiply the number of parties in a system – quite often entails interparty bargaining and coalition formation, since the electoral process usually fails to provide a political party in office with an absolute majority in parliament. In Western Europe, the heartland of parliamentarianism, almost all major countries have been governed at some point by coalitions. Actually, only Spain has never experienced such kind of governments in the post-Second World War period. Taken as a whole, about 62 per cent of all the governments that have been formed in West European countries since 1945 were formal coalitions of parties (Müller and Strøm 2000; Müller 2008).[1] Coalition governments, in other terms, represent a necessity (although a challenging one) in many countries. It is not at all surprising, therefore, that studies providing detailed empirical accounts on the politics of coalitions (interparty bargaining, coalition formation and maintenance), mostly but not only in Western Europe, have prolif-erated particularly since the early 1980s (Browne and Dreijmanis 1982; Pridham 1986; Budge and Keman 1990; Laver and Scofield 1990; Müller and Strøm 2000; Strøm *et al.* 2008).[2]

Italy has traditionally been an interesting case within this field of analysis: the first reason lies in the scope of coalitions in the Italian government system. Most of the 63 Italian governments that have been formed in Italy since 1948 (after the transitional years post-Second World War) and until the time of writing this Introduction have been based on coalitions.[3] Moreover, Italian govern-ments have been quite fragmented (formed by a considerable number of parties), and unstable (as their total number shows). Yet, only very limited alternation of parties in government occurred for more than 40 years during the period of the so-called First Republic (between 1948 and 1992), when all cabinets included the Christian Democrat (DC) party as largest coalition component and dominant party. Alternation in power, on the contrary, became the norm in the mid-1990s, with the inauguration of the so-called Second Republic (Cotta and Verzichelli 2007). Considering the large number (even in comparative terms) of coalition governments in contemporary Italy and also that coalition politics remain stan-dard politics in the country, despite the change that occurred in the political sys-tem with its transition from the First to the Second Republic, this country certainly represents a crucial case for the comparative analysis of coalition governments. Despite its shift from a party system with a dominant centrist party to one of bipo-lar competition and alternation in government, the coalition nature of the Italian government has remained unchanged.

As clearly stated by a recent and extensive literature on coalition governments, coalition politics is not institutionally free (Müller and Strøm 2000; Strøm, Müller and Bergman 2008). That is, we cannot properly understand how coalitions form, how and how well they make policy, or how and why they terminate, without taking into serious consideration the institutional environment where the coalition game takes place.

> Some of the important institutions (e.g. fundamental constitutional provi-sions) are exogenous to the coalition game in the sense that the actors in this game cannot have any realistic hope of changing them, at least in the short run. Other important institutions are endogenous, which is to say that they are rules that the party actors impose on themselves, often precisely in order to deal with the problem of coalition governance.
>
> (Müller and Strøm 2000, 4)

Along this line, it is important to note that in the last two decades, some important (both exogenous and endogenous) institutions of the coalition game have been substantially altered in Italy. Constitutional provisions remained fundamentally unchanged. Nonetheless, some other crucial (exogenous) rules and challenges for government life changed more substantially. To start with, after more than 40 years of blocked government, alternation has become fully plausible. We believe that not too many words have to be spent here to convince our readers about the magnitude and the importance of this change. 'In a well-functioning democracy, the politicians' anticipation that they will sooner or later be held to account by [citizens] is the most powerful constraint shaping their decisions' (Müller and Strøm 2008, 2). Italian government parties have not really faced this constraint during the First Republic, while accountability has become a more concrete 'challenge' for them only with the unveiling of the Second Republic.

The electoral reforms of the last 20 years, moreover, have profoundly influenced the making and functioning of government coalitions. Starting with the Mixed-Member Majoritarian (MMM) system introduced in 1993,[4] electoral rules have fostered the process of coalition formation and selection and have led to a bipolarisation of the Italian party system, frustrating the ambitions of third poles. Furthermore, new significant practices have emerged in the process of government formation. Differently from the past when all the following decisions became the main object of post-electoral transactions, parties have been induced to form pre-electoral coalitions and to indicate at the same time (in a formal way) their leader and candidate prime minister, as well as their policy programme (Cotta and Verzichelli 2007).

As repeatedly stated through the chapters of this book, all these phenomena make Italy a perfect, quasi-experimental scenario to study both causes and effects of change to consolidated patterns of government formation and life. Certainly, a main determinant of the nature of governments such as the institutional environment has changed substantially with the advent of bipolar confrontation and alternation in government. At the same time, it is our goal to assess in the book whether coalition politics in Italy has also changed. With respect to this challenge in knowledge, the contribution offered by this volume can be useful and innovative in many ways. First, our focus is on the activity of governments. The fundamental idea, in this sense, is that we can reach a better understanding of the basic dynamics (and of the effectiveness) of coalition politics, and of its transformation through time, beyond the phase of formation and through the analysis of governments 'at work'; that is, by looking at their institutional behaviour and overall performance. In order to meet this goal of moving beyond a very initial phase in government life and to analyse the most mature phases of government activity, the authors in this volume present fresh and novel analyses on various aspects of government: the formation of the government agenda and the following implementation of the government policy priorities, the management of (interparty) coalition conflicts, the relation with the parliament in the law-making process, and the government linkage with citizens.

We share with Strøm, Müller and Bergman (2008) the fundamental assumption that coalition politics must be understood as a series of interconnected events, or phases. How and how effectively a coalition government is able to avoid or manage internal conflicts, for instance, should have an impact on the ability to define a common agenda of policy priorities and to implement them through law-making. This will influence the executive–legislative relationship in the decision-making process. The policy-making capacity of the government, in turn, has a potential impact on popular support for the same government. Therefore, instead of considering these different components as if they were independent and separate from each other, this book aims at providing a dynamic and coherent perspective of all these aspects. In doing so, we bring together areas of inquiry such as government, legislative, party and public opinion studies that have been developed largely in isolation from one another by the comparative literature. In this sense, we believe that an in-depth analysis of a crucial case, such as the Italian one, could be beneficial not only to the comprehension of Italian politics, but also to comparative theories on governments and coalitions. We present in the volume a huge and up-to-date collection of empirical evidences and discuss their interconnectedness in a way that could lead to a real advancement in the comprehension of Italian politics (and of its more recent evolution), but could also become a point of reference for future works of a comparative nature.

In the remainder of this chapter we discuss in more detail the objectives of the book and the main questions that it is intended to answer. Then, we discuss the analytical approach that has been adopted and the empirical dimensions that have been analysed in the various chapters. Finally, at the end of the chapter we describe the structure of the volume.

The challenge of coalition government in a changing democracy

A general 'anxiety for change' has been said to represent one of the main silent factors for the sudden collapse of the First Republic at the beginning of the 1990s. The fragmented and polarised nature of the party system (Sartori 1976), the institutional weakness of the executive (Cassese 1980) and of the prime minister (Hine and Finocchi 1991; Elgie 1995), the blocked nature of government coalitions in the absence of any real chance of alternation[5] were the main ingredients of a rather ineffective government system that relied almost exclusively on micro-distributive (and resource-intensive) policies for survival but proved unable to promote the major reforms and re-distributive policies that were instead necessary for the system (Di Palma 1977; Cotta 1994). As a matter of fact, this system proved no more sustainable when the resources to be distributed started to run out at the end of the 1980s with the explosion of the Italian public debt which, at that point, was out of control. At the time, moreover, external challenges and constraints added to this domestic context of stagnation, such as those stemming from global economic competition and from the advancement of the European monetary convergence under the Maastricht criteria. These factors urged the Italian government to show real capacity for policy innovation and to lead an overall change in the policy paradigm in the country. Those parties that had been in government for more than 40 years proved unable to interpret this challenge their own way and to conform with the required changes; on the contrary, they remained trapped in a weak decision-making circuit affected by abundant mutual vetoes and micro-policy, but also by widespread government corruption and consequent mounting popular de-legitimation (Cotta and Isernia 1996; Di Palma *et al.* 2000).[6]

The need for a 'grand reform' was long advocated by many domestic actors who understood the fragility of the system, and by a large number of external observers, as the ultimate cure for the numerous problems of the country. Indeed, some important attempts have been made in the last 20 years to promote a transition toward an intended more majoritarian and efficient Second Republic, aiming at the simplification of the Italian party system from polarised to a bipolar multi-party type, alternation in power and, thus, the improvement of government transparency, accountability and overall performance.

The fundamental change to the previous situation concerned the creation of strong incentives to form pre-electoral coalitions with the introduction of a quasi-majoritarian (mixed-member) electoral law in 1993 (D'Alimonte and Chiaramonte 1995). Even with the re-introduction of a proportional electoral system in 2005, a number of corrections were maintained to create disproportionality of the system and a pressure on parties to form pre-electoral coalitions – such as a majority premium assigned to the winning coalition and more severe electoral thresholds for those parties that contest the elections alone – hence, although the pattern of coalition-making has changed substantially between the pre- and post-1994 period, from then on it has remained rather stable.

Not only have coalitions been encouraged to form before the elections. They have also been induced to present a common electoral programme and a leader and *de facto* candidate prime minister. The Second Republic, in this sense, has gone through two ideal-typical models of government formation. From a 'transaction' model (typical of the First Republic), which privileges bargaining on the allocation of seats and portfolios (while postponing policy decision) to a 'compliance' model aiming at the fulfilment of a programmatic platform formalised before the elections and ratified by coalition partners (Verzichelli 2003). Personalisation and even 'presidentialisation' of Italian politics have also been observed (Venturino 2001; Calise 2007)[7] under the Second Republic because the prime minister receives a more direct legitimacy from voters as leader of the winning coalition and figure mainly responsible for the implementation of the policy programme.

Pre-electoral coalitions also introduced a shift from centrist politics in the First Republic, to bipolarism and hollowing-out of the centre in the Second Republic, also due to the collapse of the Christian Democrat party in 1992–1993 which was severely sanctioned for its misconduct, corruption and policy inefficiency in the final years of the First Republic. The establishment of real alternation in power between the two main competing coalitions has introduced a sort of majoritarian turn to the Italian government system (Blondel and Battegazzorre 2002). Indeed, not only is alternation of government (or even the perception that it could occur) supposed to strengthen the prerogatives of the executive *vis-à-vis* the parliament (Zucchini 2010), it also, and foremost, changes the horizon and some basic rules of broad political competition. Only where alternation is possible are elections really contestable. After freezing the government composition for so many years during the First Republic, with the advent of the Second Republic, government accountability has become crucial and a real parameter in public assessment of the government: different party (coalition) alternatives contest the elections with a promise to really change things and voters decide about their credibility. On the contrary, with the absence of alternation, the Italian First Republic represented a paradigmatic example of *input democracy* in which the main effort of parties in this polarised system was simply to provide citizens with an 'entrance' into the circuit of representation through the parliament (Fabbrini 2000), not to give a real perspective of change in executive politics. In contrast, systems where alternation is plausible – as in the Second Republic – are *output democracies* where the government becomes a key actor and attention is paid to its capacity to provide citizens with tangible output through policies. Whereas governments in the First Republic were characterised by amorphous policy-making, mostly based on micro-policy of a clientelistic nature and by the allocation of public offices (Di Palma 1977; Motta 1985; De Micheli 1997), in the Second Republic parties and their leaders present themselves to voters as transformative forces able to deliver concrete policy change. Thus, since the advent of the Second Republic in the mid-1990s, a new generation of politicians has announced a shift in the system toward greater governmental leadership, policy innovation, government accountability and responsiveness to the citizens. Has this transition to a new system been successful?

The answer to this fundamental question cannot be fully positive. The government has, in fact, experienced frequent crises and deadlocks, policy blockades, undisciplined parliamentary majorities even in the presence of a prime minister with a clear popular mandate. The average duration of governments has increased; however, by comparative standards they remain more unstable than other governments, even of a multi-party type (Müller and Strøm 2008). The incapacity to deliver effective outputs has become more macroscopic due to the economic crisis in the late 2000s, as the government was called to make prompt and serious reforms and a real policy shift that it was actually unable to deliver. This opened the way to a series of consequences, such as the advent of a technocratic cabinet in 2011–2013 that should correct the inefficiency of political governments, an increase in electoral abstention and the rise of the protest vote, with the consequent emergence of new radical parties. So, *has the attempt to change the nature of the Italian government totally failed, or are there some achievements that should be acknowledged?* The main purpose of this volume is to address this question empirically. With this aim in mind, in the different chapters the authors provide a series of original analyses on the activity and performance of Italian coalition governments in the last two decades. We now briefly discuss the empirical dimensions that are addressed in the different chapters and the analytical frame that is common to the whole volume.

The empirical dimensions under investigation

The following chapters explore in-depth if and how the challenge of the intended shift toward a more majoritarian output democracy has been met by the Italian government. Moreover, to what extent the phenomena that we have discussed above concerning alternation, bipolarisation of the party system, presidentialisation of executive politics, changing patterns of coalition and cabinet formation have produced a more efficient and responsive government.

The very nature of the broad research question raised in this book led us to a preliminary analytical choice. We decided to focus exclusively on the performance of governments and on the results of governmental activity. Several factors reinforced our choice. First of all, quite surprisingly, the direction and the outcomes of governmental change in Italy have been little explored empirically, while more efforts have been devoted so far to the analysis of government composition, maintenance and termination (Verzichelli and Cotta 2000). The joined effort in this volume is, therefore, novel as it is specifically designed to fill this gap and to provide an in-depth empirical investigation that is rich in evidence about the inner difficulties in changing modes of governance in an established democracy.

While recent studies have focused on some specific phases of government activity during the Second Republic,[8] this book is more far-reaching as it provides an integrated analysis of different (but interdependent) aspects of government performance that have been treated separately by many former studies. Drawing largely from comparative theory (but also considering the impact of country-specific determinants), the analyses carried in the volume describe aspects of intra-coalitional conflicts and their management, policy-making, executive–legislative relationships, and government linkage with voters, and discuss their theoretical implications within the broader comparative literature.

The ability to manage conflicts among partners (either individual ministers or parties) has been argued to be a crucial challenge for coalition governments (Nousiainen 1993; Damgaard 2008). Naturally enough, it is crucial because any given government cannot easily survive high and uncontrollable levels of inter-party conflictuality and maverick behaviour of its internal components. For this reason, the analysis of intra-coalitional conflicts and conflicts management provides a useful empirical perspective to unveil coalitions' internal equilibria. In this sense, the objects of conflicts, the actors involved and the arenas and mechanisms of conflicts management are important objects of inquiry that are influenced by the very nature of governments and by the dynamics and rules of electoral competition and government formation (Andeweg and Timmermans 2008) which, as we have seen, have changed considerably with the advent of the Second Republic.[9] At the same time, the occurrence of conflicts is a thermometer of the (in-)ability of coalition members to 'stay together', to share priorities and decisions and to find a compromise on their implementation. Conflict management (or conflict avoidance), in other terms, is a necessary pre-condition for effective government decision-making.

To define a common agenda of policy priorities and objectives would actually be a major task for parties governing in coalition in the supposedly more majoritarian Italian democracy. A task that is all the more decisive when, thanks to the possibility of alternation, the incumbent government faces the urgency to provide outputs to voters (and the serious risk of being punished by them in case of poor performance). With respect to this problem, the analysis and understanding of the content and formation of policy agendas has seen great developments in recent years. This is thanks, in particular, to the joint efforts of scholars to develop theories of policy change and systematic indicators of issue attention and prioritisation within national political systems (Baumgartner and Jones 1993; Jones and Baumgartner 2005; Baumgartner *et al.* 2006). The formation of the government agenda in Italy offers, again, an ideal quasi-experimental case to be discussed within this bulk of literature. The purportedly majoritarian turn of Italian politics during the Second Republic has opened the way to pre-electoral coalitions and, thus, to pre-electoral competing coalition agendas. How are the cabinet policy priorities consequently defined? How do individual parties influence coalition cabinet agendas? And to what extent are the priorities of individual coalition parties translated into the government agenda?

In the book, we show that in the Second Republic, differently from the First Republic, the definition of the cabinet policy agenda has become a priority since the government formation stage. Yet, governments have not only to define the outputs they engage to provide. They also face the urgency to deliver these same outputs since, in the new alternational system, they are held accountable for their performance and for the goals they have been able to reach throughout the electoral cycle. The comparative literature has shown an increasing interest in measuring the capacity of governments to implement policy priorities and fulfil programmatic pledges (Dalton *et al.* 2011; Naurin 2011). Coalition agreements, in this sense, have been analysed as a form of 'contract' between parties and voters, but also (and foremost) among government partners, and, as such, as a guidance to government decision-making (Moury 2013; Müller and Strøm 2008; De Winter 2004). While in the First Republic 'transaction' model of government, coalition agreements were either non-existent or completely disregarded, with a general shift toward a 'compliance' model in the Second Republic, programmatic agreements have been progressively introduced by the party coalitions (Moury and Timmermans 2008). Whether this has taken the system to better government responsiveness and to what extent a traditionally ineffective government has managed to improve its capacity to fulfil its own pledges, is a matter of empirical investigation here.

Needless to say, government policy outputs are influenced by the behaviour and capabilities of that same government in the law-making arena. The analysis of the law-making of the executive in parliamentary democracies can profit hugely from the recent development of 'institutional theories' in legislative studies that stress the importance of parliamentary organisational features and procedural rules in shaping the relationship between executive and parliament and in influencing the legislative outputs and final policy outcomes (Döring 1995; Shepsle and Weingast 1994; Döring and Hallerberg 2004). The focus, in particular, has been on those 'devices that, on the one hand, favour majoritarian decision-making and, on the other, give protection to the rights of minority parties and to individual deputies, both at the government-opposition and at the cross-party level' (Döring

1995, 13). Italy has traditionally been characterised as a peculiar case by this stream of literature. During the First Republic, governments could only count on a very weak power to determine the parliamentary agenda (Döring 1995). Yet, government-proposed laws were most commonly of a non-conflictual and micro-distributive nature and exhibited a manifestly consensual appeal, with bills being usually approved by significant large majorities (Di Palma 1977; Cazzola 1974). One might expect, once more, that the shift to the alternational and bipolar Second Republic has resulted in more majoritarian law-making patterns. As it was argued by Zucchini (2010), the introduction of alternation should improve the parliamentary agenda power of the Italian government. The necessity for the incumbent executive to deliver policy outputs and to fulfil programmatic priorities through legislative means (i.e., laws) should lead to more adversarial approval patterns of bills. This is simply because, in alternational systems, the opposition has a (strategic) interest to denounce, block and delay those cabinet bills that are more directly linked to the policy goals and priorities of the government, and for which the incumbent parties are supposed to be held electorally accountable (De Winter 2004). In fact, scholars found that a surprising level of consensualism has survived the passage to the Second Republic (Giuliani 2008) and that Italian government laws continue to be generally approved in a consensual manner (i.e., by large majorities). We strongly believe, however, that the analysis should go beyond aggregate figures. It has already been demonstrated that there is some variance in the support received by government-sponsored legislation during the Second Republic (De Giorgi and Marangoni 2013; Marangoni 2010). An inquiry into the factors that explain this variance is necessary for a better understanding of the legislative behaviour of Italian coalition governments, and of its evolution through time.

Not only could this kind of analysis unveil basic dynamics between government and opposition, it is also useful for a better understanding of the equilibria within the same government majority in the law-making arena. As recent comparative research has demonstrated (Martin and Vanberg 2004, 2011), legislative processes and institutions are used by government parties as a tool of coalition governance (to monitor each other and to correct potential 'ministerial drift'),[10] and this can also influence the approval patterns of government bills. The analysis of the passage of government-sponsored legislation through the parliament, therefore, can effectively cast some light on the changes of the Italian government system and on the real extent of its intended evolution toward a more confrontational and government responsiveness-maximizing model. Moreover, we believe that this analysis can be extended to cover not only the enactment process, but also the post-enactment phase of government laws. Sure enough, in an ideal-typical majoritarian alternational system, incumbent governments should be more inclined to revise the laws approved by previous executives and majorities than in a pivotal party system with a blocked government as in the Italian First Republic. The study of the post-enactment phase is quite recent (Berry *et al.* 2010; Ragusa 2010; Maltzman and Shipan 2008) and it has focused almost exclusively on the American Congress. By contributing to this novel research agenda with an unprecedented in-depth analysis of the Italian case, this volume will also (start to) cover this gap and will provide an example of empirical post-enactment research in parliamentary democracies.

Finally, whatever the characteristics of the processes of conflict management, agenda formation, fulfilment of policy priorities and law-making, government face an ultimate challenge. Especially where alternation is possible, government parties need to meet citizens' satisfaction and gain their support if they aim at being confirmed in power. It has been argued that the popular expectations toward the public sector, and the public opinion's capacity to scrutinise government action (at least in the democratic world) have largely increased in more recent decades (Rothstein 2005; Radin 2000). In this regard, the analysis of cabinet popularity during the Second Republic offers a stimulating empirical perspective in the assessment of any shift of the Italian government system toward a more responsible and popularly mandated executive.

Preview of the volume

In dealing with the analytical dimensions discussed so far, this edited book presents a series of original investigations, based on new and extensive data collection on the activity and performance of Italian coalition governments in the last two decades: a period that corresponds by and large to the Second Republic.[11]

In Chapter 1, Marangoni and Vercesi provide an in-depth analysis of intra-coalitional conflictuality and its management by the Italian governments. Drawing from the comparative literature, they first measure both the intensity (number of conflicts) and the content (issues involved) of governmental conflictuality. Conflict management mechanisms and arenas are then analysed. The chapter shows some important elements of change with respect to the past, for example in terms of the object of conflicts (increasingly, the policies to be implemented by the executive) and of the mechanisms adopted by coalition partners to cope with them (increasingly centralised and internalised within the cabinet). However, equally important elements of continuity with the First Republic are highlighted by the analysis, for example some arenas that are external to government have not disappeared from the management of intra-coalitional conflicts and the overall dominance of the executive on the parliament and on the party central offices – as would be typical of majoritarian democracies – is far from being in place.

In Chapter 2, Borghetto and Carammia focus on the process of formation of the government agenda. In particular, they investigate how and to what extent the priorities of the different coalition components (i.e., parties) are accommodated in the construction of the cabinet agenda. The two authors develop their analysis through systematic content-coding of party and coalition manifestos and then contrast these results with those stemming from the analysis of governments' investiture speeches. They show that the consolidation of a bipolar pattern of party competition and the over-time variations between the First and the Second Republic[12] have really influenced the nature of the programmatic declarations of the prime ministers. These have moved, for instance, toward the inclusion of more policy-oriented content. The two authors also demonstrate that the priorities declared by the prime ministers of the Second Republic in their investiture speeches tend to be far more congruent with the policy agendas issued before the elections by their respective sponsoring coalitions, than used to be the case under the First Republic. However, the authors do not find strong evidence that the introduction of coalition agreements (as opposed to individual party platforms) has fostered the correspondence between these pre-electoral commitments and the actual cabinet priorities. On the contrary, the manifestos of individual parties sometimes translate better into the government agenda. This result seems to cast some doubts about the institutionalisation of pre-electoral programmatic agreements as underlying mechanisms of coalition governance in Italy.

Coalition agreements are specifically analysed in Chapter 3 by Conti. In coalition governments, this kind of agreement often disciplines the relationship among parties (the principal) and the executive (the agent), as the former compel the latter to a set of policy priorities, thus giving rise to expectations among voters. Public and progressively more formal coalition agreements have actually been introduced in Italy. Through the systematic analysis of both government agreements and legislative outcomes, the chapter shows that the Italian government has slowly moved toward the goal of better fulfilment of its pledges; however, this is not happening in a linear way and does not increase over time but has had some recent fall-backs. The shift of the Italian government toward a compliance model focused on fulfilment of pledges is therefore only partially satisfied.

In Chapter 4, Pedrazzani investigates the 'life' of government bills in parliament, looking in particular at the variance in the support enjoyed by government-sponsored legislation. Through the analysis of roll-call votes, the author shows that levels of consensus depend on the management of conflict between majority and opposition, and on the complexity of the bargaining environment in the parliament at the voting stage. Moreover, the presence of vote trading among legislators helps explain whether the approval of bills is more consensual or majoritarian. In addition, other features of the bills – such as their proposers and their internal complexity – are proved to influence the kind of support they gain in the end within the parliament. Finally, the length of the legislative process and the extent to which bills are modified before approval are also influential factors. The overall picture is one of a very dynamic (but also intricate) final voting stage in the parliament that does not anticipate full control by the government on the law-making process.

Chapter 5 by Borghetto and Visconti extends the analysis of the life cycle of government acts to the post-enactment phase (i.e., once government bills have become laws) through an examination of amendments to government legislation. This is a topic totally neglected by previous studies on the consequences of the evolution of the Italian political system. This contribution aims to examine how post-enactment policy change has developed from the point of view of its intensity (how much does a law change?) and pace (how long does a law last before being amended?). The two authors show that between-government changes are not greater than those introduced by the same incumbent coalition during its life cycle due to intra-coalition bargaining.

This is evidence of the fact that, despite alternation in power, policy innovation does not display at the level many would expect and that policy continuity has, instead, remained a solid feature, even after the advent of the Second Republic.

Finally, Chapter 6 by Memoli analyses patterns of popular support for the Italian government. Through the analysis of public opinion surveys, the chapter shows that policy outputs do in fact have an influence on popular support for the executive, as does the state of the economy. However, political scandals and government respect for the rule of law are also very influential and add to public support for the incumbent. Ultimately, Italian citizens seriously question not only the policy-making capacity of the Italian government (a main focus in this volume), but also its overall conduct and public image.

The main findings of the volume are summarised and the research questions raised in the introduction find answers in the Conclusion by Conti and Marangoni. Here, the results of the analyses carried in the different chapters are brought to a unified picture. Some important changes to coalition governance in Italy need to be acknowledged. However, the Italian system shows, at the same time, clear features of resistance to change of its long-run equilibria and, beyond the formal rules of the system that might really push in the direction of greater adversarial politics and government responsiveness, the way both government and opposition interpret these rules only partially fits a supposedly majoritarian democracy and a popular mandated executive. Resemblance with the mechanics of cabinet governance in the First Republic is persistent in many respects within the Italian system and its overall transformation appears characterised by lengthy adaptation to the new institutional environment and by incremental change.

Notes

1 There are of course important variations between (few) countries that have only occasionally (but not so rarely) experienced coalition governments, such as Norway (about 35 per cent of cases) and Sweden (about 29 per cent of cases), and those countries (the majority) where the formation of coalitions has proved to be a common process.
2 Together with other more theoretically driven and formal works on various aspects of coalition politics (for instance, Austen-Smith and Banks 1990; Lupia and Strøm 1995; Laver and Shepsle 1990).
3 There have been few exceptions of single-party government, especially during the First Republic, as a transitional device of very brief duration in order not to leave a vacuum in executive politics, whenever a full and public agreement could not be reached among coalition partners (Cotta and Verzichelli 2007). Technically speaking, these were minority governments supported in parliament by several parties.
4 The literature makes a fundamental distinction among mixed-member electoral system between Mixed-Member Proportional (MMP) systems and Mixed-Member Majoritarian (MMM) systems (Shugart and Wattenberg 2001). The main difference is that in the MMP system nominal and list tiers are 'linked', which basically means that in these systems, such as the one in Germany, the absolute number of parliamentary seats received by any given party is proportional to its list-tiers results. The MMP system, therefore, is intrinsically more proportional than MMM, where, conversely, the 'list and nominal tiers both allocate seats independently, not trying to maintain proportionality between seats and votes' (Thames and Edwards 2006, 2).

5 During the First Republic the power to govern never passed from the ruling majority built around the Christian Democrats (DC) to the opposition. The only possible outcome of this transfer of power would actually entail giving power to the Italian Communist Party (PCI), 'whose electoral appeal and ideological breath was second only to the DC's own. The PCI, however, was perceived (or labelled) as an "anti-system" party' (Edwards 2011, 311), and as such it was excluded from being part of executives. The result was that alternation was not even considered a realistic possibility by the main political actors and the government parties felt rather secure in this position.

6 In the early 1990s, the 'Clean hands' investigation by Milan prosecutors revealed a large web of corrupt exchanges and illegal party-financing ('Bribesville') built around political parties that had managed to politicise and control vast sectors and aspects of public life (from bureaucracy to civil society). This corruption scandal led definitively to the collapse of the then-dominant DC, together with the DC's main governing partner, the Italian Socialist party (PSI).

7 Coherently with a process that has been argued to be common to many contemporary parliamentary democracies (Poguntke and Webb 2007).

8 Typically, law-making capabilities (Marangoni 2013) and cabinet decision-making (Moury 2013).

9 A more systematic discussion of these arguments is presented in Chapter 1.

10 I.e., the possibility that individual ministers drive the content of the bills they draft closer to their (own parties) ideal point, than to the agreed-upon coalition compromise.

11 Although the time span of the analysis is extended in some chapters to cover also the final part of the First Republic, as a source of comparison.

12 From post-election coalitions with no programmatic agreement to pre-election coalitions with no programmatic agreement to pre-election coalitions with programmatic agreement.

References

Andeweg, R., and A. Timmermans (2008), 'Conflict Management in Coalition Government', in K. Strøm, W. C. Müller, and T. Bergman (eds), *Cabinets and Coalition Bargaining: The Democratic Life Cycle in Western Europe.* Oxford: Oxford University Press, pp. 269–300.

Austen-Smith, D., and J. Banks (1990), 'Stable Governments and the Allocation of Policy Portfolios', *American Political Science Review*, 84, pp. 891–906.

Baumgartner, F. R., and B. D. Jones (1993), *Agendas and Instability in American Politics*, Chicago: University of Chicago Press.

Baumgartner, F. R., C. Green-Pedersen, and B. D. Jones (2006), 'Comparative Studies of Policy Agendas', *Journal of European Public Policy*, 13, 7, pp. 955–70.

Berry, C. R., C. B. C. Burden, and G. W. Howell (2010), 'After Enactment: The Lives and Deaths of Federal Programs', *American Journal of Political Science*, 54, 1, pp. 1–17.

Blondel J., and F. Battegazzorre (2002), 'Majoritarian and Consensus Parliamentary Democracies: A Convergence Toward Cooperative Majoritarianism?', *Quaderni Italiani di Scienza Politica*, 9, 2, pp. 225–52.

Browne, E. C., and J. Dreijmanis (1982), *Governments Coalitions in Western Democracies*, New York: Longman.

Budge, I., and H. Keman (1990), *Parties and Democracy: Coalition Formation and Government Functioning in Twenty States*, Oxford: Oxford University Press.

Calise, M. (2007), 'Presidentialization, Italian Style', in T. Poguntke and P. Webb (eds), *The Presidentialization of Politics*, Oxford: Oxford University Press, pp. 88–106.

Cassese, S. (1980), 'Is There a Government in Italy? Politics and Administration at the Top', in R. Rose and E. N. Suleiman (eds), *Presidents and Prime Ministers*, Washington, DC: American Enterprise Institute for Public Policy Research.

Cazzola, F. (1974), *Governo e Opposizione nel Parlamento Italiano*, Milan: Giuffré.

Cotta, M. (1994), 'Il governo di partito in Italia. Crisi e trasformazione dell'assetto tradizionale', in M. Caciagli, F. Cazzola, L. Morlino and S. Passigli (eds), *L'Italia tra crisi e transizione*, Roma-Bari: Laterza.

Cotta, M., and P. Isernia (eds) (1996), *Il Gigante dai piedi d'argilla*, Bologna: Il Mulino.

Cotta, M., and L. Verzichelli (2007), *Political Institutions in Italy*, Oxford: Oxford University Press.

D'Alimonte, R., and A. Chiaramonte (1995), 'Il nuovo sistema elettorale italiano: le opportunità e le scelte', in S. Bartolini and R. D'Alimonte (eds), *Maggioritario ma non troppo: le elezioni politiche del 1994*, Bologna: Il Mulino, pp. 37–81.

Dalton, R. J., D. M. Farrell, and I. McAllister (2011), *Political Parties and Democratic Linkage: How Parties Organize Democracy*, Oxford: Oxford University Press.

Damgaard, E. (2008), 'Cabinet Termination', in K. Strøm, W. C. Müller, and T. Bergman (eds), *Cabinets and Coalition Bargaining: The Democratic Life Cycle in Western Europe*, Oxford: Oxford University Press, pp. 301–26.

De Giorgi, E., and F. Marangoni (2013), 'Government Laws and the Opposition Parties' Behaviour in Parliament', *Acta Politica*, advance online publication, 6 December 2013, doi:10.1057/ap.2013.34

De Micheli, C. (1997), 'L'attività legislativa dei governi al tramonto della prima repubblica', *Rivista Italiana di Scienza Politica*, 27, 1, pp. 159–96.

De Winter, L. (2004) 'Government Declarations and Law Production', in H. Döring and M. Hallerberg (eds), *Patterns of Parliamentary Behaviour: Passage of Legislation across Western Europe*, Aldershot: Ashgate, pp. 35–56.

Di Palma, G. (1977), *Surviving without Governing: The Italian Parties in Parliament*, Berkeley: UCLA Press.

Di Palma, G., S. Fabbrini and G. Freddi (eds) (2000), *Condannata al successo? L'Italia nell'Europa integrata*, Bologna: il Mulino.

Döring, H. (ed.) (1995), *Parliaments and Majority Rule in Western Europe*, New York: St. Martin's Press.

Döring, H., and M. Hallerberg (eds) (2004), *Patterns of Parliamentary Behaviour: Passage of Legislation across Western Europe*, Aldershot: Ashgate.

Edwards, P. (2011), 'Alternation? What Alternation? The Second Republic and the Challenge of Democratic Consolidation', *Bulletin of Italian Politics*, 3, 2, pp. 319–42.

Elgie, R. (1995), *Political Leadership in Liberal Democracies*, Basingstoke: Macmillan.

Fabbrini, S. (2000), *Tra Pressioni e Veti. Il cambiamento politico in Italia*, Roma-Bari: Laterza.

Giuliani, M. (2008), 'Patterns of Consensual Law-making in the Italian Parliament', *South European Society & Politics*, 13, 1, pp. 61–85.

Hine, D., and R. Finocchi (1991), 'The Italian Prime Minister', *West European Politics*, 14, 2, pp. 79–86.

Jones, B. D., and F. R. Baumgartner (2005), *The Politics of Attention: How Government Prioritizes Problems*, Chicago: University of Chicago Press.

Laver, M., and N. Schofield (1990), *Multiparty Government: The Politics of Coalition*, Oxford: Oxford University Press.

Laver, M., and K. Shepsle (1990), 'Coalitions and Cabinet Government', *American Political Science Review*, 84, 3, pp. 873–90.

Lupia, A., and K. Strøm (1995), 'Coalition Termination and the Strategic Timing of Parliamentary Elections', *The American Political Science Review*, 89, 3, pp. 648–65.

Maltzman, F., and C. Shipan (2008), 'Change, Continuity, and the Evolution of the Law', *American Journal of Political Science*, 52, 2, pp. 252–67.

Marangoni, F. (2010), 'Programma di governo e law-making: un'analisi della produzione legislativa dei governi italiani (1996–2009)', *Polis*, 24, 1, pp. 35–64.

Marangoni, F. (2013), *Provare a governare cercando di sopravvivere. Esecutivi e attività legislativa nella seconda repubblica*, Pisa: Pisa University Press.

Martin, L. W., and G. Vanberg (2004), 'Policing the Bargain: Coalition Government and Parliamentary Scrutiny', *American Journal of Political Science*, 48, 1, pp. 13–27.

Martin, L. W., and G. Vanberg (2011), *Parliaments and Coalitions: The Role of Legislative Institutions in Multiparty Governance*, Oxford: Oxford University Press.

Motta, R. (1985), 'L'attività legislativa dei governi (1948–1983)', *Rivista Italiana di Scienza Politica*, 25, 2, pp. 255–92.

Moury, C. (2013), *Coalition Governments and Party Mandate: How do Coalition Agreements Constrain Ministerial Action*, London: Routledge.

Moury, C., and A. Timmermans (2008), 'Conflitto e accordo in governi di coalizione. Il caso Italia', *Rivista Italiana di Scienza Politica*, 27, 3, pp. 417–42.

Müller, W. C. (2008), 'Government and Bureaucracies', in D. Caramani (ed.), *Comparative Politics*, Oxford: Oxford University Press.

Müller, W. C., and K. Strøm (eds) (2000), *Coalition Governments in Western Europe*, Oxford: Oxford University Press.

Müller, W. C. and K. Strøm (2008), 'Introduction', in K. Strøm, W. C. Müller, and T. Bergman (eds), *Cabinets and Coalition Bargaining. The Democratic Life Cycle in Western Europe*, Oxford: Oxford University Press.

Naurin, E. (2011), *Election Promises, Party Behaviour and Voter Perceptions*, Basingstoke: Palgrave Macmillan.

Nousiainen, J. (1993), 'Decision-Making, Policy Content and Conflict Resolution in Western European Cabinets', in J. Blondel and F. Müller-Rommel (eds), *Governing Together: The Extent and Limits of Joint Decision-Making in Western European Cabinets*, New York: St. Martin's Press, pp. 259–82.

Poguntke, T., and P. Webb (eds) (2007), *The Presidentialization of Politics*, Oxford: Oxford University Press.

Pridham, G. (ed.) (1986), *Coalitional Behaviour in Theory and Practice: An Inductive Model for Western Europe*, Cambridge: Cambridge University Press.

Radin, B. A. (2000), *Beyond Machiavelli: Policy Analysis Comes of Age*, Washington, DC: Georgetown University Press.

Ragusa, J. M. (2010), 'The Lifecycle of Public Policy: An Event History Analysis of Repeals to Landmark Legislative Enactments, 1951–2006', *American Politics Research*, 38, 6, pp. 1015–51.

Rothstein, B. (2005), *Social Traps and the Problem of Trust*, New York: Cambridge University Press.

Sartori, G. (1976), *Parties and Party Systems: A Framework for Analysis*, Cambridge: Cambridge University Press.

Shepsle, K. A., and B. R. Weingast (1994), 'Positive Theories of Congressional Institutions', *Legislative Studies Quarterly*, 19, 2, pp. 149–79.

Shugart, M. S., and P. M. Wattenberg (eds) (2001), *Mixed Member Electoral Systems: The Best of Both Worlds?* Oxford: Oxford University Press.

Strøm, K., W. C. Müller, and T. Bergman (eds) (2008), *Cabinets and Coalition Bargaining. The Democratic Life Cycle in Western Europe*, Oxford: Oxford University Press.

Thames, F. C., and M. S. Edwards (2006), 'Differentiating Mixed-Member Electoral Systems: Mixed-Member Majoritarian and Mixed-Member Proportional Systems and Government Expenditures', *Comparative Political Studies*, 39, 7, pp. 905–27.

Venturino, F. (2001), 'Presidentialization in Italian Politics: The Political Consequences of the 1993 Electoral Reform', *South European Society and Politics*, 6, 2, pp. 27–46.

Verzichelli, L. (2003), 'La formazione del governo parlamentare: tra vincoli antichi e potenziamento istituzionale', in C. Barbieri and L. Verzichelli (eds), *Il governo e i suoi apparati*, Genoa: Name.

Verzichelli, L., and M. Cotta (2000), 'Italy: From "Constrained" Coalitions to Alternating Governments', in W. C. Müller and K. Strøm (eds), *Coalition Governments in Western Europe*, Oxford: Oxford University Press, pp. 433–97.

Zucchini, F. (2010), 'Italy: Government Alternation and Legislative Agenda Setting', in B. E. Rasch and G. Tsebelis (eds), *The Role of Governments in Legislative Agenda Setting*, London: Routledge.

1 The government and its hard decisions

How conflict is managed within the coalition

Francesco Marangoni and Michelangelo Vercesi[1]

Introduction

Conflicts are intrinsic in the nature of coalitions. Government parties, in fact, are allies but, at the same time, they are organizations competing (with one another) for maximizing votes in the electoral arena (Panebianco 1988). Individual components of the executive, ministers above all, are agents of the whole cabinet, in their respective departmental policy domain, but they are also (at least some of them) representatives of their own party within the government (Andeweg 2000). A tension between centripetal and centrifugal drives, therefore, is inherent in the very nature of coalition executives: something that might be conducive to more or less frequent and serious conflicts among partners.

If intense enough, conflicts might weaken the basis of the alliance and challenge the stability of the executive. Even when less threatening, in terms of risks for government survival, intra-coalition conflicts can undermine cabinet decision-making and government performance.

It stands to reason, therefore, that conflict management is an essential commitment for coalition governments. Coalition governance, indeed, is supposed to be a matter of conflict avoidance, even more than conflict management. Coalition agreements, discussed in depth by Conti in Chapter 3, are supposed to be crucial mechanisms in this regard (Andeweg and Timmermans 2008). Unforeseen, or deferred, issues of conflicts, however, might always arise during the government *life cycle* (Strøm et al. 2008) and need to be addressed by government partners.

The analysis of conflict management, from this point of view, has proved to be a precious perspective for observing internal dynamics of coalition governments[2] and, in this respect, Italy is a very intriguing case to study. Before the 1990s, it was traditionally ruled by often conflictual and ineffective (in most of the cases coalition) governments (Di Palma 1977; Spotts and Wieser 1986). In the absence of any real chance of alternation, fragile governing coalitions were constantly formed around the Christian Democratic party (DC), which traditionally controlled the prime-ministership and the most influential cabinet portfolios (Verzichelli and Cotta 2000). On the one hand, resulting government majorities used to be fragmented and internally divided (as far as the main policy preferences are concerned). On the other, governments used not to be based on formal coalition agreements (Moury and Timmermans 2008). The attitude of Italian First

Republic governments to rely largely (if not exclusively) on arenas of conflict management and resolution that were external to the cabinet, therefore, is perfectly coherent with the arguments raised by the most advanced comparative literature on this issue. The common hypotheses, in fact, postulate that conditions like the fragility of coalitions, the bias in favor of one of the governing parties (as in the case of the DC) and the absence of any prior policy agreement among coalition partners, make government members more likely to resort to institutions that are external to the cabinet (such as a committee of parliamentary party leaders), or mixed arenas, open to both cabinet and non-cabinet actors (such as the renowned Italian 'majority summits' between ministers and party leaders), rather than to internal (and closed) arenas (i.e., the cabinet) for conflict resolution (Andeweg and Timmermans 2008).

The analysis of intra-coalitional conflicts (and of conflict management) during the Italian Second Republic, therefore, promises to be interesting and valuable. Not only because, as said, it will provide a precious empirical perspective for the observation of the government internal dynamics in an era, as emphasized in the introduction of this volume, of profound (but also uncompleted and even contradictory) transformation of the Italian political system. From a broader comparative perspective, it will also serve as a dynamic test of the same bulk of hypotheses on coalition governments and conflict management mentioned above.

It is true, on the one hand, that the evolution of the Italian political (and institutional) system between the First and the Second Republic has proved largely incomplete (Ceccanti and Vassallo 2004; Almagisti *et al.* 2014), and that traditional features (and problems) of the Italian governments have remained substantially unaltered (or become even worse) as a result. Fragmentation and heterogeneity have continued to plague government coalitions that were assembled to win the elections and to defeat the 'opposite pole', but were also unable to govern (Diamanti 2007) and to produce stable executives (Pasquino and Valbruzzi 2011). Coalition fragility and cabinet instability, moreover, have opened the way to frequent government crises and, sometimes (as in the case of the executives formed after the crisis of the Prodi I government in 1998), to more traditional – First Republic-like – patterns of government formation and coalition governance: i.e., pure parliamentary (not electoral) legitimation of majorities, no pre-electoral coalition deals and policy agreements, subordination to partisan actors outside the cabinet. Under these premises, we could hardly expect to find evidence of a diminishing intra-coalitional conflictuality.

On the other hand, however, the structure of Italian governments has experienced some evident changes in the last 15 years, that we expect to have had an impact on mechanisms of intra-coalitional conflict handling. To say the least, the new bipolar electoral competition between center-right and center-left pre-electoral coalitions (Golder 2006) has led to executives (and prime ministers) with a more direct electoral derivation (and legitimation). The new (for Italian governments) habit of drafting coalition agreements focused on policies with constraining implications on coalition governance (Moury 2012), and the increased cabinet membership rate of party leaders who, instead, used not to sit in the executive during the First Republic (Verzichelli 2009) are two of the main corollaries of this 'majoritarian turn' in Italian politics.

Drawing from the already quoted study by Andeweg and Timmermans (2008), who have found that when governing parties have prior coalition policy agreement to rely on, and when party leaders take a seat in the executive, conflicts tend to be solved within closed and internal arenas, we should expect conflict management by the Italian governments of the Second Republic to be somehow 'internalized' within the cabinet.

With the aim of verifying these general expectations, the next pages are organized as follows. We first present some basic features of Second Republic governments, with particular focus on the composition (and fragmentation) of the supporting coalitions, as these same characteristics are expected to have an impact on the dynamics of conflict occurrence and management. Intra-coalitional conflictuality is then measured for each single government (by means of an extensive newspaper analysis), as regards to both *quantity* (the number of conflicts that occurred) and *quality* (the objects of conflicts and their 'seriousness' in terms of the risks they posed to cabinet survival). Third, we provide some information about the role and the involvement of prime ministers in conflicts. The decision-making and conflict management arenas are finally examined (again using newspaper analysis as the main source of information) with particular regard to their openness or closure to actors outside the cabinet.

Government coalitions between 1996 and 2011

The starting point of the empirical investigation presented in this chapter is 1996. While we already have access to sufficient knowledge about intra-coalition conflicts and conflict management during the First Republic (Nousiainen 1993; Criscitiello 1996; Verzichelli and Cotta 2000), no systematic studies regarding more recent years are available. At the same time, we decided not to consider the period immediately following the crisis of the First Republic in 1992, as this was characterized by extreme instability of the Italian government system, and it was ruled, almost entirely,[3] by non-partisan, technocratic or quasi-technocratic executives (Fabbrini 2000).

Between 1996 and 2011 four politicians alternated as prime ministers and six coalition governments were appointed. For the sake of simplicity we treat as a single executive two governments following one another, without any change in the prime-ministership and without a general election occurring in between. According to these criteria, the six cabinets are Prodi I; D'Alema I–II;[4] Amato II;[5] Berlusconi II–III;[6] Prodi II; Berlusconi IV. Only the Amato II and Berlusconi II–III cabinets did not terminate prematurely; and only the latter lasted for the entire legislative term.[7] Table 1.1 indicates the first day in office, the date of resignation of each government, and the duration (in days) with full powers[8] of these executives. The four prime ministers, with the exception of Berlusconi, were not leaders of their own parties when in office.[9]

Table 1.1 Italian cabinets, 1996–2011

Cabinet	Date in (sworn in)	Formal resignation	Days in (with full powers)
Prodi I	18 May 1996	9 October 1998	874
D'Alema I–II	21 October 1998	19 April 2000	546
Amato II	25 April 2000	31 May 2001	401
Berlusconi II–III	11 June 2001	2 May 2006	1786
Prodi II	17 May 2006	24 January 2008	617
Berlusconi IV	8 May 2008	12 November 2011	1283

With regard to the party composition, we consider as coalition members all parties explicitly supporting the cabinet in parliament, whether or not they have any representative in the Council of ministers, or any of their members appointed as junior minister.[10] Table 1.2 reports the party composition of the coalition supporting each government, together with a measure of coalition fragmentation, computed as the number of parties that were strictly necessary to hold the absolute majority in both the Chamber of Deputies and the Senate (i.e., parties with veto power). Some coalitions were oversized, but the number of parties that were necessary to hold a majority was actually smaller.

Table 1.2 Party composition of government coalitions (at time of inauguration), 1996–2011 (including parties giving external support)

Cabinet	Coalition[a]	"Necessary" parties
Prodi I	PDS-PPI-RI-VER-*RC*	5
D'Alema I–II	DS-PPI-VER-RI-PDCI-SDI-UDR	6
Amato II	DS-DEM-PPI-VER-RI-PDCI-UDEUR-SDI	8
Berlusconi II–III	FI-LN-AN-CCD/CDU-NPSI-PRI	4
Prodi II	DS-DL-RC-RNP-PDCI-IDV-VER-Indip./PD- UDEUR-*SVP*	10
Berlusconi IV	PDL-LN-MPA-DC	2

Notes: Parties giving only external support in parliament in italics.

a Even if other very tiny parties sometimes gave external support to cabinets, only the main coalition members are indicated.

Party names: AN, National Alliance; CCD/CDU, Christian Democratic Centre/United Christian Democrats; DC, Christian Democracy; DEM, The Democrats; DL, Democracy is Freedom – the Daisy; DS, Left Democrats; FI, Go Italy (*Forza Italia*); Indip./PD, Independents for the Olive Tree; LN, Northern League; MPA, Movement for Autonomies; NPSI, New Italian Socialist Party; PDCI, Party of the Italian Communists; PDL, People of Freedom; PDS (former DS), Democratic Party of the Left; PPI, Italian People's Party; PRI, Italian Republican Party; RI, Italian Renewal; RC, Communist Refoundation; RNP, Rose in the Fist; SDI, Italian Democratic Socialists; SVP, *Südtiroler Volkspartei*, People's Party of the South Tirol; UDEUR, Union of the Democrats for Europe; VER, Greens.

Source: Marangoni (2013), revised.

Taken as a whole, data in Table 1.2 confirm that complexity and fragmenta-tion have characterized Italian government coalitions (also) during the Second Republic. There are some variations among governments, but there is not any clear pattern toward simplification of government teams. On the contrary, the most fragmented coalition was the rather recent center-left alliance supporting the 2006–2008 Prodi II executive (ten necessary parties). As we will also dis-cuss in the following pages, even the more homogeneous coalition supporting the Berlusconi IV cabinet (only two necessary parties) experienced significant troubles, due to an increasing level of internal conflictuality during the life of this government (ending up with an early dissolution of the executive).

Another aspect to be taken into careful consideration, because it is expected to have a significant impact on the attitude of governments toward conflict manage-ment, is the presence of party leaders within the cabinet. We find quite significant differences among the governments under scrutiny on this regard. Overall, the 'majoritarian' governments (those led by Prodi and Berlusconi) form a group on their own compared to the more First Republic-like governments (led by D'Alema and Amato), with the exception of the first Prodi government. Indeed, only one party leader entered this latter cabinet. On the contrary, more than half of the par-ties represented in the Berlusconi II–III and IV and Prodi II cabinets had their own leaders inside the (senior) ministerial group (Table 1.3).

Intra-coalitional conflictuality and conflict management

The level of conflictuality

In our effort to measure government conflictuality, we have first defined the con-cept of 'conflict' as any quarrel or explicit disagreement between two or more executive members and/or coalition (individual or collective) party actors.

Table 1.3 Number of party leaders in cabinet by government, 1996–2011

Cabinet	No. of coalition parties with cabinet representation	No. of party leaders in cabinet
Prodi I	4	1
D'Alema I–II	7	1
Amato II	8	1
Berlusconi II–III	4/6[a]	3[b]
Prodi II	9	5
Berlusconi IV	2	2

Notes

a NPSI and PRI obtained a representation in the cabinet only after the reshuffle of 2005.

b Initially, the cabinet comprised the leaders of FI, AN and LN. CCD and CDU merged into UDC (Union of Christian and Center Democrats) in 2002 under the leadership of Marco Follini, who entered the cabinet in 2004. The leader of LN, Umberto Bossi, had left his ministerial post some months before.

The number of (so defined) conflicts is the first indicator (rough) of the level of conflictuality a given government coalition has experienced. In this regard, we used newspaper reports as a source of information to detect single episodes of conflicts among coalition partners. Technically speaking, we operated a systematic keywords search[11] through the digital archives of two of the most relevant Italian national newspapers, *Il Corriere della Sera* and *Il Sole 24 Ore*, on all the articles (at both title and text level) published between May 1996 (the inauguration of the Prodi I executive) and November 2011 (premature end of the Berlusconi IV executive). Once we had collected the articles presenting at least one of the selected keywords, we went through a more in-depth analysis of the content of each piece, in order to find the commentaries effectively covering conflicts within government coalitions (excluding all other conflicts) and to isolate single episodes of conflicts.

At the end of this process, as reported in Table 1.4, we were able to observe more than 850 conflicts in the entire period under analysis: almost five conflicts per month, on average. Table 1.4 disaggregates data by individual governments. Interestingly, the absolute degree of conflictuality seems to vary quite independently from (or, better, not exclusively as a consequence of) coalition fragmentation and internal heterogeneity. The quite homogeneous (at least initially, before a split within the party of the prime minister) Berlusconi IV's coalition, for instance, experienced quite a high level of conflictuality (almost six conflicts, on average, per month). This was even higher than the level shown by the more fragmented Prodi II supporting coalition (on average, 4.7 conflicts per month).

As already said, however, the number of conflicts is only a rough indicator of the real level of intra-coalitional conflictuality. In fact, we cannot assume that all conflicts present the same (potential) risks for cabinet survival and for an effective and smooth functioning of government decision-making. Simply speaking, indeed, some conflicts are more 'dangerous' and serious than others. A coalition might frequently have to cope with minor internal disagreements or, vice versa, be affected by few, but very threatening conflicts. The simple observation of the frequency of conflicts can, therefore, be a good point of departure, but it is not enough for a detailed and reliable picture.

The seriousness of conflicts, therefore, needs to be carefully analyzed: a problem that we decided to consider, coherently with the literature on the topic

Table 1.4 Absolute and monthly average number of conflicts by government

Cabinet	No. of conflicts	Monthly average
Prodi I	168	5.6
D'Alema I–II	122	6.4
Amato II	57	4.1
Berlusconi II–III	186	3.2
Prodi II	98	4.7
Berlusconi IV	220	5.6
Total	851	4.7

(Nousiainen 1993; Müller and Strøm 2000; Andeweg and Timmermans 2008), by referring to the actors involved in the conflicts and the roles they perform within the government arena.

The actors in conflict

All else being equal, intra-party conflicts are commonly considered to be relatively less risky for government survival. This kind of conflict, indeed, does not directly affect the interparty cooperative basis of the coalition, unless the object of intra-party disputes is precisely the support for the government, or if internal conflicts result in party splitting (with one component leaving the majority). In these cases, even intra-party conflicts might lead to cabinet termination (Damgaard 2008; Saalfeld 2009).

Three different types of conflict do not involve (only) actors belonging to the same party: these are interdepartmental conflicts; party–government conflicts and interparty conflicts. As one might note, these different types are ordered according to the increasing involvement of partisan actors (the 'partyness' of conflicts): from conflicts where parties are not directly involved (interdepartmental conflicts) to conflicts between partisan actors (interparty conflicts). The same classification is also ordered according to increasing risks they cause to cabinet stability, as the partyness of conflicts is commonly considered a critical factor in determining the seriousness of conflicts (Huber 1996; Andeweg and Timmermans 2008).

The actors of interdepartmental conflicts are individual ministers acting as heads and in the interests of their departments, and not (purely) as representatives of their own party within the cabinet.[12] Conflicts between party and government are, instead, characterized by the actions of a coalition party (or some components of it) against the policies (even a ministry) or the overall trajectory of the government. Clearly, the prime minister is the most prominent among possible government members who can be involved in conflicts (Vercesi 2013).

The partyness of conflicts reaches its maximum strength in interparty conflicts. 'The most serious conflict in parliamentary systems generally (. . .) lies between parties (. . .) that are represented both in the government and the parliament' (Huber 1996: 270). Their dangerousness can be explained by the fact that the struggle occurs between two (or more) constitutive parts of the coalition, that is, the parties establishing a pact for government.

Each conflict in our dataset has, therefore, been classified in one (and only one) of these four categories.[13] Figure 1.1 presents the relative distribution of the episodes of conflict by type and by executive. As a whole, interparty struggles, which we mentioned as being potentially the most risky type of conflicts, cover the larger area of the figure: almost 36 per cent of the conflicts we detected can be classified in this category. Rather interestingly, we noted an exceptionally high level of interparty conflictuality with the D'Alema I–II and Amato II executives (respectively, about 56 per cent and little less than 46 per cent). These data are coherent with our expectations and can be explained when one considers the origins of these two cabinets based, like the governments of the First Republic, on

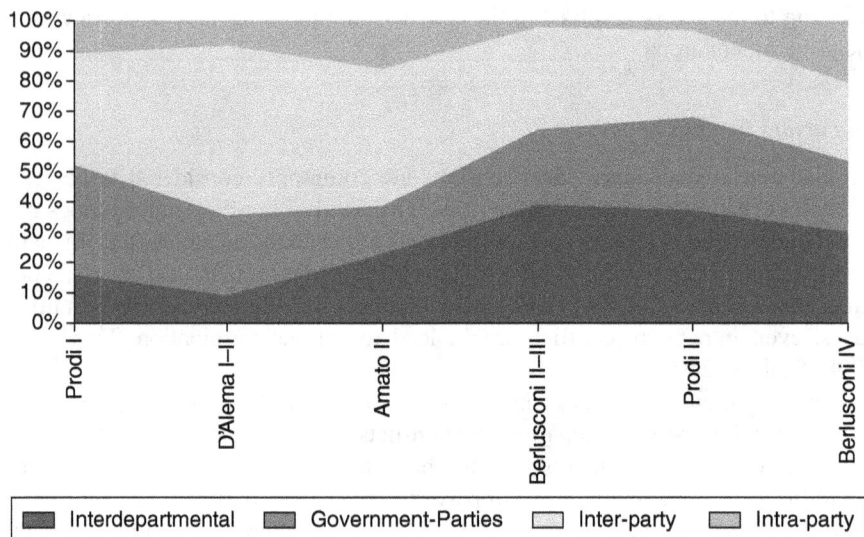

Figure 1.1 Percentage distribution of conflicts by actors involved

complex and fragile interparty bargaining and compromise in parliament after the crisis of the former executive and so under emergency conditions, rather than on electoral legitimation or a clear post-electoral agreement.

This pattern changes quite substantially with the new 'majoritarian' executives, as we define those governments resulting from pre-electoral coalitions and popular legitimacy in a context of bipolar competition (i.e., Prodi I; Berlusconi II–III; Prodi II and Berlusconi IV). The interparty conflictuality area shrinks, while conflicts progressively move into the cabinet. Interdepartmental struggles, in fact, rise from 17 per cent during the Prodi I government to almost 40 per cent during Berlusconi II–III and Prodi II governments and about 30 per cent during the Berlusconi IV.

It has been argued (Marangoni 2013) that this might be due to the relevance of the decisions taken by the executives of the Second Republic, given the tighter constraints of the EU on the Italian government and due to the fact that policy stagnation cannot be a rewarding strategy in the alternation system of the Second Republic (Curini 2011).[14] On the other hand, one might read this data as indicating the consolidation of these executives as the *locus* of party leadership. As already noted (contrary to the First Republic), in the 'majoritarian' executives the leaders of the coalition parties usually took office in the cabinet,[15] hence some interparty frictions might have boosted the interdepartmental conflicts.

The attempt by the 'majoritarian' executives of the Second Republic to play a more autonomous (from parties) and active role in the decision-making process can probably explain the high percentage of government–parties conflicts (27 per cent). At the same time, although a sign of their leadership, this type of conflict destabilized the same executives. The early termination of the Prodi I and Prodi II governments, for instance, was the consequence of open conflicts between the executive and some party components of its supporting coalition.

Naturally enough, government–parties and interparty conflicts might end up nourishing one another. The opposition of a coalition member to a given government decision can easily lead to conflicts between the former and the other party components of the majority (those more aligned with the executive). In other terms, in this kind of situation, the same government acts could become the target of interparty conflicts. This was the case, for instance, of the formal crisis ending with a reshuffle of the Berlusconi II government in April 2005 (Vassallo 2005).

An important consideration here relates to the relatively high percentage of intra-party conflicts during the Berlusconi IV government (20.5 per cent). We assumed this type of conflict is, in general, not too risky for government survival. However, sometimes intra-party conflicts can be severe enough to threaten the stability of the coalition as a whole. The Berlusconi IV executive is a perfect case in point. The increasing tensions within the People of Freedom party that ended with the decision of Gianfranco Fini (one of the founding fathers) to abandon the party[16] and to give birth in parliament to a new party (Future and Freedom) that did not support the executive, weakened the majority coalition and opened the way to a crisis in the government and to its resignation in 2011.

The objects of conflicts

Conflicts do not only differ from one another according to the actors involved. Quite evidently, the issues at stake can be of a very different nature, entailing different dynamics and risks for the government. We suggest, in this regard, classifying the issues of conflicts into three macro-categories: policy issues, structure of the cabinet, and coalitional equilibria. This latter category refers to struggles over the basic rules keeping coalition partners together: contrasts over the leadership of the coalition or on the strategies and goals to be followed by the executive are typical examples of conflicts falling in this category. Policy conflicts involve the decisions to be implemented (in terms of public policies) by the executive (the focus, therefore, is on the outputs of the government activity). Conflicts on cabinet structure are typically disagreements on the division of labor and prerogatives within the executive (starting with portfolio allocation).

Data in Table 1.5 show that, on the whole, the majority of conflicts (almost 63 per cent) concern policy issues (note that the few conflicts we have not been able to unequivocally classify into one of the three categories have been excluded). On the one hand, once again, this seems to confirm the relevance of the policy decisions the Italian executives have been called to deal with in the last two decades. On the other hand, however, these same data suggest that reaching a compromise over the policy measures to be implemented is still a difficult (and sometimes ineffective, as Conti demonstrates in Chapter 3) exercise for the Italian government coalitions.

Disaggregated data by executive are really interesting on this regard. We note, in fact, a significantly smaller percentage of policy conflicts during the D'Alema I–II and the Amato II executives (about 36 per cent and 48 per cent, respectively).

Table 1.5 Percentage distribution of conflicts by main issue (and by executive)[a]

Cabinet	Policy issues	Coalitional equilibria	Cabinet structure	No. of conflicts classified
Prodi I	62.7	23.4	13.9	158
D'Alema I–II	35.3	30.3	34.5	119
Amato II	47.9	20.8	31.3	48
Berlusconi II–III	70.8	9.4	19.9	171
Prodi II	76.1	8.7	15.2	92
Berlusconi IV	68.6	7.7	23.7	207
Total	62.5	15.5	22.0	795

Note
a Conflicts that are not unequivocally classifiable have been excluded.

This is very unlikely to be due to the more homogeneous nature of their supporting coalitions, or to their capacity to hold larger and more solid agreements (and a smoother decision-making process). The exact contrary is, instead, true. The rather composite nature of the majority coalitions, and the limited time (and policy) horizon of these two governments prevented more relevant and conflictual policy issues entering the government agenda.[17] Conflicts over the coalitional equilibria and the structure of the cabinet, somehow (numerically) residual under most 'majoritarian' executives (with the partial exception of the Prodi I), have largely characterized the life of these two governments (they make up about 65 per cent and 52 per cent of the episodes of conflict, respectively), a phenomenon echoing the typical nature of conflicts in the First Republic (Nousiainen 1993).

At this point in the analysis, we are able to combine information on the actors and issues of conflicts to produce a more complete picture of the dynamics that characterize the internal life of Italian executives, notably of the kind of relationships between different tiers of government. Interdepartmental conflicts, like those involving the cabinet (the executive inner circle) concern almost exclusively policy issues (about 89 per cent of cases), with no significant variation among governments. Quite remarkably, parties–executive (66 per cent) and interparty conflicts (53 per cent) increasingly concern policies, another sign of the relevance of policy decisions to be taken by the governments of the Second Republic. Within this context, the 'First Republic-like' D'Alema I–II and Amato II governments diverge from this general pattern, with coalition governance and executive structure and organization being more frequent issues of (extra-cabinet) conflicts between allies (in 71 per cent and 53 per cent of the cases, respectively) or between one (or more) coalition parties and the government (62 per cent and 67 per cent of this kind of conflicts, respectively).[18]

Conflicts and the internal life of cabinets: the involvement of prime ministers

In our analysis of actors and issues of intra-coalitional conflictuality a special focus is devoted to the chief executive. The Italian prime ministers were commonly considered comparatively weak by the literature on the First Republic (Hine and Finocchi 1991). However, in recent years some changes have been introduced in the role of this office with a relative strengthening of its power (O'Malley and Cavatorta 2004; Campus and Pasquino 2006; Calise 2007; Musella 2012). Our analysis of the involvement of prime ministers in intra-coalitional conflicts could contribute to shed light on this process of change and demonstrate to what extent this political figure has become more influential within the context of Italian politics.

According to our data, almost 25 per cent of all conflicts that we were able to detect involved (directly or indirectly) the prime minister, with little or no variation among governments. More than the quantity, it is the type of conflicts (particularly their contents) involving prime ministers that is of a particular interest here. Table 1.6 shows a distribution of conflicts in which prime ministers took part, by issue and cabinet. Two models seem again to emerge. On one hand, during the D'Alema I–II and Amato II executives, the conflicts involving the prime minister only rarely concerned policy issues (in no case during the Amato II government, in about 21 per cent of cases during the D'Alema I–II cabinet). The high percentage of chief-executive-engaging conflicts related to coalitional equilibria and cabinet structure suggests that these two prime ministers, deriving their legitimation from pure interparty bargaining in parliament and not from an electoral mandate (exactly like First Republic prime ministers) played primarily the role of guarantors of office allocation and balance of powers among coalition partners.

'Majoritarian' prime ministers, on the contrary, building their legitimacy on electoral (programmatic) mandate, tried to play a more active role in guiding government decision-making, even where this implied disagreement (over specific policy issues) with one or more components of the government.

Managing conflictuality: internal or external arenas?

Governments, in particular coalition governments, 'cannot survive long in an atmosphere poisoned by incessant conflicts: it is therefore important that these conflicts be resolved quickly' (Nousiainen 1993: 273).

Table 1.6 Percentage distribution of conflicts involving the prime minister (PM) by issue (and by executive)[a]

	Policy issues	*Coalitional equilibria*	*Cabinet structure*	*No. of conflicts involving the PM*
Prodi I	67.5	25.0	7.5	40
D'Alema I–II	20.9	44.2	34.9	43
Amato II	–	75.0	25.0	8
Berlusconi II–III	41.7	29.2	29.2	48
Prodi II	75.0	5.0	20.0	20
Berlusconi IV	62.5	14.6	22.9	48
Total	48.8	27.5	23.7	207

Note

a Conflicts that are not unequivocally classifiable have been excluded.

The recent comparative analysis of conflict management processes by coalition governments has mainly focused on the closure or openness of these same mechanisms to (individual and collective) components outside the cabinet. We referred to this general distinction to classify the conflict management arenas that appear to be more frequently employed by Italian governing coalitions in the period under analysis. In particular, we adopted a simplified version of the typology suggested by Andeweg and Timmermans (2008)[19] distinguishing between: interdepartmental summits between two or more ministers (internal arena); committees of ministers and leaders of the majority parliamentary groups (mixed arena); committees of ministers (usually prime ministers and other relevant ministers) and majority party leaders who do not hold any office within the executive (mixed arena); committees of parliamentary majority group leaders (external arena); interparty committees among party leaders outside the cabinet (external arena).[20]

In the same way as for measuring conflictuality, we relied on an extensive newspaper analysis to find single occurrences of the various types of conflict management arenas. We were able to isolate 261 committees and summits during the 15 years under analysis. As is reported in Table 1.7, about 66 per cent of the cases could be classified in the (mixed arena) ministers-party leaders category. These are, indeed, the so-called 'majority summits' which had already proved to be crucial decision-making arenas during the First Republic (Criscitiello 1996). About 10 per cent of the cases are ministers-parliamentary leaders committees that typically perform a 'technical' role, dealing with the parliamentary process of government bills. In almost 14 per cent of cases, the participants to the committees were non-governmental actors: the leaders of parliamentary groups (3 per cent) or majority party leaders who did not hold any office in the cabinet (more than 10 per cent).

External (and mixed) arenas, therefore, have continued to play an essential role in coordinating actions and managing conflict within government coalitions. At the same time, however, we found some evidence of the increasing importance of internal arenas for conflict management. As we show in Table 1.7, the participants to the committees were (exclusively) ministers (sometimes junior ministers) in about 11 per cent of the cases.

Quite interestingly, the latter kind of arena appears more relevant under 'majoritarian' governments (and purely external arenas not including members of the cabinet were only residual) and not under the D'Alema I–II and Amato II governments. In these two cases, on the contrary, coalition members largely resorted to external arenas, in particular interparty committees outside the cabinet: almost 27 per cent and 50 per cent of the conflict-resolution committees during the D'Alema I–II and the Amato II executives allowed as participants only those party leaders with no office in the cabinet.

Conclusion

In this chapter we have analyzed the degree of conflictuality that has characterized Italian government coalitions during the Second Republic and the mechanisms they have developed for management of conflicts.

Table 1.7 Percentage distribution of arenas by executive

	Interdepartmental summits	Committees of ministers and parliamentary leaders	Committees of ministers and party leaders	Committees of parliamentary leaders	Committees of party leaders (not holding office in the cabinet)	No.
Prodi I	4.2	16.7	62.5	6.3	10.4	48
D'Alema I–II	–	15.8	55.3	2.6	26.3	38
Amato II	–	–	43.8	6.3	50.0	16
Berlusconi II–III	20.8	3.1	72.9	1.0	2.1	96
Prodi II	9.5	9.5	76.2	–	4.8	21
Berlusconi IV	11.9	14.3	66.7	4.8	2.4	42
Total	11.1	9.6	65.9	3.1	10.3	261

We relied on extensive newspaper analysis to first detect single episodes of conflict occurring among different (individual and collective) cabinet and coalition components during the life cycle of each of the six executives in office in the period under analysis:[21] from the inauguration of the Prodi I government (May 1996) to the (early) end of the Berlusconi IV government (November 2011).

From a purely quantitative point of view, with more than 850 conflicts that we were able to identify, the high level of conflictuality confirms the complexity of government coalitions as an enduring trait of the Italian political system.

We tried, indeed, to measure intra-coalitional conflictuality not only in terms of *quantity* of conflicts, but also looking at the type of conflicts: in relation to the risks they entailed for the survival of the executive, and also to their content. As far as the first dimension is concerned, we classified single episodes of conflict into four different categories depending on the coalition (individual or collective) components who were in conflict with each other: intra-party conflicts (involving two or more actors of the parliamentary majority belonging to the same party, or two or more ministers of the same party in conflict for reasons related to the internal affairs of their own party); interdepartmental conflicts (between two or more ministers, acting as representatives of their respective departments and not as delegates of their own parties); government–party conflicts (involving one or more party components outside the cabinet and one or more members of the executive, in relation to decisions to be taken by the government); interparty conflicts (between two or more actors, belonging to two or more majority parties and not holding any office in the executive, or involving cabinet members acting in the exclusive interest of their own party).

As far as the content of conflicts is concerned, we distinguished between: policy issues (decisions and measures of public policy to be implemented by the executive); coalitional equilibria (issues related to the division of power and responsibilities among allies); and cabinet structure (issues concerning the organization of work within the cabinet).

Our results demonstrate that interparty conflicts, very often related to the 'power bases' of the coalition (that is, coalitional equilibria and cabinet structure) and the most risky ones for coalition governments according to comparative analyses, have surely characterized the life of the Italian executives during the Second Republic. Nonetheless, we also found some evidence of a process of progressive shifting of conflictuality into the cabinet and toward policy issues. This happened, in particular, during those executives that we have defined as more 'majoritarian': they were formed after the general elections on the basis of pre-electoral coalitions and their legitimacy stemmed primarily from the electoral arena.

These executives were able to claim, and partially to play, a more autonomous role with respect to their supporting parties than in the First Republic (also because, more than in the past, party leaders held ministerial responsibilities in these executives). On the one hand, the relatively large percentage of interdepartmental conflicts (mostly involving policy issues) also demonstrates the strengthening of the cabinet as a privileged arena where crucial and binding decisions are taken. On the other hand, this same percentage, together with the relatively high rate of government–parties conflicts, proves the difficulty encountered by the Italian governing parties in governing together, even when they make pre-electoral agreements.

Then, we moved the analysis to mechanisms for conflict resolution. Drawing from the most recognized comparative analyses in the field, we decided to focus our attention on the arenas mostly used by governing coalitions for conflict management. For this purpose, we relied again on newspaper analysis in order to isolate the cases of conflict management in the period that we considered. We found 261 cases that we could classify, along Andeweg and Timmermans' lines (2008), as internal (only cabinet members as participants), external (only participants who did not hold an office in the cabinet), or mixed (where both cabinet members and party actors not holding office in the executive participated) arenas.

Andeweg and Timmermans, in their comparative analysis of conflict management by coalition governments in Western Europe, further argued that

> the construction and the use of external or mixed arenas imply additional costs for the parties compared to internal arenas, and that, all else being equal, parties tend to prefer internal decision-making arenas. They will resort to external institutions when the coalition is fragile or the bargaining environment complex, when they have no definitive prior policy agreement to fall back on, or when the internal environment is likely to be biased in favour of one of the parties.
>
> (Andeweg and Timmermans 2008: 296)

Their argument can well explain the preferential (or, better, almost exclusive) employment of external and mixed arenas of conflict resolution by the governments of the First Republic (Criscitiello 1996; Verzichelli and Cotta 2000). Following the same argument, our expectation was that processes of conflict management by the coalition governments of the Second Republic would be more internalized within the executive. More precisely, we expected that: (1) a stronger (and more autonomous from parties) popular legitimacy of the government; (2) a larger presence of party leaders within the cabinet; and (3) a more articulated and formalized pre-electoral agreement of the government coalition[22] should determine greater internalization of conflict management by the executive. Our results largely confirm these expectations. In particular, we found 'majoritarian' governments to rely, much more than in the past, on internal conflict management arenas. Conflict resolution (and avoidance) processes, however, were often open (also) to actors outside the cabinet: that is, they often took place in mixed arenas. Purely external arenas, indeed, were more extensively employed by those governments (like the D'Alema I–II and Amato II executives) that proved more similar to the First Republic model of governance (Fabbrini 2000): having not a direct electoral derivation but being the result of a compromise reached in parliament by parties after the crisis of former executives, they also proved less autonomous and more party-dependent. In this sense, our analysis shows that the use of the cabinet as an arena for managing conflicts depends largely on the attitude of (governing) party leaders to be part of the executive.

In the Introduction to this volume, Conti and Marangoni question whether the advent of alternation has transformed the Italian political system toward an *outputs* democracy. Governments (and governing parties) in this new scenario face the urgency to provide and implement policy decisions, since they are fully accountable to voters. An urgency that the blocked (without alternation) governments of the First Republic did not really experience. The analysis of intra-coalitional conflicts seems to corroborate this argument. Policy decisions have become increasingly important as issues of conflict within government coalitions. On the one hand, this is an indicator of the pro-active attitude of governing actors with respect to policy-making during the Second Republic. On the other hand, the same high level of conflictuality demonstrates that Italian coalitions still encounter considerable problems in joint decision-making.

Notes

1 Michelangelo Vercesi is responsible for the first and second sections, Francesco Marangoni for the third to fifth sections, while the Introduction and Conclusion were written jointly by the two authors.
2 Although there are only a few comparative empirical studies of government conflicts, Nousiainen (1993) and the already quoted Andeweg and Timmermans (2008) are probably the two most important exceptions. But see also Miller and Müller (2010).
3 With the exception of the brief parenthesis of the first Berlusconi government between May and December 1994.
4 We count the two consecutive executives guided by Massimo D'Alema (October 1998–December 1999 and December 1999–April 2000) as a single government.
5 The first Amato cabinet was in office from 1992 to 1993.
6 We count the two consecutive executives guided by Silvio Berlusconi (June 2001–April 2005 and April 2005–May 2006) as a single government.
7 Although, as said, passing through a formal crisis.
8 I.e., not considering the period between formal resignation and formation of the new executive.
9 Massimo D'Alema resigned as national head of the left-wing party *Democratici di Sinistra* (DS – Left Democrats) soon after entering office as chief executive.
10 It is worth noting that in Italy executives need an explicit confidence vote from an absolute parliamentary majority (both at the Chamber of Deputies and at the Senate).
11 The keywords we used (in appropriate combination through Boolean operators) are: 'contrast'; 'conflict'; 'disagreement'; 'struggle'; 'against'; 'government'; 'minister'; 'majority'; 'parties'.
12 This distinction is not always easy to make. We relied, however, on a careful analysis of newspaper reports to include in this category only conflicts that have developed along interdepartmental lines.
13 As one might easily imagine, this kind of classification is not always easy or unproblematic. Some difficulties arise from individuals cumulating different roles, as in the case, for instance, of two ministers who are also leaders of their own parties. Any time these two ministers entered into conflict with each other, we distinguished whether they were in disagreement for interdepartmental reasons or, rather, they acted as leaders (and in the interests) of their parties, and then we classified single episodes of conflict accordingly.
14 On the impact of the (absence of) alternation on the agenda power and the effectiveness of Italian governments, see also Zucchini (2011).

15 With some variations among cabinets, as discussed above.
16 Formally, Gianfranco Fini was expelled by the National Steering Committee of the PDL.
17 Previous analyses, on this regard, have shown that these two governments fall significantly below the other executives of the Second Republic as far as their attitudes and capability to present significant bills to the parliament are concerned (Marangoni 2013).
18 Interestingly enough, the Prodi I executive seems closer to this model than to the other 'majoritarian' executives, in particular as far as interparty conflicts are concerned (involving extra-policy issues in more than 50 per cent of the cases). The peculiar nature of the coalition supporting this executive (with the Communist Refoundation party that was not part of the cabinet, but gave only its external support) and the fact that this government represented a first experiment of an unprecedented (and, as such, in search for some equilibrium) center-left alliance might explain this phenomenon.
19 Andeweg and Timmermans counted two different arenas for each of the three types (internal; mixed; and external). On the contrary, we grouped internal arenas into one category: the summits between ministers, irrespective of the type of the meeting.
20 It is important to note that all these different arenas might sometimes work as conflict-avoidance, rather than conflict-resolution mechanisms. In other words, they can work as decision-making arenas intended to reinforce compromise and agreement among the different components of the coalition.
21 As we mentioned above, we adopted counting criteria that differ from the official government numbering (in that we counted a new executive only when there was a change in the prime-ministership or a general election occurred).
22 See Chapter 3 on this aspect.

References

Almagisti, M., L. Lanzalaco and L. Verzichelli (eds) (2014), *La transizione politica italiana. Da tangentopoli ad oggi*. Roma: Carocci Editore.

Andeweg, R. (2000), 'Ministers As Double Agents? The Delegation Process between Cabinet and Ministers', *European Journal of Political Research* 37(3), pp. 377–95.

Andeweg, R. and A. Timmermans (2008), 'Conflict Management in Coalition Government', in K. Strøm, W. C. Müller, and T. Bergman (eds), *Cabinets and Coalition Bargaining: The Democratic Life Cycle in Western Europe*. Oxford: Oxford University Press, pp. 269–300.

Calise, M. (2007), 'Presidentialization, Italian Style', in T. Poguntke and P. Webb (eds), *The Presidentialization of Politics. A Comparative Study of Modern Democracies*. Oxford: Oxford University Press, pp. 88–106.

Campus, D. and G. Pasquino (2006), 'Leadership in Italy: The Changing Role of Leaders in Elections and in Government', *Journal of Contemporary European Studies* 14(1), pp. 25–40.

Ceccanti, S. and S. Vassallo (eds) (2004), *Come chiudere la transizione. Il sistema politico italiano tra cambiamento, apprendimento e adattamento*, Bologna: Il Mulino.

Criscitiello, A. (1996), 'Alla ricerca della collegialità di governo: i vertici di maggioranza dal 1970 al 1994', *Rivista italiana di scienza politica* 26(2), pp. 365–89.

Curini, L. (2011), 'Government Survival the Italian Way: The Core and the Advantages of Policy Immobilism during the First Republic', *European Journal of Political Research* 50(1), pp. 110–42.

Damgaard, E. (2008), 'Cabinet Termination', in K. Strøm, W. C. Müller, and T. Bergman (eds.), *Cabinets and Coalition Bargaining: The Democratic Life Cycle in Western Europe*. Oxford: Oxford University Press, pp. 301–26.

Di Palma, G. (1977), *Surviving without Governing. The Italian Parties in Parliament*. Berkeley: University of California Press.

Diamanti, I. (2007), 'The Italian Centre-Right and Centre-Left: Between Parties and "the Party"', *West European Politics* 30(4): 733–62.

Fabbrini, S. (2000), 'From the Prodi Government to the D'Alema Government: Continuity or Discontinuity', in D. Hine and S. Vassallo (eds), *Italian Politics 1998. The Return of Politics*. New York and Oxford: Berghahn Books, pp. 121–38.

Golder, S. N. (2006), *The Logic of Pre-Electoral Coalition Formation*. Columbus: Ohio State University Press.

Hine, D. and R. Finocchi (1991), 'The Italian Prime Minister', in G. W. Jones (ed.), *West European Prime Ministers*. London: Frank Cass, pp. 79–96.

Huber, J. D. (1996), 'The Vote of Confidence in Parliamentary Democracies', *American Political Science Review* 90(2), pp. 269–82.

Marangoni, F. (2013), *Provare a governare, cercando di sopravvivere. Esecutivi e attività legislativa nella seconda repubblica*. Pisa: Pisa University Press.

Miller, B. and W. C. Müller (2010), 'Managing Grand Coalitions: Germany 2005–09', *German Politics*, 19(3–4), pp. 332–52.

Moury, C. (2012), *Coalition Government and Party Mandate. How Coalition Agreements Constrain Ministerial Action*. London and New York: Routledge.

Moury, C. and A. Timmermans (2008), 'Conflitto e accordo in governi di coalizione: come l'Italia è sempre meno un "caso differente"', *Rivista italiana di scienza politica* 38(3), pp. 417–42.

Müller, W. C. and K. Strøm (2000), 'Conclusion: Coalition Governance in Western Europe', in W. C. Müller and K. Strøm (eds), *Coalition Governments in Western Europe*. Oxford: Oxford University Press, pp. 559–92.

Musella, F. (2012), *Il premier diviso. Italia tra presidenzialismo e parlamentarismo*. Milan: Egea.

Nousiainen, J. (1993), 'Decision-Making, Policy Content and Conflict Resolution in Western European Cabinets', in J. Blondel and F. Müller-Rommel (eds), *Governing Together. The Extent and Limits of Joint Decision-Making in Western European Cabinets*. New York: St. Martin's Press, pp. 259–82.

O'Malley, E. and F. Cavatorta (2004), 'Finding a Party and Losing Some Friends: Overcoming the Weaknesses of the Prime Ministerial Figure in Italy', *Contemporary Politics* 10(3–4), pp. 271–86.

Panebianco, A. (1988), *Political Parties: Organization and Power*. Cambridge: Cambridge University Press.

Pasquino, G. and M. Valbruzzi (2011) (eds), *Il potere dell'alternanza. Teorie e ricerche sui cambi di governo*. Bononia University Press: Bologna.

Saalfeld, T. (2009), 'Intra-Party Conflict and Cabinet Survival in 17 West European Democracies, 1945–1999', in D. Giannetti and K. Benoit (eds), *Intra-Party Politics and Coalition Governments*. London: Routledge, pp. 169–86.

Spotts, F. and T. Wieser (1986), *Italy, a Difficult Democracy. A Survey of Italian Politics*. Cambridge: Cambridge University Press.

Strøm, K., W. C. Müller, and T. Bergman (eds) (2008), *Cabinets and Coalition Bargaining: The Democratic Life Cycle in Western Europe*. Oxford: Oxford University Press.

Vassallo, S. (2005), 'The Constitutional Reforms of the Center-Right', in C. Guarnieri and James Newell (eds), *Italian Politics. Quo vadis?* Oxford and New York: Berghahn Books, pp. 117–35.

Vercesi, M. (2013), 'Party, Coalition, Premiership: The Role of Silvio Berlusconi in Coalition Dynamics and its Determinants', *Contemporary Italian Politics* 5(3), pp. 292–308.

Verzichelli, L. (2009), 'Italy. The Difficult Road Towards a More Effective Process of Ministerial Selection', in K. Dowding and P. Dumont (eds), *The Selection of Ministers in Europe: Hiring and Firing*. London and New York: Routledge, pp. 79–100.

Verzichelli, L. and M. Cotta (2000), 'Italy. From 'Constrained' Coalitions to Alternating Governments?', in W. C. Müller, and K. Strøm (eds), *Coalition Governments in Western Europe*. Oxford: Oxford University Press, pp. 433–97.

Zucchini, F. (2011), 'Government Alternation and Legislative Agenda Setting', *European Journal of Political Research* 50(6), pp. 749–74.

2 Party priorities, government formation and the making of the executive agenda

Enrico Borghetto and Marcello Carammia[1]

Introduction

In parliamentary democracies, the after-election confidence vote represents the foundational moment of governments. It sanctions the accountability relationship between a legislative majority and a cabinet. As in other countries, even in Italy a speech of the appointed Prime Minister (PM) precedes the vote of confidence, laying down the policy priorities of the cabinet for the rest of the mandate.[2] Investiture speeches have historically represented the key venue where Italian PMs officially outline their policy agendas. However, while the evolution of their format and substantive contents has been studied (Villone and Zuliani 1996), less is known of how the priorities spelled out in investiture speeches are formed, and notably how each coalition member's priorities, as expressed at the time of elections, are merged into the executive agenda.

The congruence between the policy content of party platforms and the government agenda should, by definition, be high in single-party government. Most of the policy priorities emphasised during the electoral campaign (and condensed into the party manifesto) should automatically become the blueprint for government action. In turn, one should expect the mechanisms of agenda definition to be more complex in multiparty governments. The cabinet agenda represents the outcome of a compromise between coalition members, and how this compromise is reached depends on the format of the coalition and the rules governing its formation.

With few exceptions, Italy has been governed by party coalitions for the last thirty years of its republican history. The formation and governance of these coalitions, however, has changed markedly over this period. Before a change of the electoral law in 1993 and the shift toward the so-called Second Republic, governing coalitions always included a dominant party, Christian Democracy (DC), in alliance with a varying set of medium sized (the Socialist Party, PSI) and small parties. Most importantly, coalitions were formed after elections, usually after secretive negotiations among party leaders. In most parliamentary democracies, the outcome of negotiations are formalised in coalition agreements, consisting in statements on policy matters and procedural rules 'inducing shared expectations and cooperation between coalition partners' (Strøm and Müller 1999: 266). In Italy's First Republic, however, those agreements were never made public.

The replacement of a pure proportional electoral system with a new mixed system created strong incentives for political parties to form pre-electoral coalitions. Post-1994 party competition (at least up to the 2013 elections) revolved around two coalitions alternating in power. Whereas in the early years of the Second Republic these coalitions did not undersign formal coalition agreements, the 2001 elections marked a watershed with the introduction of coalition manifestos by the main competitors. The second electoral reform introduced in 2006, an atypical party-lists proportional representation system prescribing electoral thresholds and a strong majority premium for the relative majority coalition, consolidated the practice of pre-electoral coalitions held together by a shared programmatic platform.

The last thirty years of Italian history provide an ideal background against which to analyse the impact on the government agenda of variations in coalition politics. Toward this end, this chapter takes an agenda-setting approach and looks at the congruence between the distribution of policy priorities in party manifestos and in government investiture speeches. The analysis of the congruence between distribution of priorities – or *policy agendas* – permits us to test the claims of mandate theory. Following mandate theory, we should expect a greater congruence between pre- and post-electoral agendas when a credible threat of being sanctioned by voters at the next elections for not fulfilling the mandate is introduced. Accordingly, the empirical section of this chapter explores whether the passage to a bipolar competition after 1993 increased the extent to which the cabinet agenda relates to the priorities that coalition parties communicated to voters during election campaigns. The analysis relies on data on party manifestos and investiture speeches coded according to the policy content coding system of the Italian Policy Agendas Project.

The chapter is organised as follows. The next section provides an overview of the changes in coalition governance that have occurred in Italy over the last thirty years, reviews the literature, and outlines some theoretical expectations about the impact of the change in coalition governance on the formation of the government agenda. A discussion of the data and research design follows. The empirical analysis proceeds in two steps. Sections 4 and 5 focus on the evolution in the format of, respectively, electoral manifestos and PMs' investiture speeches at an aggregate level, while section 6 analyses the formation of government agendas. The findings are reappraised in the conclusions.

The politics of coalitions in Italy between the First and Second Republics

Until the beginning of the 1990s, the creation and dismissal of Italian governments occurred within a party system and party competition model that Sartori notoriously called 'polarised multipartism' (Sartori 1976). Pre-1994 elections were formally run as an everyone-against-everyone contest to get the absolute majority of seats in parliament. However, no single party ever achieved the votes needed to form a single-party government. The relative majority party (the DC) only occasionally formed single-party minority governments, and these were generally very short-lived.[3] In the large majority of cases, governments had to rely on the support of party coalitions. In addition, the range of possible coalition partners for the DC was relatively predictable, because the Communist Party (PCI, the biggest party of the left) and the post-Fascists of the Italian Social Movement (MSI) were considered as anti-system forces with scarce democratic credentials. As a result, until the 1994 elections, most Italian governments relied on the support of party coalitions, with a limited alternation of some relatively small and medium parties around the pivotal Christian Democracy party.

The lack of proper alternation in government and the strongly proportional electoral rule encouraged coalition partners to bargain the division of government spoils and policy platforms after the polls were closed and each party could measure the respective electoral weight. While the distribution of government posts has undergone extensive scrutiny in the scholarly literature (see Ceron 2014 for a review), the study of coalition agreements has lagged behind. This is largely due to the fact that whereas coalition agreements have become standard practice in post-war parliamentary systems (Strøm *et al.* 2008), Italian coalitions never formalised the outcome of their negotiations. In practical terms, the lack of any text or declaration summarising the terms of the compromises reached limited the possibility of scholarly analysis.

The exclusion of anti-system parties from the range of 'coalitionable' parties (Sartori 1976) resulted in 'constrained coalitions' (Verzichelli and Cotta 2000). Membership, however, was perhaps the only element of stability of coalition governments. The inclusion of parties with distinct ideological profiles and policy priorities, coupled with the lack of institutionalised mechanisms for the definition and enforcement of shared agendas, resulted in extremely unstable governments, marked by continuous negotiations between (and within) coalition members in search of ad hoc agreements on a decision-by-decision basis. The concurrence of multiple shocks made an apparently stable system collapse suddenly in the early 1990s (Cotta and Isernia 1996). The joint action of the *Mani Pulite* (Clean Hands) investigations on political corruption, the end of the Cold War, and the budgetary and fiscal crisis of the early 1990s, precipitated a longer-term trend of growing dissatisfaction with the functioning of Italian politics.

Central to the dissatisfaction was the governance of coalition cabinets, generally understood as a crucial weakness of the system. The renewed social activism supporting the transition from the First to the Second Republic was catalysed by the 'Referendum Movement'. Its core argument, which soon escalated into general consensus, was that the 'transmission belt' between public demands and government's output was malfunctioning; and that a plurality rule would lead to a more direct connection between voters and governments, thus improving government performance in terms of both responsiveness and accountability. Since the party system showed resistance to change, this was to be achieved through the tools of direct democracy. The Referendum Movement eventually won its battle, and the parliament passed a new electoral law in 1993.[4] In practice, grafting a quasi-majoritarian law within a fragmented and polarised party system did not result in a change toward bipartism, but rather in further fragmentation. As will be discussed in the next section, however, a key departure from the old system was achieved with the creation of incentives for political parties to form pre-election coalitions (Golder 2006).[5]

Summing up, multiparty coalitions have been central to the Italian Republic experience since the post-war years, but until 1993 the terms of their agreements were never formalised. They were, rather, the object of constant bargaining among coalition members, throughout entire legislative terms. This affected coalition governance, which was generally rather inefficient, resulting in instability and limited governing capacity. To this, one must also add the lack of responsiveness of governing parties, which were perceived to disregard public priorities. The lack of transparency, effectiveness and accountability of First Republic coalitions was a crucial weakness of the system. The architects of the Second Republic tried to establish the new system on different premises. Key to this goal was the construction of coalitions around a common and publicly known set of policy positions.

This chapter tests empirically the operation of the above mechanisms between the First and Second Republics. It does so by exploring the congruence between party manifestos and government speeches. It focuses on the genesis of coalition priorities, looking at the agenda of multiparty coalition cabinets as spelled out during investiture speeches in front of parliaments, and contrasting them to the priorities made public by political parties during election campaigns. In focusing on declarations instead of decisions or public policy outputs, the analysis bypasses the operation of a number of constraints to the implementation of the government mandate, such as the difficulties in passing a legislative bill or the lack of funding available for a policy. Moreover, in looking at the genesis of coalition agendas, we restrict our focus on the transmission of priorities from political party manifestos to coalition government agendas as expressed in investiture speeches. While pre-electoral coalitions will clearly negotiate their preferences before elections, preference formation that occurs prior to the beginning of the legislative term falls beyond the scope of the analysis. Similarly, we do not explore whether those preferences reached at the pre-electoral stage remain stable or change over time. In a sense, we look at pure agenda-formation – those processes preliminary to the policy decisions and law-making activities that are analysed in other chapters of this volume – and we narrow our focus on the constituent moment of government formation.

Our core expectation is that the shift to the Second Republic increased the correspondence between the agenda of coalition governments on the one side, and the priorities spelled out by political parties during election campaigns on the other side. The shift from post- to pre-election coalitions made the Italian system similar to those with directly elected executives, which generally show higher degrees of responsiveness (Persson *et al.* 1997). The public discussion of the programmes of coalition parties has indeed been central to the election campaigns of the Italian Second Republic. In addition, the advent of (perfect) alternation to government introduced real electoral contestability, which is associated with higher responsiveness (Hobolt and Klemmensen 2008) because cabinets become sensitive to the possibility of future electoral sanctions. Against a political discourse and a public mood increasingly focused on the respect of the political mandate, the clear allocation of political responsibility to pre-electoral coalitions should have pushed governments toward incorporating electoral priorities into government agendas. Moreover, a number of formal and informal changes increased the decision-making power of the government vis-à-vis the parliament,[6] improving agenda control. Therefore, we expect that Second Republic coalition cabinets should not move too far from their electoral priorities when they take office and declare their agenda.

Of course, even in the Second Republic, coalition agendas should not be expected to be the mere reproduction of electoral platforms. Besides difference in format and language between the two agendas, a number of factors can make PMs' priorities deviate from party manifestos, including the personality of leaders or the propensity to uptake some of the priorities of the opposition. Yet, overall, there are strong reasons to expect an increase in the translation of electoral priorities into cabinet priorities from the First to the Second Republic. The system change of the 1990s provides an ideal opportunity to explore the functioning of coalition governance under different settings. While coalition cabinets have long been the subject of scholarly interest, the main focus has mainly been on issues related to the formation of coalition governments and the allocation of government portfolios among coalition members (Laver and Shepsle 1996; Riker 1962; specifically on Italy see Giannetti and Laver 2001). The governance of coalition cabinets, in turn, is a more recent object of study – not least because of the difficulty in analysing the actual functioning of coalitions. To address this question, studies of coalition governance have looked into the 'keys to togetherness' (Strøm and Müller 1999): the coalition agreements that hold together individual political parties. The study of coalition agreements has furthered the understanding of coalition governance. By permitting the crucial problems of bargaining and delegation to be addressed (Strøm and Müller 1999: 256; Strøm *et al.* 2008), agreements reduce policy conflict among coalition parties (Timmermans 2003, 2006). Recent research has gone even farther than that. In a comparative study of four countries, Moury (2013) found systematic evidence that agreements work as contracts among coalition members and are implemented to a significant extent.

The small number of observations limits the possibility to pursue a comprehensive statistical test. However, beside the degree of transposition of electoral priorities into government agendas, our analysis also explores how individual parties contribute to setting the agenda of the coalition. In particular, it explores the agenda-setting role of small and large parties, the influence of the *formateur*, and the impact of the introduction of coalition agreements on the coalition government agenda. Different roles for individual (types of) parties in the formation of the agenda mean different models of coalition agenda-building. A pure *mandate model* would imply that single parties' influence on the coalition agenda should be proportional to their electoral share (Warwick 2001, 2011). If the main party of the coalition – which in Italy has the median position in the coalition's ideological space – has a dominant influence on the coalition agenda, then a *median party mandate model* would apply (McDonald and Budge 2005). A *proposer* or *formateur model* would result in a greater influence for the party of the PM (Baron and Ferejohn 1989). Finally, a veto-player model would assign disproportionate agenda-setting power to small parties (Tsebelis 2002).

Data and research design

The empirical analysis relies on data collected and coded within a larger research project, the Comparative Agendas Project (CAP). All sentences and quasi-sentences of all manifestos and PM investiture speeches (those immediately following the election of a new parliament) between 1983 and 2006 were attributed to one of the twenty-one topic codes making up the Italian Policy Agendas codebook (see appendix A and Borghetto *et al.* (2014)). Trained coders, working in pairs, double-coded each sentence or quasi-sentence independently. In case of disagreement, codes were discussed under the supervision of the authors until an agreed solution was reached. Inter-coder reliability reached over 90 per cent in both manifesto and speech data collection. While most research on party manifestos uses the Comparative Manifesto Project (CMP) datasets (Budge *et al.* 2001), CAP data provide a better resource for our study because they apply the same coding scheme also to other policy agendas, making the study of the relationship between different arenas possible.

The coding of sentences in PM investiture speeches used a variable indicating whether statements actually had policy content. Those statements referring to the government-formation process or to some very general point about government lacking substantive agenda relevance were excluded from the study. The datasets of party manifestos and PM investiture speeches contain some 41,000 and 7,000 content-coded sentences, respectively.

In the next two sections, we map the general empirical picture of both types of agendas. We show aggregate-level findings for party manifestos and investiture speeches, and briefly discuss their meaning. Then we move to the analysis of the congruence between the priorities set in manifestos and in the PM speeches during the eight legislatures under examination.

Evolution of party agendas: manifesto data

One of the most evident elements of change between the First and Second Republics was the replacement of individual party manifestos with pre-electoral coalition agreements. Before 1993, party manifestos fulfilled their purpose by reinforcing the elements of identification of voters to specific parties. The predisposition to vote for one party instead of another was then traditionally based on social identities and political cleavages (mainly religion and class) rather than on either the content of policies on offer, the reputation of the candidates or the competence shown in government (Segatti and Bellucci 2010). Nothing precluded these documents from including references to concrete measures to be taken once elected in office, but party elites knew from the outset that voters could hardly hold them accountable for not fulfilling their promises. The heterogeneity of

Italian coalitions and, above all, the blocked system of government formation (with a dominant centrist party and alternation virtually impossible, hence little incentive for government performance) prevented voters from sanctioning or rewarding their representatives through a retrospective assessment of their action.

The new electoral system brought about a (gradual) change in the political supply. Berlusconi won the 1994 elections by creating a coalition of 'variable geometry', with right-wing forces in the South and with regionalist separatist parties in the North of the country. Faced with different and untested rules of the game, parties adopted a conservative strategy: no official coalition manifesto was drawn up to sanction the alliances. At the next elections in 1996, centre-left forces joined behind Prodi's leadership and created the *Ulivo* (Olive Tree) coalition, which won the elections. Their manifesto was the first instance of a large programmatic platform, but it did not find an equivalent in the centre-right camp. The reasons underlying these different approaches were mostly rooted in post-electoral rather than on pre-electoral calculations. Since the beginning of the Second Republic, the creation of electoral cartels was needed on the left camp because of the high degree of fragmentation and the lack of a unifying leadership emerging from the ranks of the predominant party (Prodi himself was initially a technocrat and a political outsider). Conversely, the right was unified under the strong leadership of Berlusconi, at the helm of the larger coalition party, *Forza Italia*, dealing with a lower number of satellite coalition partners.

The 2001 election campaign put strong emphasis on party manifestos. Berlusconi set the tone of the campaign with his unorthodox use of media, which culminated in the symbolic 'Contract with Italians', a document signed during a television show where he committed himself to respect the five most salient measures of the manifesto of his coalition (*Casa delle Libertà*, House of freedom [CDL]). Finally, the 2006 elections saw a renewed confrontation between the 1996 candidates for the two poles, Prodi and Berlusconi, but the new electoral law and its majority premium provided new incentives for building even larger coalitions. While Berlusconi opted for a condensed programmatic platform, the centre-left had to deal with problems of internal fragmentation. The severe problems of coalition-management resulted in a large and articulated coalition manifesto. In fact, specifying the details of each policy commitment would permit coalition partners to later keep ministers accountable in case they decided to deviate too widely from what was agreed in the manifesto. This is consistent with a key function of coalition agreements, which is to allow coalition partners to minimise agency losses when delegating to ministers of other parties (Moury 2013).

The evolution of the electoral agendas of political parties, as captured by party manifestos, is described through a range of indicators in Figure 2.1.[7] First, the introduction of coalition manifestos is associated with a significant increase in the size of these documents. The upward trend starts from the XII Second Republic legislative term, and increases over time. The trend peaks in coincidence with the XIV and XV terms, where manifestos were, respectively, one and two times

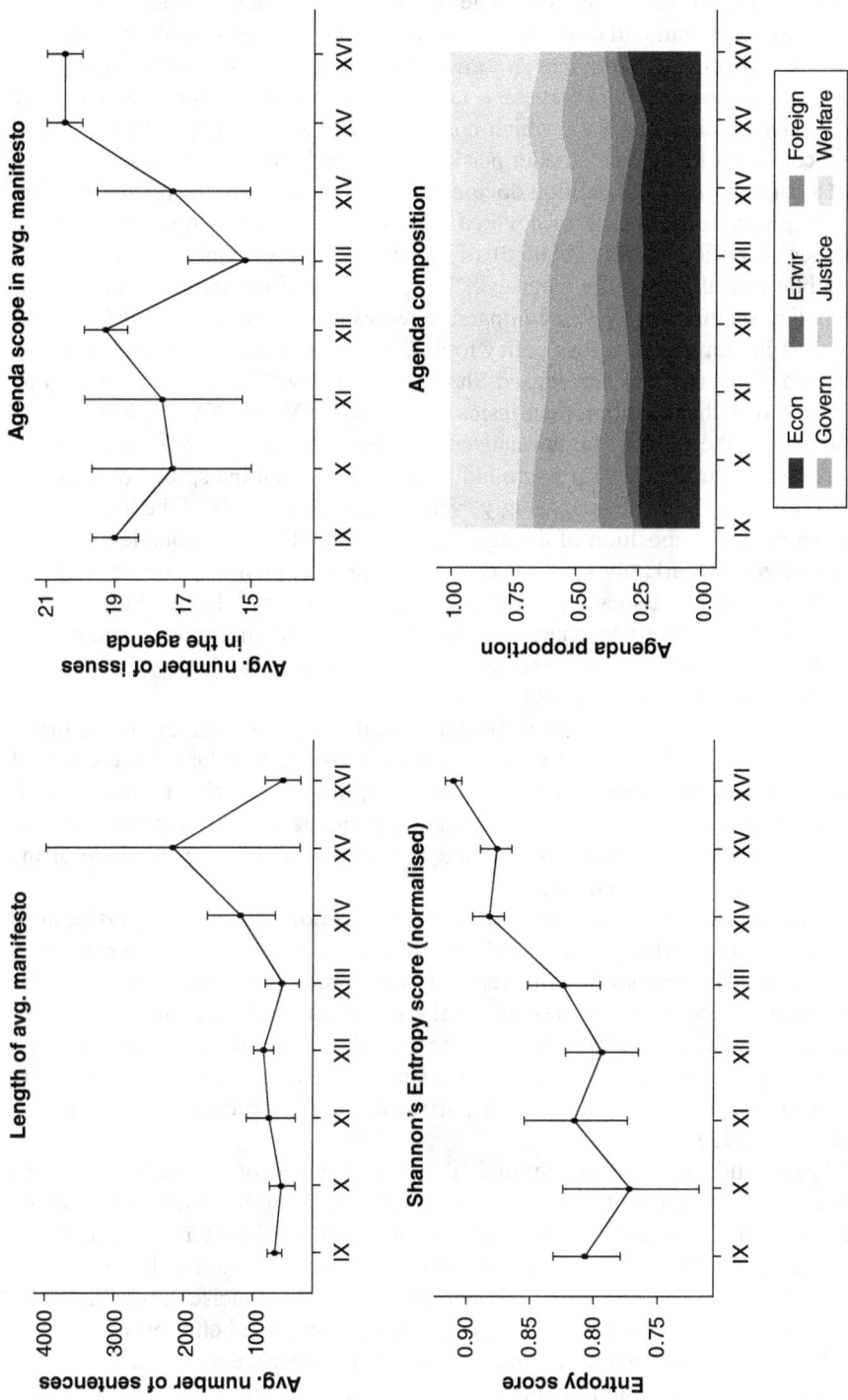

Figure 2.1 Evolution of party/coalition manifestos by legislatures

longer than in previous elections. The XV legislature stands out as well for the extremely large standard deviation in the length of documents, resulting from the centre-left manifesto being eleven times longer than the centre-right one (346 vs 3,960 quasi-sentences). The average length of manifestos then decreases in the last analysed term, the XVI, which coincided with an attempt by both left and right coalitions to exclude smaller parties and simplify the system.

The higher detail of coalition documents is not necessarily the result of higher heterogeneity in the range of covered policies. The policy scope (the absolute number of policy issues included) of an average party manifesto in the First Republic was already quite extensive. This, however, does not imply that different policy sectors were given comparable relevance. To analyse the diffusion of attention in manifestos across policy topics, we use a measure of agenda concentration or diversity: the normalised Shannon's entropy.[8] The analysis of entropy clearly shows that coalition manifestos of the XIV, XV, and XVI legislatures are in a class of their own. The normalised Shannon's entropy score increases from an average of around 0.8 up to around 0.95, meaning that the spread of attention across all issues became increasingly even. Finally, an analysis of the longitudinal change in the composition of the agenda reveals that the most notable change in an otherwise remarkably stable agenda is the proportional increase in attention devoted to welfare issues (see also Conti in this volume).[9] Topics like employment, health, culture and education, the integration of immigrants, community development, housing issues and, in general, help for disadvantaged social categories gained more space in the manifestos.

A combined reading of these indicators reveals the profound mutation of manifesto documents. Confronted with the necessity to speak to larger audiences of voters and win the support of the median voter, the two cartels of parties broadened their policy supply to a level unknown in the past. They widened the coverage of policies in their platforms, and allocated a more balanced share of the agenda space to individual issues.

In the new era of government alternation, elections rather than parties after elections decide who gets into office. Manifestos are one of the weapons in the hands of large coalitions to reach an electorate that is diverse, given the heterogeneity of partners making up the coalition, and gives increasing relevance to valence factors. In other terms, the evaluation of candidates is increasingly based on the evaluation of party leaders, their effectiveness in government, and the policies that parties commit to pursue once in power (Bellucci 2012).

Against this general background, there is evidence of a divergence in the approach of single coalitions. Coalition manifestos being the minimum common denominator among different party profiles, and being in the interest of party leaders to keep the commitment with their voters to a manageable level, the expectation is that the lower the level of fragmentation, the more concise the document. In this respect, leaders of the centre-right coalitions were in a better position, given the lower degree of internal fragmentation and the presence of a clear leadership in their camp. The same remarks do not apply to the centre-left, whose internal heterogeneity resulted in longer documents laying down in more detail the terms of the compromise.

Evolution of cabinet agenda: government declarations

Italian cabinets in the First Republic did not use to issue a clear cabinet programme or commit to a specific set of policies in front of their electors (Verzichelli and Cotta 2000). In truth, the requirement for the designated PM to deliver a speech in front of both chambers before the confidence vote, existed from the first years of the Republic. Yet, the main addressees of that speech were not voters or administrators, but rather fellow coalition parties (Villone and Zuliani 1996). A content analysis of government declarations from the period shows that they were largely filled with symbolic and generic references aimed at sanctioning the (loose) post-electoral pact among coalition partners. Decisions on specific measures were left to other arenas – either informal meetings of party leaders or parliamentary committees, where deals could be brokered not only with coalition partners but also with the opposition (Di Palma 1977).

The relative scarcity of programmatic references in one of the most publicised and significant interventions of the PM in parliament is indicative of its peculiar weight in the balance of power characterising the first forty years of republican history, when Italy was an emblematic case of strong party government (Vassallo 1994). Parties played a pivotal role by filling political institutions with their members, but also by directly influencing executive decision-making processes.[10] Given these conditions, the leadership role, formally bestowed on the PM by the Constitution,[11] varied extensively depending on the presence of multiple factors: their own and the ministers' respective political stature, minister portfolios, the political leverage of their party and the political support they enjoyed within it. As a result, Italian PMs were traditionally considered weaker than other heads of governments (Hine and Finocchi 1991).

It has been argued that the majoritarian turn of the early 1990s contributed to strengthening the PM's position, both in its positive power of policy direction and in its negative power of limiting ministerial discretion (Verzichelli 2006). The PM can now rely on a direct mandate from electors as the leader of an electoral cartel – so much so that some scholars speak of a presidentialisation of Italian politics (Venturino 2001). Three further factors might have contributed to this unprecedented visibility. A series of reforms[12] provided the PM with new tools to control the cabinet agenda and coordinate the actions of ministers. Second, the personalistic and centralising interpretation of the role of PM by Berlusconi created a strong precedent. Third, the greater frequency of European and international meetings between heads of government increased the need for strong and durable leaders representing the country.

We can use a range of indicators to read the evolution of the instrument of the PM's speech (see Figure 2.2). The analysis which follows compares the first two (IX and X, illustrating First Republic speeches) with the last four legislatures

(XIII to XVI, illustrating Second Republic speeches). The XI and XII legislatures are considered legislatures of transition and will be dealt with separately. In terms of length, the average number of sentences shifts from 224 in the First to 359 in the Second Republic. The only exception is Berlusconi who opened his fourth government during the XVI term with an exceptionally short speech. Second, speeches cover a considerably wider range of policies: the average agenda scope is almost twice as large in the Second Republic (from around twelve to more than eighteen). Third, the average distribution of attention across policy sectors measured by the normalised Shannon's entropy rises from 0.65 to around 0.8. Finally, similarly to manifestos, there is a decrease of attention to foreign policy issues, while domestic matters such as the welfare state receive more emphasis. Overall, PMs' speeches became not only longer and larger in scope, but also more balanced in the distribution of attention to different topics. The evidence shows a change over time in their format, taking increasingly the shape of articulated accounts of the cabinet's stance on a variety of issues – exactly what one would expect from programmatic platforms in a majoritarian democracy.

Reported scores point to a significant increase in many indicators already in the XI legislature. These increases largely resulted from the exceptional circumstances characterising those years. Italy had just signed the Maastricht Treaty and was under constant pressure from international markets and European partners to keep its national debt under control. Meanwhile, the national currency, the *Lira*, was undergoing a period of wild fluctuation, which eventually led to its withdrawal from the Exchange Rate Mechanism in September 1992. Finally, traditional political parties were weakened by both the unsatisfactory results obtained in the last elections and the allegations of corruption against a large number of their most prominent members.

It may be argued that these extraordinary conditions both constrained and gave a freer rein to the Amato government in setting the agenda. On the one hand, Amato had to implement a range of budget cuts and austerity reforms required by the market and the European partners. Their presentation as externally imposed conditions made it easier for Amato to introduce them in the agenda. On the other hand, the dire state of the political forces supporting his government might have pushed him to present a more articulated speech, where he tried to tie coalition partners (DC, PSI, PSDI and PLI) and external supporters (PRI) to the mast in support of his 'weak' cabinet (that would eventually last only ten months). The exceptional character of the period stands out if one considers the dramatic change that occurred in the subsequent legislature, the XII: the speech delivered by the new PM Berlusconi exhibited lowest scores in all indicators, and anticipated most of the features of the new format of government declarations in the Second Republic.

The formation of government agenda

This section focuses on the link between the issues attended in party/coalition manifestos and those discussed at the moment of the government investiture.

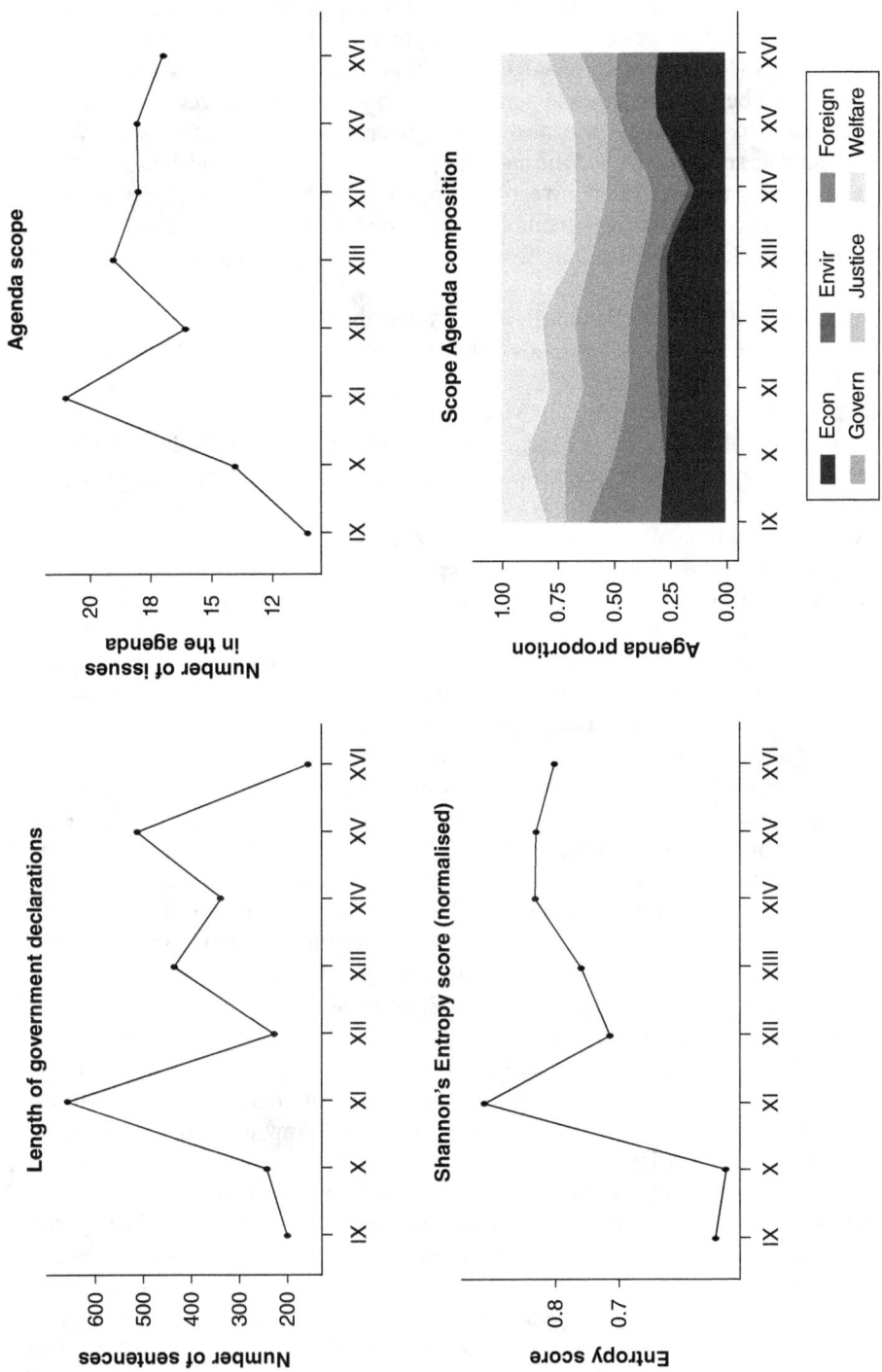

Figure 2.2 Evolution of government speeches

Previous works have examined this link from a positional perspective, asking whether the preferences expressed in party manifestos are reflected in the cabinet agendas (McDonald and Budge 2005; Warwick 2011). Here, we look at the congruence between the pre-electoral policy priorities of parties/coalitions on the one side, and the policy priorities of the government on the other side. While the previous sections showed the metamorphosis in the format and content of both party manifestos and PMs' investiture speeches, this section explores whether and how the passage to the Second Republic affected the congruence between the priorities declared in party manifestos and those set by PMs at the beginning of the legislature.

In order to quantify the similarity between the two agendas we applied the measure of 'issue convergence' developed by Sigelman and Buell (2004).[13] The maximum level of congruence is 1: for example, a score of 0.5 would indicate a 50 per cent overlap between the two agendas.

Since the first four government coalitions under observation did not issue a common manifesto before elections, to measure their electoral agendas we aggregated single-party manifestos. We computed three different versions of this artificial measure of coalition agendas. In this way, we can capture different models of agenda-building. First, 'formateur' represents the agenda of the party which is called to form the government, namely the party of the PM. According to the 'proposer' model delineated by Baron and Ferejohn (1989), the formateur is in a more favourable position with respect to coalition partners and thus will get a greater payoff in terms of cabinet posts. We explore this hypothesis in the setting of the cabinet agenda (see also Curini and Ceron 2013).[14]

Second, we measure the coalition agenda as the sum of (relative share of) salient policies in each party manifesto. Here, all party agendas are considered as having equal importance, irrespective of the size and relevance of each party in the coalition. In so doing, this approach over-represents the agendas of smaller parties. The idea behind this measure can be related to a veto-player view of coalition politics, where all actors are assumed to have the same relevance (Tsebelis 2002).

Finally, we consider the coalition agenda as the sum of (relative share of) salient policies in each party manifesto, but adding a weight to each party agenda based on its share of parliamentary seats. Smaller parties are considered here, but the relevance of their programmes is weighted to take into account their leverage within the coalition (Warwick 2001, 2011). This measure of coalition agendas captures the variation in the 'blackmailing power' of smaller coalition parties, which can threaten to exit from the coalition and withdraw their support from the government (Sartori 1976).[15]

Figure 2.3 illustrates the longitudinal variation of issue convergence between our three measurements of coalition agenda on the one side, and the cabinet agenda outlined in the investiture debate on the other side. The first remarkable finding is the leap in the issue convergence score between the last two legislatures of the First Republic and the subsequent period. The dismantling of the old party system (XI and XII) first, and then the establishment of a system of bipolar alternation in government (XIII, XIV, XV and XVI) introduced a shift in the pattern of

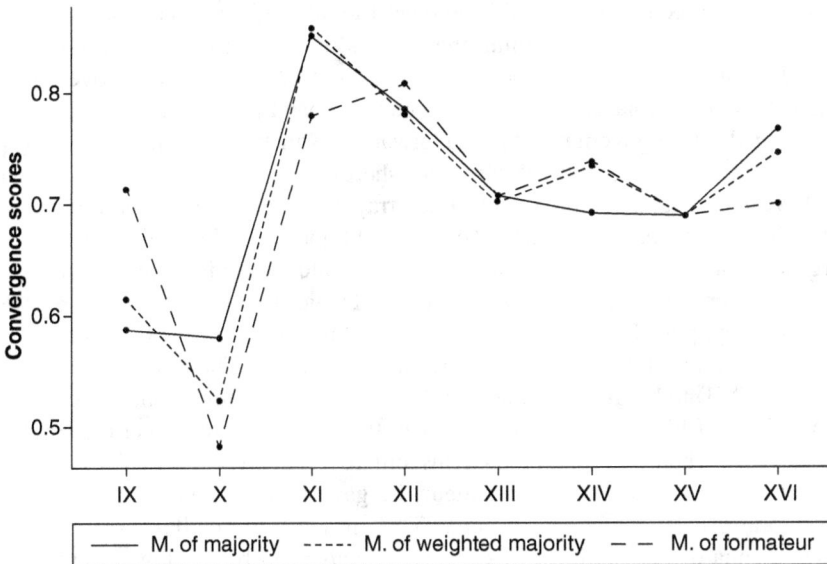

Figure 2.3 Convergence scores between party agendas and government agendas over time

agenda-formation. After the 1993 reform of the electoral law, citizens expressed a preference not only for a party but also for a governing coalition which shares a common leader and often also a common programme. In addition, as we argued above, the PM has evolved toward a role of coalition leader rather than mediator.

An analysis by legislature permits us to comment on the differential impact of the three distinct measurements of majority coalition priorities on the cabinet agenda. In the IX legislature, the highest convergence score is associated with the agenda of the formateur, the manifesto of the Socialist Party led by Bettino Craxi. This finding is clearly consistent with accounts of the strong interpretation of the premiership role by the PSI leader (Hine 1986). His 'presidential' approach, in conjunction with the creation of a core executive (an inner cabinet composed of the party leaders), strengthened his political coordination of the executive.

The low convergence score recorded during the X legislature, a re-edition of the previous five-party coalition, is strikingly representative of the disconnection between the issues debated in party manifestos and the government agenda. Aware of its 'political weakness' the government, headed by the Christian Democrat leader Goria, opted for a low-profile speech, avoiding the discussion of the most critical issues.

Although the Amato government (XI legislature) could rely on a similarly weak parliamentary majority, the high convergence scores (the highest in the period covered in our study) might be the result of 'external' factors. Recall that the speech delivered by Giuliano Amato is an outlier according to most of our indexes. Its length, heterogeneity and more even distribution across many policy topics makes it more comparable to a written platform than to a traditional parliamentary speech. Arguably, this atypical format originated the outstandingly high convergence scores. Explaining the reasons underlying the preference for a long and complex executive agenda is more difficult. As mentioned above, there might be two main explanations. One could be the strong European and international pressures on Amato's government to push forward a restructuring of the Italian budget (something he actually carried out during his short term in office). The other reason could have to do with the state of political disarray that Italian party elites were experiencing in those dramatic months (end of the First Republic), which might justify the emergence of a PM with a well-defined mandate written in conjunction by coalition partners (higher scores for majority and weighted majority scores).

Remarkably, post-1992 congruence scores did not go below the 0.7 level, irrespective of the measure of coalition agenda that we use. The strong imprint of Berlusconi (XII) to his first cabinet agenda is visible in the high congruence with the manifesto of his own party (0.81). Even though the overall level of convergence is lower when we look at the Berlusconi government of the XIV legislative term, we still find that, as the formateur, he gave much higher prominence to the electoral priorities of his own party. The influence of smaller parties in the cabinet agenda of his coalition was lower, as evidenced by the lower degree of convergence between the cabinet agenda and the unweighted electoral agenda of coalition parties. It is when we weight the relevance of parties in the construction of the coalition manifesto, thus assigning a larger role to big parties and a smaller role to smaller parties, that we find a higher correspondence. We read the comparatively lower score of the unweighted manifesto priorities in the second Berlusconi executive as evidence of his presidential style and of the lower level of fragmentation of his coalition. In turn, the last Berlusconi government, appointed after the 2008 elections, shows opposite evidence: the smaller coalition party – in that case, the only ally formally separated from the Berlusconi party was the *Lega Nord* (Northern League) – enjoys a disproportionate agenda-setting power when compared to the main coalition party. This was the result of the *Lega Nord*'s capacity to mainstream some key points of its programme, such as immigration and federalism, in the cabinet agenda (see also Conti in this volume).

When we look at centre-left governments, both Prodi's speeches (XIII and XV) share a strong proportion of priorities with the two manifestos of the centre-left coalition. During the first Prodi government (XIII), the left-wing *Ulivo* coalition enjoyed external support from the Communists, which issued an autonomous electoral manifesto. Interestingly, when we add the priorities of the Communists to the coalition agenda, the convergence between the cabinet agenda and that of the *Ulivo* neither increases nor decreases markedly. This indicates that in his investiture speech Prodi incorporated the priorities of the external supporting party, resulting in similar convergence scores of the three versions of coalition agenda.

The centre-left coalition that won the 2006 elections (XV term) issued a single coalition manifesto. This makes it impossible to explore the influence of individual parties in the coalition agenda. What is interesting here is the striking similarity between the degrees of manifesto-speech convergence for the two centre-left governments. This indicates that, even though the introduction of a public pre-election coalition agreement moved negotiations to the pre-election stage, it did not substantially affect the translation of electoral priorities on the government agenda.

In sum, we found strong support for our main expectation. In comparison with the First Republic, the priorities that political parties adopt in their election campaign are taken into much higher consideration by the coalition cabinets of the Second Republic. This holds consistently for all governments, with the partial exception of the formateur appointed at the beginning of the IX term, Bettino Craxi, who managed to have his own party dominate the cabinet agenda.

On the contrary, we did not find evidence for our expectation that the introduction of coalition agreements would increase the correspondence between party electoral agendas and cabinet agendas. While the overall congruence is higher during the Second Republic, it is not related to the existence of coalition agreements. This comes out when we compare centre-right coalitions – which either did not present a coalition manifesto or complemented it with the manifestos of their individual party components – with centre-left coalitions which always presented a coalition manifesto: the correspondence between electoral and government priorities is systematically higher for centre-right governments.

When we look at the way the coalition agenda is 'built' – relating it more closely to the role of the formateur/large/median party, or rather to the veto-power of smaller parties – we do not find a clear pattern. During the First Republic, the Socialist leader Bettino Craxi managed to give his own (medium size) party a disproportionate influence on the government agenda. In contrast, the formateur appointed after the 1987 elections came from the largest party and had very little influence on the cabinet agenda. We find inconsistent evidence for Second Republic governments too. In two cases (XII and XIV legislatures), Berlusconi's party was successful in dominating the government's agenda, as was clearest in the XIV term when the 'Contract with Italians' was formalised during the election campaign. In other cases, the *Lega Nord* acted as a veto player and exercised a disproportionate influence. In contrast, when it won the elections, the centre-left always presented a pre-election coalition manifesto, but its congruence with government priorities was always lower than it was for the centre-right. The lack of a consistent finding seems to point to the establishment of ad hoc equilibria in the governance of individual coalitions, rather than to systematic patterns of agenda-building.

Conclusions

This chapter has analysed how the priorities of coalition members set the agenda of Italian governments. Italy represents an ideal case to explore the dynamics behind the formation of coalition agendas in a quasi-experimental context. Before 1993, each party used to run its own electoral campaign with a distinct portfolio of priorities. The failure of single parties to win an absolute majority of seats led to the post-election creation of oversized coalition governments, or more rarely (Christian Democrat-led) minority governments. The programmatic platform of Italian governments was therefore negotiated by party leaders only after the elections. In the early- to mid-1990s, the consolidation of a bipolar pattern of party competition and alternation in government made governments more accountable to voters. This had a strong impact on how coalition governments and their policy priorities are formed, resulting in the shift from post-electoral coalitions with no coalition agreements to pre-electoral coalitions with (pre-electoral) agreements, increasingly incorporated in coalition manifestos.

We first explored the consequences of this change for the structure and content of both party and coalition agendas, looking respectively at party (and later coalition) manifestos and investiture speeches. We found that both changed in a way consistent with the context and institutional background. From the First to the Second Republic, party manifestos became longer in size, which is coherent with their evolution toward pre-electoral coalition agendas. The changing function of party manifestos also affected their policy scope, which became broader, reflecting the consolidation of a bipolar pattern of competition and the related need to catch larger portions of the electorate. Finally, party manifestos gradually moved toward the inclusion of more policy-oriented contents. We found similar changes in the structure and contents of investiture speeches. Moving from a largely symbolic role mainly addressed to coalition members during the First Republic, investiture speeches increased in length and in the breadth of the policy issues covered, and the distribution of attention across policy topics became more even.

We also explored a hypothesis about the translation of party policy priorities on to the agenda of coalition governments. We expected that the combination of the shift to public, pre-electoral coalition agendas, and the increased public accountability of governments, would increase the congruence between the policy priorities of coalition parties' agendas as made public during election campaigns on the one side, and the priorities of coalition governments declared in investiture speeches on the other side. The findings corroborate our expectations: in comparison to the governments of the First Republic, the distribution of priorities declared in the investiture speeches of Second Republic governments is more congruent with the (coalition) party agendas issued for the elections. Under the Second Republic, governments appear to evolve toward an electoral mandate model, with closer connection between the priorities spelled out during the election campaign and the agenda announced by the PM during the investiture speech. As the other chapters in this volume show, problems of implementation arise at later stages of the decision-making process.

When we explored the agenda-setting power of individual coalition parties, we did not find consistent evidence for any model of agenda-building. We found differences within, rather than between, the First and Second Republics. We also found differences within blocks in the Second Republic. Finally, when both single party and coalition manifestos were issued before the elections and we could compare the relevance of pre-election priorities with those of individual parties in influencing the coalition cabinet agenda, we did not find consistent evidence for an increased transposition of the priorities issued in the coalition manifesto. This suggests that, in their search for congruence with their electoral priorities, the Italian coalition cabinets did not follow any systematic agenda-setting pattern but, rather, pursued ad hoc equilibria.

APPENDIX A

The 21 Policy topics and the six macro topics in the Italian Policy Agendas Codebook

Code	Policy	Macro policy
1	Domestic macroeconomic issues	Economy
2	Civil rights, minority issues, and civil liberties	Justice
3	Health	Welfare
4	Agriculture	Environment
5	Labour, employment	Welfare
6	Education	Welfare
7	Environment	Environment
8	Energy	Economy
9	Immigration	Welfare
10	Transportation	Economy
12	Law and crime	Justice
13	Social welfare	Welfare
14	Community development and housing issues	Welfare
15	Banking, finance, and domestic commerce	Economy
16	Defence	Foreign policy
17	Space, science, technology and communications	Economy
18	Foreign trade	Foreign policy
19	International affairs and foreign aid	Foreign policy
20	Government operations	Government
21	Public lands and water management	Environment
23	Culture policy issues	Welfare

APPENDIX B

Legislature	Election date	Prime Minister	Number of days (since start of the cabinet)	Confidence vote (Chamber of Deputies)	Coalition manifestoes included in the analysis
IX	1983-06-26	Craxi I	1094 (1983-08-04)	1983-08-12	DC–PSI–PRI–PSDI–PLI
X	1987-06-14	Goria	260 (1987-07-28)	1987-07-30	DC–PSI–PSDI–PLI
XI	1992-04-05	Amato I	304 (1992-06-28)	1992-07-04	DC–PSI–PLI–PSDI
XII	1994-03-27	Berlusconi I	252 (1994-05-11)	1994-05-20	LN–AN–FI
XIII	1996-04-21	Prodi I	887 (1996-05-18)	1996-05-31	ULIVO, PRC, Verdi, PPI
XIV	2001-05-13	Berlusconi II	1412 (2001-06-11)	2001-06-21	CDL, Lega-Polo Agreement, CCD/CDU
XV	2006-04-09	Prodi II	722 (2006-05-17)	2006-05-23	UNIONE
XVI	2008-04-13	Berlusconi IV	1287 (2008-05-08)	2008-05-14	PdL–LN

Notes

1 This article is a joint effort of the two authors. Sections 2, 3 and 4 were mainly written by Marcello Carammia, Sections 5 and 6 by Enrico Borghetto. The Introduction and Conclusions were written jointly by the two authors.

2 The speech is then followed by a debate where representatives of party groups are given the chance to reply to the PM.

3 The single-party DC governments were (duration of days in parenthesis): Leone I 1963 (137); Leone II 1968 (148); Andreotti I 1972 (9); Fanfani VI 1987 (11); De Gasperi VIII 1953 (12); Pella 1953 (141); Fanfani I 1954 (12); Zoli 1957 (397); Segni II 1959 (374); Tambroni (116) and Fanfani III 1960 (556); Andreotti III 1976 (536); Andreotti IV 1978 (325).

4 Laws n.286 and 287.

5 This also explains why the move back to a proportional law in 2005 did not result in a major change to the pattern of coalitions. Not only had this law an in-built disproportionality which is rarely found in proportional representation systems; it also provided powerful incentives for the formation of pre-electoral coalitions, such as a system of thresholds that favoured pre-election aggregations, the indication of coalition leaders, and the presentation of coalition manifestos.

6 Formal changes included, for example, the strengthening of the Presidency of the Council of Ministers (Law 400/1988) and of the Minister of the Treasury, culminating in the creation of the Super-Minister of the Economy. Informal changes resulted from increased legitimacy of the government and the PM, as a consequence, in turn, of the more direct connection with the electorate that pre-electoral coalitions and 'candidate Presidents of the Council' enjoyed.

7 See Appendix B for a list of party platforms included in the analysis.

8 This score varies between 0 and 1 and it increases as the spread of attention across all issues evens out. Assuming a maximum of twenty topics in the agenda, it will get: a 1 if each topic receives exactly 5 per cent of the attention; a 0 if the speech deals with just one topic. It is calculated as follows:

$$ShannonsHnorm = \frac{-\sum_{i=1}^{n} p(x_i) * lnp(x_i)}{ln(N)}$$

where x_i represents an issue, $p(x_i)$ is the proportion of total attention the issue receives, $lnp(x_i)$ is the natural log of the proportion of attention the dimension receives and N is the total number of issues.

9 To improve the understanding of the graph, the 21 CAP issue areas were collapsed into six macro-categories. See Appendix A.

10 For instance, they could do so by 'opposing initiatives of ministers from another party, or defending explicitly the action of "their" ministers during a conflict with the PM about a specific policy competence' (Verzichelli 2006: 449).

11 Article 95 of the Italian Constitution states that the President of Council of Ministers conducts and is responsible for the general policy of the government. He is to ensure the unity and consistency of the political and administrative programme 'by promoting and coordinating the activity of ministers'.

12 E.g. law 400/1988 on the structure of the Presidency of the Council.

13 The Sigelman/Buell index was developed within the study of party competition in US presidential campaigns. It is measured as follows:

$$1-(\sum_{n}^{i=1} | PercM - PercS|)/2$$

where *PercM* and *PercS* are the percentages of the total attention devoted to a particular issue respectively in manifestos and speeches, and the absolute differences between them are summed over all *n* of the potential issues. For an application of this measure to agenda-setting research on executive speeches, see Mortensen *et al.* (2011).

14 The formateurs in the seven legislatures under observation were, respectively: IX(PSI), X(DC), XI(PSI), XII(Forza Italia), XIII(Ulivo), XIV(Casa delle Libertà), XV(Ulivo).
15 The three measures coincide in the XV legislature where only the centre-left and centre-right coalitions issued a manifesto.

References

Baron, D. P. and J. A. Ferejohn (1989), 'Bargaining in Legislatures', *American Political Science Review* 83(4, December), pp. 1181–206.

Bellucci, P. (2012), 'Government Accountability and Voting Choice in Italy, 1990–2008', *Electoral Studies* 31(3), pp. 491–97.

Borghetto, E., M. Carammia and F. Zucchini (2014), 'The Impact of Party Policy Priorities on Italian Law-Making from the First to the Second Republic (1983–2006)', in S. Walgrave and C. Green-Pedersen (eds), *Agenda Setting, Policies, and Political Systems*. Chicago: Chicago University Press, pp. 164–82.

Budge, I., *et al.* (2001), *Mapping Policy Preferences: Estimates for Parties, Electors, and Governments 1945–1998*. Oxford: Oxford University Press.

Ceron, A. (2014), 'Gamson Rule Not for All: Patterns of Portfolio Allocation among Italian Party Factions', *European Journal of Political Research* 53(1), pp. 180–99.

Cotta, M. and P. Isernia (1996), *Il Gigante Dai Piedi D'argilla*. Bologna: Il Mulino.

Curini, L. and A. Ceron (2013), 'Parties' Influence during Government Policy Negotiations: Parliamentary Dynamics and Spatial Advantages in the First Italian Republic', *The Journal of Legislative Studies* 19(4), pp. 429–49.

Di Palma, G. (1977), *Surviving without Governing: The Italian Parties in Parliament*. Berkeley: University of California Press.

Giannetti, D. and M. Laver (2001), 'Party System Dynamics and the Making and Breaking of Italian Governments', *Electoral Studies* 20(4), pp. 529–53.

Golder, S. N. (2006), *The Logic of Pre-Electoral Coalition Formation*. Ohio: Ohio State University Press.

Hine, D. (1986), 'The Craxi Premiership', in R. Leonardi and R. Nanetti (eds), *Italian Politics: A Review*. Boulder, CO: Westview Press.

Hine, D. and R. Finocchi (1991), 'The Italian Prime Minister', *West European Politics* 14(2), pp. 79–96.

Hobolt, S. and R. Klemmensen (2008), 'Government Responsiveness and Political Competition in Comparative Perspective', *Comparative Political Studies* 41(3), pp. 309–37.

Laver, M. and K. A. Shepsle (1996), *Making and Breaking Governments: Cabinets and Legislatures in Parliamentary Democracies*. Cambridge: Cambridge University Press.

McDonald, M. D. and I. Budge (2005), *Elections, Parties, Democracy: Conferring the Median Mandate*. Oxford: Oxford University Press.

Mortensen, P. B., C. Green-Pedersen, G. Breeman, L. Chaques-Bonafont, W. Jennings, P. John, *et al.* (2011), 'Comparing Government Agendas: Executive Speeches in the Netherlands, United Kingdom, and Denmark', *Comparative Political Studies* 44(8), pp. 973–1000.

Moury, C. (2013), *Coalition Government and Party Mandate: How Coalition Agreements Constrain Ministerial Action*. London: Routledge.

Persson, T., G. Roland and G. Tabellini (1997), 'Separation of Powers and Political Accountability', *The Quarterly Journal of Economics* 112(4), pp. 1163–202.

Riker, W. H. (1962), *The Theory of Political Coalitions*. New Haven, CT: Yale University Press.

Sartori, G. (1976), *Parties and Party Systems: A Theoretical Framework.* Cambridge University Press: Cambridge.

Segatti, P. and P. Bellucci (eds) (2010), *Votare in Italia: 1968–2008: Dall'appartenenza Alla Scelta.* Bologna: Il Mulino.

Sigelman, L. and E. H. Buell (2004), 'Avoidance or Engagement? Issue Convergence in U.S. Presidential Campaigns, 1960–2000', *American Journal of Political Science* 48(4), pp. 650–61.

Strøm, K. and W. C. Müller (1999), 'The Keys to Togetherness: Coalition Agreements in Parliamentary Democracies', *The Journal of Legislative Studies* 5(3), pp. 255–82.

Strøm, K., W. C. Müller and T. Bergman (eds) (2008), *Cabinets and Coalition Bargaining : The Democratic Life Cycle in Western Europe.* Oxford: Oxford University.

Timmermans, A. (2003), *High Politics in the Low Countries: An Empirical Study of Coalition Agreements in Belgium and the Netherlands.* London: Ashgate Publishing, Ltd.

Timmermans, A. (2006), 'Standing Apart and Sitting Together: Enforcing Coalition Agreements in Multiparty Systems', *European Journal of Political Research* 45(2), pp. 263–83.

Tsebelis, G. (2002), *Veto Players: How Political Institutions Work.* Princeton, NJ: Princeton University Press.

Vassallo, S. (1994), *Il Governo Di Partito in Italia (1943–1993).* Bologna: Il Mulino.

Venturino, F. (2001), 'Presidentialization in Italian Politics: The Political Consequences of the 1993 Electoral Reform', *South European Society and Politics* 6(2), pp. 27–46.

Verzichelli, L. (2006), 'Italy: Delegation and Accountability in a Changing Parliamentary Democracy', in K. Strøm, W. Müller and W. Bernhard (eds), *Delegation and Accountability in Parliamentary Democracies.* New York: Oxford University Press, pp. 445–76.

Verzichelli, L. and M. Cotta (2000), 'Italy: From "Constrained" Coalitions to Alternating Governments', in W. Müller and K. Strøm (eds), *Coalition Governments in Western Europe.* Oxford: Oxford University Press, pp. 433–97.

Villone, M. and A. Zuliani (eds) (1996), *L'attività Dei Governi Della Repubblica Italiana (1948–1994).* Bologna: Il Mulino.

Warwick, P. V. (2001), 'Coalition Policy in Parliamentary Democracies: Who Gets How Much and Why', *Comparative Political Studies* 34(10), pp. 1212–36.

Warwick, P. V. (2011), 'Voters, Parties, and Declared Government Policy', *Comparative Political Studies* 44(12), pp. 1675–99.

3 From words to facts

The implementation of the government agreement

Nicolò Conti

The context

The comparative literature shows the relevance of government agreements for the life and stability of coalition cabinets. Agreements often discipline the relationship among parties (the principal) and the executive (the agent), as through this arrangement the former compel the latter to a set of policy priorities, thus giving rise to definite expectations among voters against which to evaluate the performance of the government. According to Katz (1986), it is this process of delegation – from citizens to parties to executives – that makes most governments (especially those of a parliamentary type) work as *party government*, where parties play a role of gatekeepers of public policy and then respond to the citizens on policy outcomes on the occasion of the elections. Budge and Hofferbert (1990) argue that through this process of delegation, citizens assign a specific mandate to government based on a bounded policy repertoire. In comparative research, the evidence shows that the influence of coalition agreements on multi-party governments and on policy-making is rather effective (Dalton *et al.* 2011; Müller and Strøm 2008; Naurin 2011; Strøm 2000). Recent studies show that Italy, too, is moving in same direction (Moury 2011; Moury and Timmermans 2008). This is not only because the system has become more focused on bipolar competition, real alternation and supposedly greater accountability compared to the First Republic, when the same parties were in government for very long cycles in a context lacking real alternation. Party organisation has changed as well, the party central office and the party in public office tend to overlap more than was the case in the First Republic and there is a shift of authority from the central party office to the latter party faces (Bardi *et al.* 2007). In turn, the policy preferences of parties in the Second Republic should be more internally coherent and harmonised than was the case in the past, under the guidance of the party in public office.

In Italy, government agreements have long been either non-existent or completely disregarded, while the focus of government activities was placed primarily on office allocation and clientelistic policies (see also Borghetto and Carammia in this volume). However, in the recent past, thanks to the bipolarisation of the Italian political competition, parties and coalitions have contested the elections on the basis of more developed programmatic platforms and pledges. According to Verzichelli (2002), in the Second Republic the Italian government marked a discontinuity compared to the past with a shift of its focus from transaction (based on negotiation among coalition partners with the main goal of office allocation) to pledge fulfilment. This may have contributed to the overall responsiveness of parties and of governments, as they might have become more attentive to citizens' demands and to formulate their pledges accordingly, taking their fulfilment into serious consideration in order to maximize the popular support (Laver and Budge 1992). The empirical corroboration of this prospect is a main goal of the volume and the core aim of this chapter.

With the exception of the period after 2011, when cabinets have been based on post-electoral oversized coalitions, the Second Republic has been characterised by pre-electoral coalitions in the context of bipolar competition. These coalitions committed to a set of pledges with a promise that these would then be inserted in the government agenda. Borghetto and Carammia (in this volume) show that under the Second Republic when the government agenda has been announced there has been closer connection with the priorities spelled out by the winning coalition during the election campaign. What happens after the phase of investiture of cabinets? Have the Italian governments been able to fulfil the pledges they have been voted in for? If this congruence with pledges could be confirmed beyond the phase of investiture and throughout cabinet governance, then the Italian government would resemble a popularly mandated executive. This chapter will address these questions.

The comparative literature shows that single-party cabinets, like the British ones, are among those most engaged with pledge fulfilment (Table 3.1). However, some minority governments (Sweden), as well as post-electoral coalitions (Ireland, Netherlands), can reach high levels of implementation too (Costello and Thomson 2008; De Winter *et al.* 2000; Naurin 2009; Thomson 2001). Thus, the number of parties and the pre- or post-electoral nature of their agreement do not seem to influence the capacity of governments to fulfil their pledges. For this reason, the nature of coalition governance in Italy (largely based on formal pre-electoral coalitions with written agreements) cannot, alone, be considered a guarantee for stronger/weaker capacity to fulfil pledges, and empirical verification of such capacity becomes necessary. The analysis carried in this chapter shows

Table 3.1 Fulfilment rates of government pledges in different countries

	At least partially fulfilled (%)
Sweden 1994–2002	89
United Kingdom 1974–1997	85
United States 1976–2000	65
Norway 2001–2005	60
France 1997–2007	60
Netherlands 1986–1998	57
Spain 1993–2000	55
Ireland 1977–2007	52
Czech Republic 1992–2006	45

Source: Own elaboration of the data presented in Naurin (2009)

that despite the expectation that the pre-electoral nature of coalition agreements should induce early resolution of conflict and of transaction costs among the coalition partners, the Italian government actually lags behind other governments in terms of pledge fulfilment.

This chapter complements Chapter 2 on the making of the government agenda and Chapter 4 on the approval of government bills by the parliament. The main goal of this part of the research is to analyse to what extent the Italian government has actually fulfilled its pledges and whether this has moved toward an electoral mandate model establishing a strong linkage between government pledges and policy-making. Moving beyond the phase of investiture of cabinets (Borghetto and Carammia in this volume), and through the analysis of law-making, this chapter looks towards the next step in the coalition governance process. Ultimately, the chapter shows that the Italian government has slowly improved its capacity to fulfil its pledges, however, this has not progressed in a linear way and has not necessarily increased over time; on the contrary, there have been some set-backs throughout the process.

As was extensively discussed in Chapter 2, only recently have the Italian parties started to contest the elections with policy-salient programmatic platforms. These were sometimes proposed as coalition manifestos, other times as the platforms of the individual parties. Compared to other countries were policy-oriented coalition agreements can rely on a longer tradition and have been shown to be very effective in reducing conflict and transaction costs within the governing coalition (De Winter 2004; De Winter *et al.* 2000; Müller and Strøm 2008) and to have real influence on decision-making, in Italy this kind of tradition is lacking. However, the research in this volume shows that in Italy, too, the programmatic platforms of parties and coalitions have gradually become more articulate and cover more policy fields than in the past. Past research has showed that starting at least from 1996, the efforts of the Italian government to fulfil its pledges have become more evident, particularly through legislation initiated by the cabinet (Marangoni 2010a) and through the acts passed by the parliament (Moury 2001; Moury and Timmermans 2008). These results anticipate the evolution of the Italian system from a situation of dominance of micro-policy of a clientelistic nature that was typical of the First Republic (Capano and Giuliani 2001; see also the Introduction to this volume), to representation via mandates that guide governments in their actions. This chapter analyses the most recent popularly mandated government, the Berlusconi IV (2008–2011) that was based on a pre-electoral coalition, a case that has not yet been examined with the same level of depth as the past cabinets (see Moury 2011). I will examine the level of fit between the pledges of this government and their actual fulfilment through legislation. A comparison with the other cabinets of the Second Republic will allow us to test empirically whether the Italian government has definitely embraced a mandate model in the longer term. Indeed, the analysis of this cabinet will be inserted in the broader analysis of the executive in the period 1996–2011, when all cabinets were based on pre-electoral coalitions voted for by citizens.[1] Due to the impact of the economic crisis and of the inconclusive results of the 2013 parliamentary elections, the following cabinets led by Monti, Letta and Renzi did not have same characteristics and were, instead, based on left/right post-electoral coalitions of diverse ideology and nested interests.

The chapter is structured as follows. This introduction is followed by a section on the methodology applied in the analysis of pledge fulfilment of the Italian government. Then, a section is devoted to the description of the contents of the coalition agreement of the Berlusconi IV government. This will be followed by two sections where I analyse in-depth what parts of the coalition agreement were actually fulfilled. Then, through longitudinal analysis, the Italian government is inserted in a longer time perspective. Finally, the concluding remarks summarise the main results of the analysis and assess the level of congruence of the Italian government with the mandate model of democracy.

Method

The comparative literature has defined pledges as those statements explicitly supporting concrete institutional acts or policy outcomes. When referring to government pledges these are defined as clear actions or goals that will be met during the government term (Moury 2011; Naurin 2009; Thomson 2001). In the definition of pledges, unambiguous support refers to commitments that are not conditional on the hypothetical occurrence of given circumstances (e.g. GDP growth, or the end of the economic crisis) but are instead absolute and firm. Under the point of view of the operationalisation of the concept of pledge, it is important that there is an empirical matching part that allows pledge fulfilment to be verified and assessed. In other terms, the actions that will be taken or the goal that will be strived for in order to fulfil a pledge should be verifiable. A specific government or parliamentary act, but also a quantifiable outcome (e.g. reduce the unemployment below a certain rate) allow the testability of pledges. According to these criteria, it is possible to separate the programmatic statements between, on the one side (1) broad statements, (2) descriptions of former or current situations, (3) evaluations of past governments, (4) general rhetorical statements, (5) simple enunciations; and, on the other side (6) fully fledged pledges.

Within the research agenda on party and government pledges and on their fulfilment, the contents of the programmatic platforms of the Italian cabinets during the 1996–2011 period were systematically classified following a standardised coding procedure. The first step was to classify pledges and other statements; after this first classification, the second step consisted of the analysis of the legislation passed by the parliament in order to establish how many pledges were followed by real institutional action by this main decision-making body. The cabinet can indeed initiate legislation, however this always needs the approval of the parliament in order to become law. In this volume, Borghetto and Carammia show that Italian government has become increasingly embedded into pledge fulfilment at the time of its investiture. Other studies show that the pledge-conforming initiative of the Italian government has sometimes been high (Marangoni 2010b). However, has the government been able to influence the whole legislative process and to bring its pledge-related initiatives to success within the parliament? In pledge studies this is a fundamental question, as pledge fulfilment is highly dependent on the interaction between executive and legislative powers and this could prove far from unproblematic, especially in the presence of coalition cabinets. Hence, if the investiture speeches and the legislative initiative of the government are precursors to pledge fulfilment, their actual completion can only be assessed against the legislation subsequently passed by the parliament. In the case of pledges with broad scope (such as to reduce unemployment, or to induce enterprise at a given annual rate) the official statistics were also examined.

A method based on the analysis of the final legislative output not only completes the picture provided in the volume, it is also more reliable and empirically viable than other methods of analysis of pledge fulfilment. For example, research shows that the analysis of public opinion, specifically how much citizens think governments fulfil their pledges, shows a permanent underestimation of the achievements compared to the analysis of legislation and is, therefore, representative of popular sentiments, not necessarily of reality (Naurin 2009). Other methods that have been tried include the analysis of the distribution of public expenditure and how this fits the government pledges. However, this attempt can document only in part the real commitment of the government as, many times, pledge fulfilment implies regulatory policies with limited (or no) costs (Budge and Hofferbert 1990). Finally, an in-depth policy analysis aimed at testing pledge fulfilment (and possibly their efficacy) is bound to be narrow in scope if referred only to one policy (as the pledges supplied by a government usually cover several policy fields) or, otherwise, is very costly; moreover, some past attempts to carry out this kind of analyses showed serious problems of standardisation among policies and also among countries (Imbeau *et al.* 2001) that have not found solution in scholarly research so far. Finally, to test pledge fulfilment against the legislation passed by the parliament seems a method inclusive and parsimonious enough to give a full account of the pledge achievements of a government across all policy fields.

The data on the 2006–2011 period presented in this chapter have been collected within the comparative project on *Party Pledges and Democratic Accountability* of the Iscte-Iul of the University of Lisbon. For the longitudinal analysis of past governments I refer to secondary data presented in past works (Moury 2011; Moury and Timmermans 2008). I will also make reference to studies on the legislative initiatives of the government in order to compare the final legislative output with cabinet activation at an earlier stage of the legislative process (Cotta *et al.* 2008, 2011).

Case study: the contents of the government agreement of the Berlusconi IV cabinet

As already discussed by Marangoni and Vercesi in this volume, thanks to a large electoral victory of its supporting coalition, the Berlusconi IV cabinet (2008–2011) could rely on the support of only two *necessary* parties. Of these two parties, one had a much larger representation in government and in the parliament

(People of Freedom (PDL), 37.4 per cent of votes in the lower Chamber com-pared to 8.3 per cent of the allied party Northern League (LN)), including Prime Minister Berlusconi. Maybe for this reason, the government agreement of this cabinet replicated the party manifesto of the PDL of the 2008 elections that was immediately ratified by the LN who had contested the same elections in coali-tion with the PDL, but with its own manifesto. Despite the evident difference in size of these two parties, the fact that this time they did not issue a joint coalition agreement before the elections, and that after the elections there was no official negotiation on the government programme but only ratification of the manifesto of the PDL by LN, shows that the making of coalition agreements in Italy is not completely institutionalised yet and it often follows context.

The main goal of this section is to describe the contents of this coalition agree-ment and to define the set of pledges against which the analysis of fulfilment in the following sections will be performed. As has been discussed by Borghetto and Carammia (this volume), in the Second Republic the government-announced agenda moved toward inclusion of more policy-oriented contents and the length and breadth of the policy issues covered increased as well. The Berlusconi IV government was no exception; its programme had a wide distribution of attention across policy topics although some clear prioritisation could be seen. In particular, an effort to balance aspects of the economy and the welfare state is evident. Past research shows that these two broad domains had already been central to party competition in the past and that convergence toward a stance in favour of a social market economy has been in place in Italy starting from the 1990s, with a gradual broad convergence of the cen-tre-right and centre-left camps on these issues (Conti 2008). This convergence should not be surprising because, beyond the dramatic tones of confrontation between these two opposite camps in the electoral campaign and in political discourse in general, the ideological distance among the most relevant parties of the Second Republic has reduced, as is normal in the context of bipolar competition (Budge 2001: 82) where parties tend to differentiate on some limited issues where they exert a sort of issue ownership (Budge 1982: 49), as was the case in Italy between left and right on issues of justice, immigration, morality and minority rights.

Moving to a closer inspection of the government programme, Figure 3.1 shows that this consists of seven sections with the following headings recurring in these proportions (number of statements): economic development (24.4 per cent) and finance (6.1 per cent); family welfare (26 per cent) and public services for all citi-zens (15.7 per cent);[2] law and order (18.1 per cent); reference to problems in the underdeveloped regions of the South of Italy (6.1 per cent); the internal federalisa-tion of the country (3.1 per cent).

In terms of deepness of the statements, it should be noted that 78.8 per cent of the manifesto was made of pledges (a total of 100 statements) and the remaining part consisted of broad statements. The number of pledges of this cabinet was lower than in the preceding cabinets: Prodi I in 1996–1998 (274 pledges), Prodi II in 2006–2008 (294) and Berlusconi II–III in 2001–2006 (183).[3] This difference in size and the consequent cut in the total number of pledges by the Berlusconi IV cabinet could be a sign of greater accuracy in definition of the government goals

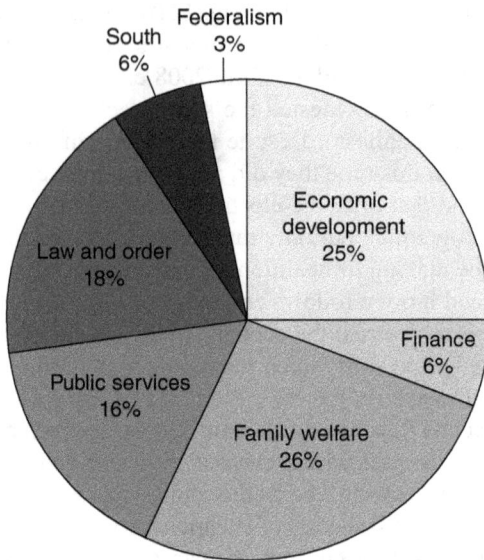

Figure 3.1 Government agreement with the Berlusconi IV cabinet by policy area

and in favour of their testability, a strategy that fits well with the mandate model of democracy. Indeed, we should remember that no past government was reconfirmed after the elections and that the popularity of the executive was always declining throughout the term because of the perceived inefficacy of the government. As Memoli (in this volume) shows, the popularity of the government is influenced (although not exclusively) by its perceived efficiency and capacity to deliver outputs and the nature of pledges announced by the government certainly influences those expectations. Those pledges that are too broad or over-ambitious could create expectations among citizens that are equally large and unrealistic. For example, a frequent criticism of the Prodi II government was that its pledges were too broad to monitor (as the total number of pledges shows), too comprehensive to be fulfilled within a limited time span (the cabinet only lasted 18 months) and that they were bound to generate a sense of confusion and discontent among voters. The reading of this over-detailed coalition agreement was particularly arduous and complicated, as it was composed of a very large number of statements (717) of which only a part consisted of real pledges (294 = 41 per cent), while the majority consisted of other statements (423). The Prodi II cabinet was often attacked, especially by the media, for the complexity and indirectness of the coalition agreement and this certainly contributed to the rapid deterioration of its support. The case of the coalition agreement of the Berlusconi IV cabinet was exactly the opposite. It was shorter in size, but very purposeful and pledge-oriented (around 80 per cent of its contents were pledges). Hence, with respect to the past cabinets of the Second Republic, this cabinet was very attentive in shaping proposals that were more limited in number, but at the same time more focused and recognisable.

Transposing the government agreement

Although the programmatic platform of the Berlusconi IV cabinet fits the mandate model better than those of past cabinets, the efforts of the government to transpose it into acts and translate pledges into reality was actually much more limited. In a previous study based on the examination of the legislative initiative of this cabinet (Cotta *et al*. 2011), it was shown that the government initiative that was congruent with its announced pledges was intense (over 60 per cent of all government initiatives) only during its first months of life; then, it declined rapidly and reached record low levels (29 per cent) by the time of its resignation. Hence, two conjectures could be raised in order to interpret this phenomenon: either pledge fulfilment was very successful in the initial phase of life of this government and left little to be fulfilled in the following phases, or the cabinet was not very committed to pledge fulfilment. It is necessary to move beyond the analysis of the legislative initiative of the government and to examine actual legislation in order to assess how many pledges were fulfilled in the end.

Following the coding method presented in the previous section, first of all I have excluded from the analysis those statements that cannot be defined as pledges. This classification is crucial for the results of the analysis, as I will contrast the total level of fulfilment only against the pledges, not against broader statements. For those platforms (such as that of the Prodi II cabinet) that presented a very large number of broad statements, the analysis of pledge fulfilment is therefore limited to a (minor) part of the platform and the rates of fulfilment could be inflated consequentially. This is not the case of the Berlusconi IV cabinet (100 pledges out of 127 total statements), but it is important to consider the inner differences in the very nature of the government agreement when comparing different cabinets.

The analysis of the overall legislation under the Berlusconi IV cabinet (as found in the official records of the Parliament)[4] shows that after 43 months, out of 100 pledges only 47 were (at least partially) fulfilled. This is a rate of less than 50 per cent and clearly not fully adequate for conformity with the mandate model. Moreover, this calculation is rather generous as it includes even those pledges that were only partially fulfilled, without distinction between complete and unfinished execution.[5] Certainly, the early termination of this cabinet was a main cause of such partial achievement. However, as is shown later in this section, a lack of coordination between pledges and parliamentary acts was already visible well before termination and was, therefore, a major characteristic of this government.

It is useful to complement the analysis with the data presented by Cotta *et al*. (2011) on the legislative initiative of this cabinet. Their data show that (with the exclusion only of proposals of ratification of international treaties that are usually consensual in nature and do not find any real opposition within the parliament), 42.2 per cent of the statements in the government agreement were actually followed by a legislative proposal that was issued by the cabinet.[6] This is a proportion very similar to that registered for parliamentary acts (47 per cent) in this study.[7] Although the objects of the analyses (government legislative initiative and parliamentary acts) are different in the two studies, the similarity of results is rather striking and suggests that despite the overall limited record, the cabinet and the parliament actually worked in strict cooperation in order to translate the pledge-oriented government initiative into parliamentary acts. However, this needs to be further specified. It is true that during the first half of its life (until 2009), the cabinet was able to coordinate the works of (its majority in) the parliament. As was found by Cotta *et al.* in the same study, this was a period of high mobilisation of the cabinet in favour of fulfilment of its own pledges. It was also the time of most intense commitment of the parliament; in the same period I was able to find 81 parliamentary acts converging with government pledges.[8] However, this record declined shortly after when pledge fulfilment was almost completely abandoned: in 2010 and 2011 only 10 and 5 convergences between parliamentary acts and government pledges could be found, respectively. This evidence corresponds with and confirms the finding of Cotta *et al.* of gradual disengagement of the cabinet from pledge implementation during its term. Conversely, the activity of the parliament did not cease as a whole, the total number of bills passed by the parliament was 43 in 2008, 79 in 2009, 72 in 2010 and 86 in 2011. It is only pledge-related legislation that went in a different direction and toward substantial attenuation. The above findings lead to the conclusion that during the first half of its life, particularly in the initial months of its term, the Berlusconi IV cabinet was really committed to pledge fulfilment and mobilised all the decision-making structures with this aim. The parliament gave support in the attainment of this goal and so the executive and the legislative branches worked in agreement and tended to harmonise with a mandate model of democracy. However, this situation was not stable during the cabinet term and things deteriorated quite rapidly. The pledge-related legislative initiative of the cabinet declined substantially, but its success rate within the parliament declined even more suddenly, as is proved by the small number of pledge-transposing bills passed by the parliament in 2010 and 2011.

It is important to describe the context where this U-turn took place. Despite the small number of parties supporting the government, the parliamentary majority proved very unstable and the main coalition party (PDL) went through a party split with the splinter group led by the speaker of the parliament, Gianfranco Fini, creating a new party (Future and Freedom) and moving to opposition. In order to survive and secure a majority, the cabinet opened to some individual MPs of the opposition who decided to support the government. From this point on, the initial government programme lost centrality, and the government activity embraced a transaction mode mainly focused on office allocation (since a number of offices were left vacant after the exit of Future and Freedom from the coalition), as was typical of the First Republic.

There could be several reasons why the focus of the government agreement moved so much during the cabinet term. I have already discussed the difficult political context where problems of internal cohesiveness arose making survival very uncertain for the cabinet. One could add problems related to the international financial crisis and to the consequent economic problems in the country which, in this period, were severe. However, beyond these factors pertaining to the domestic and international context, the focus of the analysis now moves to another factor: the different nature of the real preferences of the Berlusconi IV cabinet compared to its announced pledges.

Issue prioritisation

When we have a closer look at the pledges fulfilled by the Berlusconi IV cabinet, we find a clear pattern of prioritisation of different issues. The level of fulfilment is not equally distributed among pledges, instead some policy fields were prioritised compared to some others, none was completely neglected. In particular, the project of *federalism* consisted of a unique pledge within the platform, but an extremely ambitious one. The underlying principle was one of decentralisation of competences and resources in Italy from the state to the regional level. The works of the executive and of the parliament during the first phase of cabinet life were really characterised by the efforts to pass a bill that would make the Italian state more decentralised. This was not an easy task as this would imply a major reform of territorial politics in the country. Also, this goal should be pursued without changing the Italian constitution, as this would not find the support of the opposition that was necessary to reach the quorum required to pass constitutional amendments without a popular confirmatory referendum. Moreover, this government-sponsored project grew in a climate of reciprocal distrust with the opposition, especially because it was put forward by a majority including the Northern League, a regionalist party that in the past called for disaggregation of the country and independence of its northern regions. In the end, the majority was able to pass a broad bill (nr. 42/2009) that authorised the above decentralisation. Under the new regime, the local level of government would be financially independent from the state and should keep a considerable share of taxation locally to finance a wide set of policies.[9]

The other policy area that was most relevant in terms of pledge fulfilment was *law and order* (63.2 per cent at least partially fulfilled), followed by *economic development* (56.7 per cent), *the South* (50 per cent), *family welfare* (34.3 per cent), *public services for all citizens* (30 per cent), *finance* (25 per cent).

It is interesting to note that the programmatic platform of the government was very balanced between pledges concerning the economy and others in support of the welfare state. However, the data show that when fulfilling the pledges the main focus of the majority was actually on issues of internal federalism and law and order (Table 3.2). I have already discussed the achievements in the former field, while in the latter many measures were passed for the defence of public order, to enhance the fight against illegal immigration and crime, and to prevent violence (especially against women). The cabinet and the parliamentary majority also passed bills against legal prosecution of political leaders including the prime minister,[10] but they were removed later, after the intervention of the Constitutional Court and a popular referendum, or they were simply stopped throughout the process due to pressure from public opinion. The economy was also relevant, particularly the fulfilment of measures in support of economic development was higher than the average pledge fulfilment of this cabinet and they concerned measures to induce enterprise and to promote Italian-made goods. The balance was much less favourable with respect to the financial sector, particularly the pledges promising a reform of the state budget to reduce taxation. Certainly, the economic crisis induced a completely different trajectory onto the country from the one announced by Berlusconi and his cabinet in 2008. What is most interesting, however, is that despite the emphasis given in the government programme, the pledges concerning welfare (both family welfare and public services for all citizens) had comparatively very low levels of fulfilment.

When we compare the data in Table 3.2 on pledge fulfilment through legisla-tion with the results of the analyses carried by Cotta *et al.* (2011) concerning the legislative initiative of the government, we find again a high level of congruence. Within the cabinet, there was a strong group of ministers who influenced gov-ernment activity by proposing a large number of initiatives: the Prime Minister (who signed, or co-signed 35 per cent of initiatives), the Minister of the Economy (22 per cent), the Minister of Justice (17 per cent), followed by the Minister of Defence and the Minister of the Interior.[11] Law and order and the economy were also policy fields were we found the highest levels of fulfilment of pledges in the works of the parliament. Finally, there is high convergence between the two data sets, as the work of Cotta *et al.* shows that the legislative initiative of the govern-ment was highest in those areas where the fulfilments of the parliament were also highest. For example, the low level of fulfilment in the field of welfare corre-sponds to a low level of mobilisation of the relevant minister. In other words, the achievements of the Berlusconi IV cabinet appear very structured and respond to a precise pattern of issue prioritisation by the government and its majority.

In the end, considering the whole picture, it appears that under the Berlusconi IV cabinet the announced pledges and their actual fulfilment were very differ-ent. The government and its supporting majority were rather distant from the underlying principles of a popularly mandated executive bound to achievement of a publicly declared programme. It would be difficult (and it was not the aim of this chapter) to estimate whether the change in the policy direction of the

Table 3.2 Fulfilment rates of the pledges of the Berlusconi IV cabinet by policy area

	Pledges	At least partially fulfilled (%)
Federalism	1	1 (100)
Economic development	30	17 (56.7)
Law and order	19	12 (63.2)
Family welfare	32	11 (34.4)
South	4	2 (50)
Public services for all citizens	10	3 (30)
Finance	4	1 (25)
Total	100	47 (47)

government compared to its announced pledges was beneficial and even necessary in order to address the most urgent problems of the country. Furthermore, the economic crisis might have introduced more severe constraints on this cabinet than was the case at the time of its investiture. For our purposes and for the problems addressed in this volume, it was important to document that during its life cycle this cabinet abandoned any resemblance with the mandate model, and even those policy fields that present relevant achievements were actually very unbalanced and distant from the weight given to them in the official government programme. One could argue that the coalition led by Berlusconi contested the elections on the basis of a platform, which was also formally adopted by the new government at the time of its investiture, but this was deeply modified and finally abandoned during cabinet governance. In the electoral campaign, a specific emphasis was given to those social issues cherished by the centre-left voters, but when the centre-right won the elections and after the investiture of the new government, the actual policy-making privileged those policy issues more sensitive for centre-right voters (federalism, law and order, measures to induce enterprise), before losing any tie with the announced pledges toward the second half of the cabinet term.

A longitudinal and comparative perspective

In order to insert the analysis of the Berlusconi IV cabinet in a broader perspective, in this section I compare the results pertaining to this cabinet with those on previous cabinets in Italy and in other countries. To start with, the data show that the process of pledge fulfilment and the overall adherence to the mandate model of democracy of the Italian government was not at all incremental as past literature hypothesised. On the contrary, the Berlusconi IV cabinet marked a discontinuity compared to the past, as the XVI Italian legislature was the one with lowest levels of pledge fulfilment in the analysed period (Table 3.3). To be precise, the fact that I could only consider for this legislature the Berlusconi IV cabinet, not the technocratic cabinet led by Monti that followed immediately after and lasted until the end of the legislature, certainly contributed to this negative record. For the past legislatures (XIII–XV), I could consider the whole period and the different cabinets they included (Prodi I, D'Alema I and II and Amato II in the XIII legislature; Berlusconi II and III in the XIV legislature), because they largely reflected the same majority coalition voted for by citizens in the elections (contrary to the emergence of the technocratic government of Monti that was supported by a grand coalition that was not popularly mandated).

The past legislatures experienced mean levels of pledge fulfilment around 54 per cent, higher in the XIV (58.5 per cent) and lower in the XV legislature that was also very short (52.7 per cent). Particularly in the latter case, it should be noted that despite the government failing to survive its internal differences and uncohesiveness (that were also evident in the coalition agreement), the Prodi II cabinet managed to fulfil 155 pledges, evenly distributed during its life time between 2006 and 2007,[12] at

Table 3.3 Fulfilment rates of government pledges in different Italian legislatures (actual number of pledges fulfilled in parentheses)

	XIII legislature (1996–2001)	XIV legislature (2001–2006)	XV legislature (2006–2008)	XVI legislature (2008–2011)
At least partially fulfilled	Legislature 56.9% (156) Prodi I (1996–1998) 40.9% (112)	58.5% (107)	52.7% (155)	47% (47)
Not fulfilled	Legislature 43.1% (118) Prodi I (1996–1998) 59.1% (162)	41.5% (76)	47.3% (139)	53% (54)
Total	100% (274)	100% (183)	100% (294)	100% (100)

Source: the data on 1996–2006 were adapted from Moury (2011).

a pace comparable with that of the previous cabinets and triple in absolute terms that of Berlusconi IV. Even in the presence of narrow and diverse majorities, the cabinets led by Prodi were able to mobilise on a large number of pledges. Even when the overall success rate of the government initiated legislation was low due to the uncohesiveness of the majority in the parliament (it was only 35 per cent for Prodi II; see Cotta *et al.* 2008), the final achievements were far from negligible. Probably, it was this greater activity and the better rates of pledge fulfilment of the past executives that pushed other authors (Moury 2011; Moury and Timmermans 2008; Verzichelli 2002) to anticipate the turn of the Italian government toward the mandate model of democracy.

The longitudinal analysis of the Italian case actually raises many doubts as to the correctness of the above argument. It is possible to confirm that attention was paid to pledge fulfilment in those cases where the cabinet was made up of the same coalition winning the elections and was led by its recognised leader (Prodi I and II; Berlusconi II, III and IV). On the contrary, any change to the composition of the coalition supporting the government, or to the figure of the chief executive, resulted in a shift of the government toward a transaction model similar to what happened in the First Republic (as was the case of D'Alema I–II and Amato II in 1998–2001, and also of Berlusconi IV after a change to its parliamentary majority). In the end, there is not a linear tendency that could characterise the Italian case as moving toward a mandate model of democracy and greater responsiveness of its government on formally declared commitments. On the contrary, the Italian government appears to switch between a mandate and a transaction model: the overall capacity to propose a well-defined agenda at the time of the elections and of investiture has improved, but at the same time this improved capacity has to coexist with the most centrifugal pressures of the system (such as the undisciplined behaviour of the coalition partners and consequent changes to the majority). Although this chapter has mainly focused on the in-depth analysis of a single cabinet (Berlusconi IV), the data presented in this section show that these problems not only concerned this cabinet but also others in the previous legislatures. Government agreements, even in the form of pre-electoral coalition agreements, did not solve the problem of transaction costs within the winning coalition (Berlusconi II–III),[13] nor the most serious internal conflicts that resulted in the exit of some internal party components (Prodi I–II and Berlusconi IV). Not only were government agreements not considered mandatory by parties, also they were not considered binding enough by the cabinet that changed the ranking of issue prioritisation (Berlusconi IV), losing adherence with the original commitment with the citizens.

It is useful to compare the Italian government with the tendencies that emerged in other consolidated democracies, in order to have a more objective view on this case study. We have seen that the efforts to fulfil pledges are very evident in the United Kingdom, but also in Sweden and in countries as different as the United States, Norway and France (Table 3.1). Compared to these countries, the record of pledge fulfilment in Italy is not particularly high. In fact, the chapter documents a tendency toward deterioration of pledge fulfilment in recent times in Italy. This may certainly be due to the negative impact of the economic crisis that has unquestionably changed the government agenda and its scope of manoeuvre. However, even in the period before, the achievements of the Italian government were usually poorer than those in the other countries, although they were certainly higher than in the First Republic where pledge fulfilment was not even measurable due to the extreme vagueness of the government agenda. From an explanatory point of view, it should be noted that the reasons behind the achievements of governments that are so diverse remain largely unknown. The literature has mainly focused on the making of coalition agreements (Müller and Strøm 2008), but the determinants of their success and failure remain rather mysterious. With reference to the Italian case, this chapter has documented that the pre-electoral nature of the coalition and of the chief executive (the leader of the winning coalition at the time of the elections) positively influenced the fulfilment of pledges. However, in a similar vein to the analyses carried in the other chapters, this chapter has demonstrated that the culture that was rooted in the political environment of the First Republic has not been completely abandoned and there are several signs of continuity in the Second Republic. The fact that parties and cabinets do not consider the government agreements so binding could be a reflection of past habits, against which there have been gradual alterations but not real transformations.

Final remarks

This chapter has documented the achievements of the Italian government in pledge fulfilment and argued that Italy has not moved toward a more responsive government and has not embraced a mandate model of democracy where the government makes efforts to meet its own policy promises. There have certainly been improvements compared to the First Republic where pledges were either non-existent or very limited in number and were not necessarily conceived in order to be fulfilled. However, in the Second Republic the pattern is still very uncertain. A rescue of the transaction model typical of the First Republic – where the office-seeking orientation of parties and cabinets prevail over their policy-seeking and pledge-conforming conduct – was at the horizon of every single legislature, while intense mobilisation in favour of government pledges was confined to the early phase of the legislature.

The analysis of the Berlusconi IV cabinet was particularly informative in this respect. This cabinet could rely on an initial large majority and two necessary parties, but the centrifugal tendencies within the coalition prevailed shortly after its investiture. In the end, although this government was very accurate in definition of its pledges, their fulfilment was far from exceptional and was concentrated in the first year and a half of cabinet life. Moreover, achievements were not evenly distributed among the policy fields that were announced in the government agenda, but a clear issue prioritisation was forwarded by the cabinet and this turned into very unbalanced fulfilment of the government programme.

Finally, the results of the analysis that was carried in this chapter tend to converge with those in the other chapters. Although many differences with the First Republic are visible, the political background of Italy is still very influential in shaping the behaviour of parties and governments in the Second Republic. Some attempts to move toward an output democracy embedded in a mandate model have been visible, however these coexist with pressures of opposite sign that aim at keeping the transaction model into existence. In the end, the path from the First to the Second Republic has been long and rich in innovation, but less conducive to real change.

Notes

1 Some asymmetries between the pre-electoral and the actual government coalitions should be noted in legislature XIII (1996–2001), as the communist party *Rifondazione comunista* split in 1998 and only one faction continued to support the government, while at the same time some centrist MPs elected with the opposition became part of the majority.
2 This category actually includes 2/3 of references to public health and education and 1/3 to protection of the environment.
3 The data for the Berlusconi IV and Prodi II cabinets are original and were collected specifically within this project, while I refer to Moury (2011) for calculations on the other cabinets. All data were collected making use of a homogeneous coding scheme.
4 Available at http://www.camera.it.
5 The analysis of pledge fulfilment usually does not separate complete from partial fulfilment, as this level of depth is often difficult to reach.
6 In their study, Cotta *et al.* did not distinguish between pledges and other statements, therefore their calculations include all 127 statements of the government agreement.
7 This proportion was, instead, calculated only against pledges (100).
8 It is important to note that every pledge can be transposed into more than one bill, this is the reason why the total number of pledge/bill convergences is higher than the total number of fulfilled pledges (47). At the same time, a single bill could transpose more than one pledge.
9 However, most of these goals remained unachieved because in order to be implemented the bill required many decree laws to be issued, but the resignation of Berlusconi in 2011

came too early in the process and so the task was not completed. The following cabinets, in particular Monti's, took a different direction in support of re-centralisation, so the process of devolution started by the Berlusconi IV cabinet has regressed in the following years.

10 This was a particularly sensitive issue for Berlusconi, who was under trial while in office under several allegations including fiscal fraud, abuse of *office* and having paid for sexual services with an underage girl.

11 The Minister of Foreign Affairs is not included in the calculation as most of his initiatives concerned ratification of international treaties and were technical acts of a consensual nature.

12 The government received a no confidence vote on 24 January 2008.

13 The Berlusconi III cabinet was not so different from the Berlusconi II and could rely on the same majority. It mainly consisted of a reshuffle of the previous cabinet, with generous rewards in office allocation paid to the most recalcitrant coalition partners.

References

Bardi, L., Ignazi, P. and Massari, O. (eds.) (2007), *I Partiti Italiani*, Milan: Università Bocconi Editore.

Budge, I. (1982), 'Electoral Volatility: Issue Effects and Basic Change in 23 Post-war Democracies', *Electoral Studies*, 1(2), pp. 147–168.

Budge, I. (2001), 'Theory and Measurement of Party Policy Positions', in I. Budge *et al.* (eds) *Mapping Policy Preferences. Estimates for Parties, Electors, and Governments 1945–1998*, Oxford: Oxford University Press.

Budge, I. and Hofferbert, R.I. (1990), 'Mandates and Policy Outputs: U.S. Party Platforms and Federal Expenditures', *American Political Science Review*, 84(1), pp. 111–131.

Capano, G. and Giuliani, M. (2001), 'Governing Without Surviving: An Italian Paradox', *Journal of Legislative Studies*, 7(4), pp. 13–36.

Conti, N. (2008), 'The Italian Parties and their Programmatic Platforms: How Alternative?', *Modern Italy*, 13(4), pp. 451–464.

Costello, R. and Thomson, R. (2008), 'Election Pledges and their Enactment in Coalition Governments: A Comparative Analysis of Ireland', *Journal of Elections, Public Opinion and Parties*, 18(3), pp. 239–256.

Cotta, M., Marangoni, F. and Verzichelli, L. (2008), *Rapporto sul governo*, Centre for the Study of Political Change (CIRCaP), University of Siena, available online at http://www.circap.org/government-reports.html.

Cotta, M., De Giorgi, E., Marangoni, F. and Verzichelli, L. (2011) *Rapporto sul governo*, Centre for the Study of Political Change (CIRCaP), University of Siena, available online at http://www.circap.org/government-reports.html.

Dalton, R.J., Farrell, D.M. and McAllister, I. (2011), *Political Parties and Democratic Linkage: How Parties Organize Democracy*, Oxford: Oxford University Press.

De Winter, L. (2004), 'Government Declarations and Law Production', in H. Döring and M. Hallerberg (eds), *Patterns of Parliamentary Behaviour: Passage of Legislation across Western Europe*, Aldershot: Ashgate, pp. 35–56.

De Winter, L., Timmermans, A. and Patrick, D. (2000), 'On Government Agreements, Evangelists, Followers and Heretics', in W.C. Müller and K. Strøm (eds), *Coalition Governments in Western Europe*, Oxford: Oxford University Press, pp. 300–355.

Imbeau, L.M., Pétry, F. and Lamari, M. (2001), 'Left☐right Party Ideology and Government Policies: A Meta-analysis', *European Journal of Political Research*, 40(1), pp. 1–29.

Katz, R.S. (1986), 'Party Government: A Rationalistic Conception', in F.G. Castles and R. Wildenmann (eds), *Visions and Realities of Party Government*, Berlin: De Gruyter, pp. 31–71.

Laver, M.J. and Budge, I. (1992), *Party Policy and Government Coalitions*, New York: St. Martin's Press.

Marangoni, F. (2010a), 'Programma di governo e law-making: un'analisi della produzione legislativa dei governi italiani (1996–2009)', *Polis*, 1, pp. 35–64.

Marangoni, F. (2010b), 'The First Two Years of Berlusconi's Fourth Government: Activity and Legislative Performance', *Bulletin of Italian Politics*, 1, pp. 121–136.

Moury, C. (2011), 'Italian Coalitions and Electoral Promises: Assessing the Democratic Performance of the Prodi I and Berlusconi II Governments', *Modern Italy*, 16(1), pp. 35–50.

Moury, C. and Timmermans, A. (2008), 'Conflitto e accordo in governi di coalizione: il caso Italia', *Rivista Italiana di Scienza Politica*, 38(3), pp. 417–442.

Müller, W.C. and Strøm, K. (2008), 'Coalition Agreements and Cabinet Governance', in W.C. Müller, K. Strøm and T. Bergman (eds), *Cabinets and Coalition Bargaining*, Oxford: Oxford University Press, pp. 159–199.

Naurin, E. (2009), *Promising Democracy, Parties, Citizens and Election Promises*, Gothenburg: Gothenburg University Press.

Naurin, E. (2011), *Election Promises, Party Behaviour and Voter Perceptions*, Basingstoke: Palgrave Macmillan.

Strøm, K. (2000), 'Delegation and Accountability in Parliamentary Democracies', *European Journal of Political Research*, 37(3), pp. 261–289.

Thomson, R. (2001), 'The Program to Policy Linkage: The Fulfilment of Election Pledges on Socio-Economic Policy in the Netherlands, 1986–1998', *European Journal of Political Research*, 40(2), pp. 171–197.

Verzichelli, L. (2002), 'La formazione del governo parlamentare: tra vincoli antichi e potenziamento istituzionale', *Quaderni di Scienza politica*, 9(1), pp. 145–181.

4 Looking beyond the aggregate figures

An investigation of the consensual approval of Italian government bills

Andrea Pedrazzani

Introduction

Policymaking in contemporary parliamentary democracies appears to be dominated by executives. The vast majority of legislative proposals are drafted in governmental offices, and most of these bills become laws (see Andeweg and Nijzink 1995; Gamm and Huber 2002). Still, legislatures seem to retain a fundamental role in the lawmaking process. Legislative bodies are not merely 'rubber stamps' for governmental proposals. As a growing research programme has illustrated, during the legislative process, parliamentary institutions are employed by coalition parties to manage the tensions arising among them and make joint policy (Martin and Vanberg 2004, 2005, 2011). Moreover, all major policy initiatives normally require the final approval of parliament, and hence investigating what happens in the precise stage when parliamentary approval is given can be extremely informative. Which is the outcome of the parliamentary voting stage? Are bills supported by a scanty majority of legislators, or do they enjoy the votes of very large portions of the assembly? Most of all, are bills backed just by the representatives forming the legislative majority, or do they (also) receive the votes of members of the opposition?

Analysing the parliamentary voting stage can thus be useful for an evaluation of the level of cooperation among the legislators (and the parties) that are present in the assembly, as well as for a deeper understanding of the dynamics between executive and legislative and the relationships within the legislative majority.[1] Undoubtedly, the topic is especially relevant for government-sponsored legislation. In the case of the bills initiated by the executive, a wide support in the assembly means that at least part of the opposition is voting with the majority.

The study of the parliamentary support for government legislation seems particularly interesting in Italy's Second Republic. As commonly acknowledged, despite harsh confrontation between parties in the public debate, Italian legislation (including government bills) has usually been approved by very large parliamentary majorities (e.g., Di Palma 1977; Giuliani 1997), and the consensualism characterizing Italian lawmaking seems to have survived even the end of the First Republic and the shift to the alternational and (would-be) majoritarian Second Republic (Capano and Giuliani 2001a, 2001b, 2003).

Up to now, the literature on Italy has primarily focused on the aggregate figures of the degree of support gained by laws at the final voting stage in the parliament, while the internal differences between more and less consensual processes remain a rather understudied topic (Giuliani 2008). However, a deeper inspection reveals that not all the bills introduced by the Italian governments are approved in a consensual manner. Their approval can be more universal in some cases, and more strictly majoritarian in others.

Aiming to investigate such a variance, this work will analyse data on the legislative production of Italian governments over a relatively long period of time (1988–2008). The chosen time span thus covers four Second Republic legislatures and, as a point of comparison, two First Republic parliamentary terms.

This chapter is organized as follows. The next section presents the Italian case, focusing on the consensual patterns of lawmaking emphasized in the literature, and in particular on the remarkable degree of support that, on average, legislation receives in the Italian parliament. Trying to go one step further, the third section discusses a number of theoretical explanations that can account for variation in the level of consensus through which government legislation is passed in parliament. The considered explanatory hypotheses are drawn both from the comparative research on parliamentary systems and from the literature on the U.S. Congress. This work also assesses the impact of two original factors that are specifically related to the processes through which bills are approved: the length of the legislative process and the extent to which bills are modified in parliament before approval. Taking into account these two important process-related aspects that are particularly relevant in the Italian case contributes to explaining what happens at the final voting stage in the parliament.

The fourth section introduces the dataset and describes the dependent variables employed in my analyses, while the operationalization of the independent variables is discussed in the fifth section. The results of the analyses are illustrated in the sixth section, and concluding remarks are presented in the final section.

Lawmaking in the Second Republic: consensus in a (wished-for) majoritarian setting

The consensual nature of Italian lawmaking has quickly become common wisdom in the literature.[2] Starting from the first contributions in the 1960s and 70s, scholars have documented that cooperative practices have been extensively employed throughout the legislative process in Italy. Consensualism has characterized the introduction of legislation, the amendatory process, the assignment of bills to parliamentary committees, and the final voting (Allum 1973; Blondel 1988; Cotta 1994; Di Palma 1977; Furlong 1990; Hine 1993; Hine and Finocchi 1991; Spotts and Wieser 1986). As for the last aspect, which is the primary concern of the present work, Italian legislation has generally been approved by very large parliamentary majorities, and this has been true also for the laws introduced by the cabinet. In spite of this consensualism, government and opposition parties have usually confronted each other fiercely in public debates and electoral campaigns, behaving as ideologically irreconcilable adversaries.

In his seminal work, Di Palma (1977: 85–89) found that the laws approved in the 1948–1972 period obtained, on average, 81 per cent of favourable votes (see also Cazzola 1975).[3] Moreover, more than 70 per cent of the legislation tabled by the government was adopted with the favourable vote of the largest opposition party (i.e., the Communists), and this percentage increases to 80 per cent taking abstentions into account.[4] In addition, permanent committees became the main arena for consensual practices: a large part of legislation was adopted in committee (see Della Sala 1993), and the opposition parties only rarely opposed the decision to endow a committee with direct legislative powers, thus showing a clearly cooperative attitude towards the government (Di Palma 1977: 90, 260 ff.).[5]

More recently, De Micheli's (1997) analysis of the effectiveness of Italian executives confirmed these traits. The author showed that the tendency on the part of Italian opposition to sustain government legislation persisted in the last period of the First Republic (1983–1994), and that this cooperative style, which was typical of the works of parliamentary committees, was increasingly adopted also on the floor (see also Morisi 1992).

In order to measure consensual lawmaking in the Italian parliament, Giuliani (1997) proposed a cumulative index that adds together the proportion of laws directly passed by committees and the proportion of laws approved on the floor with only minor opposition (i.e., fewer than 30 votes against). As shown in later works, over the last three decades the portion of laws adopted in a non-consensual manner by the Italian parliament has never exceeded 30 per cent. In particular, consensual practices have survived the shift from the First to the Second Republic by simply changing their institutional setting. They have just moved from the committees to the floor of the assembly: since the beginning of the 1990s the portion of laws adopted by committees has decreased, while in the same period there has been an almost equivalent increase in the portion of laws approved on the floor by very large majorities (Capano and Giuliani 2001a, 2001b; Giuliani 2008).[6]

The persistence of consensualism in the Italian parliament is striking if we take into account the major changes that occurred in the mid-1990s, which were expected to move Italy towards a more majoritarian direction: the adoption of a quasi-plurality electoral system in 1993 (D'Alimonte and Chiaramonte 1995; Katz 1996), the establishment of a bi-polar party system (Newell 2000), the emergence of clear electoral majorities after elections (Bartolini and D'Alimonte 1998), and the emergence and consolidation of government alternation (Zucchini 2013). Although these fundamental changes should have had some impact on the level of parliamentary consensus when government bills are voted on, Giuliani (2008: 65–66) reports that, in the XIII and XIV legislatures (i.e., from 1996 to 2006), legislation was approved with an average 91.7 and 88.7 per cent of favourable votes, respectively.[7] Hence, in the analysis of the degree of support that Italian government legislation enjoys at the final voting stage, we should observe no particular differences in the parliamentary majority supporting governmental laws between the First and the Second Republics.

Accounting for variation

If research on Italian lawmaking suggests we should expect fairly high levels of parliamentary support when government legislation is voted on even in the Second Republic, important studies on parliamentary systems and the literature on the U.S. Congress can help us explain the possible variation in such levels of consensus, identifying the conditions under which voting outcomes can be strictly majoritarian. First of all, the degree of consensualism that characterizes the approval of governmental laws may depend on the conflict between majority and opposition, and, more generally, on the complexity of the bargaining environment at the voting stage in the parliament. The support that government bills gain when they are voted on in parliament may be affected also by the proposer's ability to build consensus in the assembly. Second, as highlighted by the literature on the Congress, whether the approval of bills is universal or strictly majoritarian can be related to the presence of vote trading among legislators, and to the need to reach rapid decisions. Third, process-related factors, such as the length of the legislative process and the extent to which bills are modified in parliament, can also account for variation in the outcomes of the voting stage.

Opposition, parliamentary bargaining environment and technical ministers

Unsurprisingly, parliamentary studies have identified government–opposition relations as one of the main factors explaining legislative outcomes. In parliamentary government systems, the endogenously generated discipline of legislative parties allows the executive to rely on the votes of a (quite possibly ever-changing) parliamentary support coalition (Laver 2006). Since the parties supporting the cabinet are reasonably likely to vote for governmental initiatives, the approval of government bills by very large legislative majorities thus indicates that at least part of the opposition has voted with the government. The members of the opposition may have various reasons to support bills sponsored by the government: generally speaking, time is extremely scarce in legislatures (Döring 1995b; Cox 2006), and the parliamentary minority might extract some concessions from the cabinet in exchange for not delaying the approval of government legislation. Therefore, although controlling too few votes to block governmental initiatives, opposition parties can use their delaying powers to secure some benefits for their respective constituencies. Several important comparative studies highlight the influence that, due to its ability to use parliamentary procedures, the opposition exerts in parliamentary lawmaking (e.g., Döring 1995a; Müller and Strøm 2000; Powell 2000; Saalfeld 2000) and, in the Italian case, opposition parties have been commonly described as particularly effective in conditioning legislative outcomes and delaying legislation (Strøm 1990; Cox *et al.* 2008). For the purposes of the present work, we can argue that the lower their policy distance from the government position, the more likely opposition members will be to vote with the government. As a consequence, we can expect that: *The higher the conflict between government and opposition, the narrower will be the majority approving government legislation (Hypothesis 1).*

More generally, the probability that government legislation is approved by a very large parliamentary majority (in the extreme case, by the unanimity of the assembly) may depend on the complexity of the bargaining environment in parliament. The more complex it is to bargain in the assembly, the less likely it is to reach broad agreements on legislation. In Strøm *et al.*'s (2008) bargaining-based framework of coalition governance, which the authors apply to the entire coalition's life cycle, bargaining complexity is defined as a situation where actors are faced with a relatively high number of options – i.e., many possible alternative coalitions appear viable (see also Laver and Schofield 1990: 162).[8]

As the literature on coalition politics has pointed out, bargaining complexity stems from the number of parties, their size, and their policy preferences (Laver and Schofield 1990; Warwick 1994; Strøm and Müller 1999; Grofman 1989; Taagepera and Grofman 1985). In the legislative process, the higher the number of parties, the higher the array of possible parliamentary coalitions supporting legislation and approving it. A high number of parliamentary parties is also likely to extend the range of preferences that must be taken into account if comprehensive agreements are pursued, and to increase the dimensionality of the potential legislative coalition. Of course, the number of parties is related to the distribution of resources in the parliamentary party system, and the seat shares of parties determine their respective bargaining powers. As for party preferences, bargaining complexity is likely to increase the wider the policy divisions in the parliament, and the higher the number of relevant policy dimensions involved in the decision. With regard to this last point, when government legislation addresses more than one policy domain, then both debate and deliberation in the parliament take place in a multidimensional policy space, where the final outcome is not easily predictable by anyone (Plott 1967; McKelvey 1976; Schofield 1978). In the Italian case, the complexity of parliamentary bargaining has been shown to affect both legislative outcomes and government formation (see, e.g., Di Palma 1977; Zucchini 2001).

Summing up, when the parliamentary party system is highly fragmented, ideological divergence in the legislature is particularly severe, or parliamentary debate involves many policy dimensions, broad agreements on legislation encompassing parties from both the government and the opposition become unlikely. In this situation, parliamentary voting on government bills will probably reflect the divide between government and opposition.[9] In other words: *The majority approving government legislation will be narrower the more complex is the parliamentary bargaining – i.e., the higher the fragmentation of the parliamentary party system, the wider the ideological divisions in parliament, the higher the number of policy dimensions involved (Hypothesis 2).*

Parliamentary scholars are recently devoting growing attention to technical members of the cabinet. The topic has become particularly relevant during the Second Italian Republic, where technocrats have been more often appointed as ministers and two fully technocratic governments were formed – the last one in late 2011 (see, e.g., Verzichelli and Cotta 2012). Unlike their partisan colleagues, who represent the party they belong to in the cabinet, technical ministers are assigned portfolios because of their competence in a certain policy area. For our purposes: *We should expect larger majorities supporting governmental bills when these bills are introduced by technical ministers (Hypothesis 3).*

This can happen for a couple of reasons. First, technical ministers are usually acknowledged experts in the policy domain on which they have jurisdiction, and are reasonably expected to draft legislation according to their expertise. Hence, the bills introduced by technical ministers are likely to be viewed as programmes devised on the basis of merely technical considerations, and not on the basis of partisan preferences. This should induce both the parties in government and those in the opposition to support technical ministers' legislation. Second, the parties forming government coalitions are subject to position-taking incentives (Huber 1996), and ministers initiate legislation also for the purpose of communicating with voters and maximizing support for their own party (Martin and Vanberg 2011). However, this is not true for technical ministers, who neither represent a certain political party or constituency, nor do they seek to be re-elected. Parties can thus be quite sure that the legislation they are voting on does not constitute a partisan message delivered to the electorate.[10]

Logrolling and legislative patience

The type of outcome in the legislative voting stage has been explicitly studied by the literature on the U.S. Congress. This fundamental body of scholarship has traditionally employed a distributive approach on legislative organization, whereby public policy is conceived as the result of the conflicting interests of representatives with geographically based constituencies, and is thus studied as a distributive problem among districts (e.g., Shepsle 1979a, 1979b; Shepsle and Weingast 1981; Weingast *et al.* 1981; Weingast and Marshall 1988; Baron and Ferejohn 1989). One of the concerns in these studies has long been whether legislative equilibria are strictly majoritarian or universal. A strictly majoritarian equilibrium would allocate benefits to a minimal majority, thus reflecting the majoritarian nature of the voting rule. This is what Riker's (1962) theory of minimal winning coalitions predicts. By contrast, a universal equilibrium would imply unanimous passage of legislation and universal distribution of benefits, and this is predicted by Weingast's (1979) model of legislative game.

In a seminal article, Weingast, Shepsle and Johnsen (1981) highlight that universalism and logrolling are the typical legislative practices when policymaking concerns distributive issues. Distributive bills concentrate benefits in some specific districts and spread costs through generalized taxation, and are used by politicians for their re-election purposes (Wilson 1973: 333–334). When the legislature examines a bill providing particularistic benefits for some geographical constituency or for a certain interest group, such a proposal is unlikely to be supported by a legislative majority. However, a set of distributive bills can be approved with very large majorities because of mutual exchanges of votes among parties (or any other groups of legislators), with each party supporting other bills in exchange for votes on the bill it is most interested in (Tullock 1981; Collie 1988; see also Carrubba and Volden 2000; Crombez 2000).[11] *We thus should expect broader majorities supporting governmental bills when these bills are distributive (Hypothesis 4).*[12]

Indeed, the Italian parliament has been traditionally considered as an appropriate setting for the application of a distributive perspective, and the pork-barrel nature of Italian legislation is emphasized also in recent studies (see, e.g., Cotta 1994; Golden and Picci 2008).

In illustrating their model of legislative bargaining, Baron and Ferejohn (1989) identify another condition under which the voting equilibrium in the legislature can be universal: legislative actors' preference to reach agreements quickly rather than slowly. According to the model, under an open rule the voting outcomes depend on the level of impatience in the legislature: if delay in the passage of legislation is not so costly, the outcome is majoritarian, with benefits allocated to a minimal majority; if, instead, immediate passage of legislation is a necessity, the benefits may be distributed among a supermajority.

Being impatient means discounting the utility of future payoffs, and, for elected politicians, approaching a new election is the major reason to be impatient. At the beginning of the term, legislative actors reasonably expect to have enough time to pass legislation. As the term proceeds, the time for approving bills gets shorter and shorter, and hence the value that is assigned to future benefits or policy achievements progressively decreases. When the end of the term is near, such a value is very close to zero. Therefore, as new elections approach, the legislative majority supporting the government can be more inclined to make concessions to opposition parties in order to assure the approval of its bills. In other words: *We should expect larger majorities supporting governmental bills when patience is lower in the legislature (Hypothesis 5).*

Length of legislative process and parliamentary changes

The theoretical arguments discussed so far consider as explanatory factors some particular attributes of the parliamentary party system (number, size, preferences of parties), some features of the context in which the debate takes place (number of policy dimensions involved, level of impatience), or certain characteristics of the bills (distributive nature, type of proposer). As suggested in the literature, all of these may help explain why the approval of government bills is more universal in some cases, and more strictly majoritarian in other cases. However, none of these explanations takes into account explicitly what happens to legislation during the parliamentary process – i.e., between the introduction of bills in parliament and the final voting stage. This section discusses two factors that are specifically related to the legislative process: its duration and the extent to which legislation is modified in parliament before being approved.

Reasonably, both many days spent in parliament and huge changes undergone before approval should result in large majorities, involving also the opposition, when government bills are voted on. Long parliamentary processes might indicate that legislative actors are spending time and effort to reach broad agreements. When parties (both from the government and the opposition) negotiate a lot in the legislature, they slow down the entire process, but the policy they finally agree on is likely to be acceptable to a large portion of the legislature, and will probably be passed with the support of a wide legislative majority. Similarly, if a bill introduced by a certain cabinet minister is heavily altered in parliament, we can imagine that, for some reason, the government is trying to involve the opposition in rewriting the initial proposal. Hence, extensively amended bills should be approved by large majorities. Based on these arguments: *We should expect larger majorities supporting governmental bills the longer the legislative process (Hypothesis 6a) and the more governmental bills are altered in the legislature (Hypothesis 7a).*

Remarkably, recent research on policymaking in multiparty executives suggests a different interpretation of both the length of the legislative process and the parliamentary changes made to government bills. Focusing on delegation relationships in coalition cabinets, Martin and Vanberg (2004, 2005, 2011) show that coalition parties use parliamentary institutions to monitor each other. More precisely, the authors find that coalition members scrutinize the bills proposed by ministers from other coalition parties, which results in longer processes and larger changes to the initial drafts.[13] In this view, both legislative time and parliamentary changes are considered as instruments handled only by the governing parties. The opposition is not expected to be involved, and government legislation should be approved just by the legislative majority supporting the cabinet. According to this perspective, *we should expect narrower majorities supporting governmental bills the longer the legislative process (Hypothesis 6b) and the more governmental bills are altered in the legislature (Hypothesis 7b).*

Measuring consensus

The data used for my empirical analysis of the degree of support that governmental legislation enjoys at the final voting stage in Italy include four Second Republic legislatures (1994–1996, 1996–2001, 2001–2006, 2006–2008) and, as a term of comparison, two First Republic legislatures (1987–1992, 1992–1994). The chosen time period starts in 1988, when the requirement of a secret ballot for the final vote on bills was abolished in the Chamber of Deputies, and thus covers 20 years of the legislative production of Italian governments.[14]

The dataset tracks the parliamentary history of all laws introduced by Italian cabinets in the Chamber (as first reading), and approved on the floor with open roll call in the considered period.[15] Some particular types of government laws have not been included in the dataset. Besides removing bills directly adopted by committees and those approved with secret voting, I excluded constitutional laws, budgetary laws, annual Community Acts implementing EU legislation, and laws ratifying international treaties and agreements. The former three are approved according to legislative dynamics that are different from the rest of the government legislation. Ratifying laws, instead, is often nothing more than the formal endorsement of international treaties and agreements on highly technical or purely symbolic issues. Given their politically neutral nature, these bills are usually approved by a unanimous but unconcerned assembly (Giuliani 2008: 71). As already noted, their inclusion would probably inflate the degree of parliamentary consensus observed at the final voting stage. All that said, the final dataset used for my empirical analysis comprises 522 government-sponsored laws.

The aim of the present chapter is to investigate the variance in the support enjoyed by government-sponsored legislation in Italy. Operationalizing the level of parliamentary consensus for each law thus requires a measure based on the votes cast by legislators at the final voting stage. However, simply counting the percentage of ayes over the number of MPs who are in the assembly when legislation is approved would pose a couple of problems in the Italian case. The first deals with abstentions, which in the Italian Chamber of Deputies cannot be considered as a neutral behaviour. According to the rules of the Chamber, abstentions are counted for calculation of the majority of legislators required for the vote to be valid (i.e., the quorum), but they are not considered for calculation of the majority of votes necessary to pass a bill. In other words, abstentions are an instrument for indirectly aligning with the prevailing voting behaviour in the Chamber: abstentions can be considered as positive votes if there is a majority of ayes, and negative votes if there is a majority of nays. Therefore, when just approved laws are considered, as in the present case, abstentions should be counted as favourable votes. The second problem regards absences, which can be used by parliamentary parties to hinder the formation of a legislative majority or to communicate with voters. When all, or almost all, the members of a parliamentary group are absent, this can indicate an explicit attempt to prevent the assembly from reaching the quorum, or the decision to signal an absolute disapproval of the bill.

To deal with these problems, I built my dependent variable following Curini and Zucchini (2010: 12). More precisely, abstentions are counted as positive votes. The absence of a legislator is instead considered as a negative vote when his/her party is entirely absent, or when his/her party is almost entirely absent (90 per cent) and the few who are present vote nay or abstain.[16]

Hence, my dependent variable, the DEGREE OF PARLIAMENTARY SUPPORT, is calculated as the number of MPs who vote aye or abstain over the total number of MPs who are present in the assembly, and is corrected for absences as explained above.[17] This variable is thus a proportion, whose lower and upper limits correspond to two extreme outcomes of the final voting stage: approval by a minimal majority (50 per cent plus one MP) and approval by unanimity (100 per cent of MPs), respectively.[18] As displayed in Table 4.1(a), the average degree of parliamentary support enjoyed by the governmental laws in the considered time period is 86 per cent, which is a fairly high value. Consistent with the literature on Italian lawmaking, the parliamentary consensus on government legislation has not decreased in the Second Republic. The average parliamentary support was 83 per cent in the X legislature, and the highest values are found during the transition from the First to the Second Republic: in the XI and, especially, the XII parliamentary terms. During the XII legislature, in particular, government

Table 4.1 Degree of parliamentary support (a) and degree of opposition support (b) of government bills in Italy (1988–2008), by legislature

Legislature	N.	(a) Degree of parliamentary support				(b) Degree of opposition support			
		Mean	St. Dev.	Min.	Max.	Mean	St. Dev.	Min.	Max.
X (1988–1992)	82	0.829	0.174	0.550	1	0.571	0.441	0.000	1
XI (1992–1994)	62	0.894	0.122	0.569	1	0.784	0.263	0.036	1
XII (1994–1996)	79	0.921	0.118	0.568	1	0.840	0.282	0.070	1
XIII (1996–2001)	148	0.864	0.154	0.517	1	0.705	0.336	0.090	1
XIV (2001–2006)	127	0.836	0.191	0.521	1	0.619	0.440	0.031	1
XV (2006–2008)	24	0.834	0.189	0.529	1	0.619	0.453	0.032	1
Entire sample	522	0.863	0.163	0.517	1	0.690	0.383	0.000	1

Source: Author's own elaboration based on the ILMA data archive (Borghetto et al. 2012)

laws were passed with the average support (either through explicit ayes or through abstention) of 92 per cent of the members of the Italian Chamber.[19] Thereafter, the level of consensus has decreased, gradually approaching the value observed in the X legislature.

These aggregate figures are exactly what research has mainly focused on up to now. However, a deeper inspection of the data reveals that not all the bills introduced by the Italian governments are approved according to a consensual process. Under certain circumstances, parliamentary approval can be strictly majoritarian. As Figure 4.1(a) illustrates, the distribution of the dependent variable displays two peaks, reflecting two different voting outcomes. One peak corresponds to quasi-unanimity and is much higher. The lower one corresponds to strictly majoritarian approval. In any case, the number of governmental bills adopted in a non-consensual manner is not negligible: the figure shows that about 30 per cent of the laws in my sample are approved with the support of fewer than 80 per cent of MPs.

Since this chapter focuses on government legislation, on which we can reasonably assume that the legislative majority will always vote in favour,[20] consensual approval should indicate that the opposition decides to join the majority. In other words, whether the outcome of the parliamentary voting stage is more or less consensual should depend precisely on the opposition's behaviour. To check for this, I built a second variable: the DEGREE OF OPPOSITION SUPPORT. This is the number of opposition MPs who vote aye or abstain over the total number of opposition MPs who are present in the assembly. Table 4.1(b) shows that the laws initiated by Italian executives receive relatively high support from the parliamentary opposition: on average, 69 per cent of opposition MPs sustain government-sponsored legislation. Remarkably, both the trend over time and the distributional form of the opposition support closely reflect those of the overall parliamentary support.[21] The degree of opposition support has increased up to the XII legislature, when on average 84 per cent of opposition MPs voted aye or abstained on government legislation, and then has gradually decreased, settling down to a value of 62 per cent in the last two legislatures included in the sample. Moreover, as Figure 4.1(b) shows, although government bills are very often backed by a large part of the opposition, about 30 per cent of them are passed with the support of fewer than 50 per cent of the opposition MPs.

Explanatory variables

Let us now turn to the operationalization of the independent variables included in the analysis. The first of the explanatory hypotheses discussed in the third section of this chapter deals with the opposition's ideological distance from the government. To measure this distance, I used data from Laver and Hunt's (1992) and Benoit and Laver's (2006) expert surveys, which provide policy positions and saliency scores for parties in a number of policy domains.[22] I proceeded as follows. After assigning each governmental bill to one of these policy areas, I computed the absolute distance between the government mid-range and the farthest opposition party.[23] I did not consider opposition parliamentary groups with

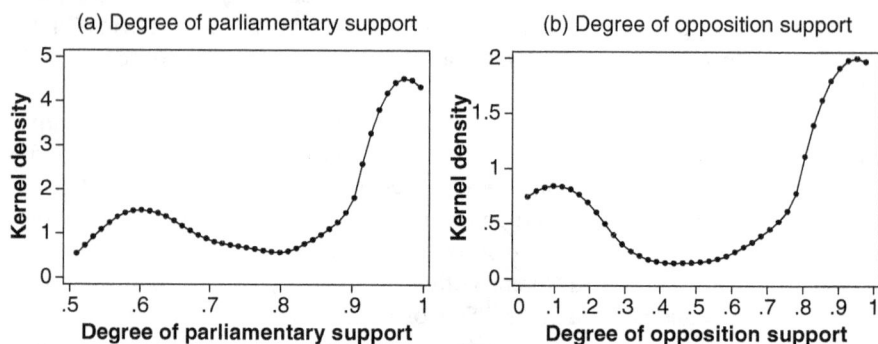

Figure 4.1 Distribution of the degree of parliamentary support (a) and of the degree of opposition support (b) for government legislation (1988–2008)

Source: Author's own elaboration based on the ILMA data archive (Borghetto *et al.* 2012).

fewer than 20 members, because these parties are usually constrained in their ability to influence parliamentary proceedings (e.g., they do not participate in the *Conferenza dei capigruppo*, where legislative business is planned). The distance between government and opposition is then weighted by an issue-specific mea-sure of salience, which allows us to capture whether the opposition's propensity to join the majority is lower on more salient dimensions.[24] The resulting variable is called OPPOSITION CONFLICT.

According to my second hypothesis, the opposition is unlikely to support gov-ernment bills when the parliamentary party system is highly fragmented, ideo-logical conflict in the assembly is particularly severe, or the debate on legisla-tion involves many policy areas. I therefore constructed three variables. First, I calculated Laakso and Taagepera's (1979) effective number of parties (ENP), which has become the standard numerical measure of fractionalization for the analysis of party systems. This measure takes into account both the number of parties and their relative weights, which I computed using the parties' shares of seats in the Chamber of Deputies. Second, I operationalized policy divisions in the parliament as the range between the two most extreme parties in the Chamber (RANGE PARL). Third, I measured the multidimensional nature of legislation by counting the number of consulting committees to which the bill was referred in the first reading (MULTIDIM). Indeed, since each committee has jurisdiction over a specific policy domain, when a bill deals with multiple policy areas more than one committee is in charge.

My third hypothesis involves technical ministers, whose bills should be backed by larger majorities than partisan ministers' bills. I identified technical ministers using Verzichelli and Cotta's (2000) data on the distribution of cabinet minister-ships in Italy, and consulting the websites of the Italian government and parliament for the following years. Then, I created the dummy TECHNICAL MINISTER, which is 1 if the first signatory of the bill is a minister who does not represent any party, and 0 otherwise.

With regard to the two hypotheses that I derived from the literature on the U.S. Congress, the distributive nature of legislation is operationalized with the dummy DISTRIBUTIVE, whose value is 1 when the bill contains at least one pork-barrel clause. More precisely, I checked whether the bill includes benefits for particular professional categories, interest groups, organizations, territories or people. Legislative patience is measured as the number of days between the introduction of the bill and the end of the legislative term (PATIENCE).

My last hypotheses involve two process-related factors: the length of the legislative process and the degree to which legislation is modified in parliament before being approved. The former is operationalized simply as the total number of days a bill spends in parliament, from its introduction to the final vote (DURATION). Measuring the latter requires some comparison between the final text of the bill approved in parliament and the original draft introduced by the government. I employed the variable DEGREE OF CHANGE, which is constructed as follows. Looking at the most basic units in the text of bills, I counted the number of words that were changed – i.e., added, deleted, or modified – during the legislative process (see Pedrazzani and Zucchini 2013). Then, I divided the obtained quantity by the number of words in the original text of the bill introduced by the government. The resulting variable is a fraction and is bounded from below by 0.[25]

As summarized in the second section of this chapter, research on Italian lawmaking has shown that, despite the shift from a pivotal to an alternational party system (Strøm 2003) that occurred in Italy towards the mid-1990s, the Second Republic is not characterized by narrower legislative majorities approving government initiatives. In any case, in order to control for the possible variation over time, in my analyses I included the dummy SECOND REPUBLIC. This variable takes the value 1 for bills approved during the XII, XIII, XIV and XV legislatures (1994–2008), and 0 for bills approved during the X and XI legislatures (1988–1994).

I introduced the minority status of governments and the policy area addressed by legislation as control variables. As to the former aspect, those executives that are not supported by a stable legislative majority might systematically try to build oversized majorities in order to push their projects forward within the parliament. I hence included the dummy MINORITY, which has the value 1 if the government introducing the bill does not control more than 50 per cent of seats in the Chamber.[26] Concerning the latter factor, some policy domains might happen to be more intrinsically consensual than others. Certain pieces of legislation can be less controversial because, for example, they deal with commonly shared values or politically neutral issues, or because in that policy area there are no outside interest groups harshly opposing each other. Therefore, I incorporated fixed-effect indicators, one for each policy domain, that are based on the classification of the Comparative Agendas Project.[27]

Table 4.2 summarizes the explanatory hypotheses that I will test in the next section, and provides descriptive statistics for the corresponding independent variables. Descriptive statistics for the indicators of policy domains are given in Table 4.3.

Table 4.2 Independent and control variables (1988–2008)

Variable		Description	Min.	Median	Max.	Mean	St. Dev.
INDEPENDENT VARIABLES							
H.1	OPPOSITION CONFLICT	Distance minister–farthest opp. party (saliency–weighted)	1.942	9.414	16.582	8.763	2.479
H.2	ENP	Laakso and Taagepera's (1979) effective no. of parties	4.355	6.140	8.705	6.146	1.169
	RANGE PARL	Distance between the two extreme parliamentary parties	9.800	14.600	17.790	14.371	1.476
	MULTIDIM	No. of consulting committees	0	4	13	4.588	2.672
H.3	TECHNICAL MINISTER	1 if proposed by a technical minister	0	0	1	0.220	0.415
H.4	DISTRIBUTIVE	1 if at least one pork barrel clause	0	0	1	0.372	0.484
H.5	PATIENCE	No. of days between introduction of a bill and end of legislative term	53	740	1844	867.956	531.333
H.6a, b	DURATION	No. of days between introduction and final approval of a bill	6	56	1287	126.854	193.661
H.7a, b	DEGREE OF CHANGE	No. of added, substituted and deleted words / no. of words in the initial bill	0	0.227	10.333	0.482	0.826
CONTROL VARIABLES							
	SECOND REPUBLIC	1 if bill discussed between 1994 and 2008	0	1	1	0.724	0.447
	MINORITY	1 if minority cabinet	0	0	1	0.257	0.437

Table 4.3 Policy domains in government bills (1988–2008)

Policy domain (Comparative Agendas Project)	No.	Per cent
Agriculture	28	5.36
Banking, Finance, and Domestic Commerce	27	5.17
Civil Rights, Minority Issues, and Civil Liberties	10	1.92
Community Development and Housing Issues	10	1.92
Culture Policy Issues	16	3.07
Defence	32	6.13
Domestic Macroeconomic Issues	62	11.88
Education	21	4.02
Energy	11	2.11
Environment	21	4.02
Foreign Trade	8	1.53
Government Operations	79	15.13
Health	30	5.75
Immigration	6	1.15
International Affairs and Foreign Aid	36	6.90
Labour, Employment	24	4.60
Law and Crime	58	11.11
Public Lands and Water Management	5	0.96
Social Welfare	2	0.38
Space, Science, Technology and Communications	3	0.57
Transportation	33	6.32
Total	522	100.00

Analysis and findings

Since my dependent variable – the degree of parliamentary support obtained by government legislation – is a typical fractional response variable, employing a standard linear model would be problematic.[28] In my analyses I thus used the fractional logit model, which was proposed as the most appropriate technique for this kind of variable by Papke and Wooldridge (1996, 2008).[29]

Table 4.4 shows the results from fractional logit regressions on the degree of parliamentary support for government legislation. A first interesting point is that all the three variables measuring bargaining complexity in parliament (Hypothesis 2) have a strong and statistically significant impact. Yet, one of them has not the expected sign (Model 1). On the one hand, as expected, RANGE PARL and MULTIDIM have a negative effect on the size of the legislative majorities that support government bills: when ideological divisions in the assembly are severe and the debate on legislation involves many policy domains, bargaining in parliament becomes particularly complex, and this leads to narrower majorities approving government bills. On the other hand, ENP has an unexpectedly positive sign, suggesting that the fragmentation of the parliamentary party system favours the formation of oversized legislative majorities. The presence of a particularly high number of parties in parliament makes the passage of government legislation less sure, thus leading the executive to build super-majorities.[30]

Policy divisions between cabinet and opposition (Hypothesis 1) have the expected impact. In Model 2 and subsequent models, OPPOSITION CONFLICT is negative and strongly significant, indicating that the approval of government legislation is less universalistic the farther the opposition is from the government.[31]

By contrast, the degree of parliamentary consensus when government bills are voted on does not seem to depend on whether the proposer of legislation is a technical minister or a partisan minister (Hypothesis 3). Although it has the expected sign, the dummy TECHNICAL MINISTER is not significant in any model. In other terms, government technicians do not prove to be particularly able to build consensus in the assembly.

Both the hypotheses drawn from the literature on the U.S. Congress are confirmed by my data on the legislative production of Italian governments. The variables DISTRIBUTIVE and PATIENCE have significant coefficients with the expected sign: the parliamentary majorities supporting government bills are larger when bills have a distributive nature (Hypothesis 4) and, as predicted by Baron and Ferejohn (1989), when there is little patience in the legislature (Hypothesis 5). The approval is more strictly majoritarian if legislation does not contain any pork-barrel clause or if the end of the legislative term is a long way off in the future.

Remarkably, the two process-related variables included in my analyses affect the degree of parliamentary support for government legislation, but with opposite signs: the coefficient is positive for DURATION (Hypothesis 6), and negative for DEGREE OF CHANGE (Hypothesis 7). While longer processes result in broader supporting majorities, more extensive changes in the text of government bills lead to more strictly majoritarian approval. Legislative time is thus used to build wide majorities, involving members of the opposition. By contrast, the parliamentary changes made to government legislation appear to be used as intra-coalitional monitoring tools. This seems in line with recent research on multiparty policy-making, according to which the bills introduced by cabinet ministers are reviewed just by coalition partners, with the aim of restoring the coalition compromise (Martin and Vanberg 2004, 2005, 2011). Therefore, the more government legislation is altered in parliament, the higher the probability that parliamentary voting will reflect the divide between government and opposition.

The situation is indeed more complex. As shown in Model 3, where DEGREE OF CHANGE is interacted with the dummy SECOND REPUBLIC, the impact of parliamentary changes seems to depend on certain general features of the political system. More precisely, the positive and significant coefficient on DEGREE OF CHANGE indicates that, under the pivotal system of the First Italian Republic (SECOND REPUBLIC = 0), more modifications made to government bills resulted in more universal approval in parliament. Fewer than one third of the bills in my sample (144 out of 522) were passed as laws during the First Republic. The coefficient on DEGREE OF CHANGE during the Second Republic (SECOND REPUBLIC

(a) Degree of parliamentary support   **(b) Degree of opposition support**

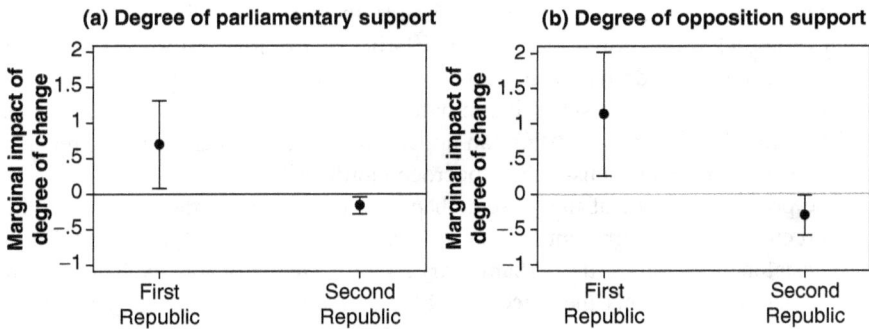

Figure 4.2 Marginal impact of parliamentary changes on the degree of parliamentary support (a) and on the degree of opposition support (b) in the First and Second Republics

Note: The markers indicate the marginal impact of DEGREE OF CHANGE on the dependent variables, along with 95 per cent confidence intervals. The dependent variable is DEGREE OF PARLIAMENTARY SUPPORT in panel (a), and DEGREE OF OPPOSITION SUPPORT in panel (b).

= 1) is instead significant and negative,[32] implying that, during the alternational Second Republic (378 bills), more parliamentary changes made to government-sponsored bills resulted in narrower legislative majorities (for a graphical illustration, see Figure 4.2(a)). These findings seem to suggest that, while in the former period parliamentary scrutiny of government legislation was employed by opposition parties, in the latter period it was an instrument at governing parties' disposal.[33]

It is worth noting that, unlike DEGREE OF CHANGE, the other process-related variable included in my analyses does not interact with the type of party system. As Model 4 shows, the interaction term DURATION × SECOND REPUBLIC is not statistically significant.

As expected, the type of party system (pivotal versus alternational) does not exercise an influence on its own. It just interacts with the degree of parliamentary modifications. Indeed, the significant effect of SECOND REPUBLIC displayed in Model 2 disappears once the interaction term is incorporated.

As for the other control variables, the analyses provide some evidence that minority cabinets (MINORITY) tend to build oversized majorities to push their bills through parliament, while an examination of the coefficients on policy domains allows us to identify which areas are intrinsically more consensual. More precisely, in comparison to 'Domestic Macroeconomic Issues' (the baseline category), government laws receive broader support when they deal with subjects such as freedom of speech, discrimination based on race, sex, age or disability, protection of minorities ('Civil Rights'), with nutrition programmes, assistance to the elderly and the disabled, youth care ('Social Welfare'),[34] or with court administration, crime prevention, prisons ('Law and Crime').[35] On these issues, which are typically excluded from political competition in Italy, parliamentary parties are likely to share common positions. The same is true for foreign aid, international organization, terrorism ('International Affairs and Foreign Aid'), export promotion, trade negotiations ('Foreign Trade'), culture, works of art, publishing ('Culture'). These are politically neutral issues, through which the Italian government promotes the national interest. Legislative majorities tend to be large also in the 'Agriculture' domain, on which, very often, governmental laws contain subsidies and hence are distributive in nature. Quite surprisingly, some evidence is found that bills on immigration, an apparently highly contested issue, receive more parliamentary consensus than macroeconomic bills.

The primary concern of the present chapter is to investigate the variance in the support enjoyed by government-sponsored legislation in the Italian parliament. Since the legislators belonging to the parliamentary majority are reasonably likely to support government bills, whether the outcomes of the parliamentary voting stage are more

Table 4.4 Fractional logit estimates of the degree of parliamentary support for government legislation (1988–2008)

Explanatory variables	Model 1 Coeff. (robust s.e.)	Model 2 Coeff. (robust s.e.)	Model 3 Coeff. (robust s.e.)	Model 4 Coeff. (robust s.e.)
OPPOSITION CONFLICT		−0.135*** (0.031)	−0.132*** (0.031)	−0.134*** (0.031)
ENP	0.226** (0.101)	0.370*** (0.106)	0.363*** (0.104)	0.368*** (0.105)
RANGE PARL	−0.165*** (0.062)			
MULTIDIM	−0.133*** (0.020)	−0.140*** (0.020)	−0.144*** (0.020)	−0.140*** (0.020)
TECHNICAL MINISTER	0.149 (0.168)	−0.023 (0.163)	−0.026 (0.163)	−0.028 (0.163)
DISTRIBUTIVE	0.321** (0.126)	0.303** (0.126)	0.329*** (0.125)	0.307** (0.126)
PATIENCE	−0.000*** (0.000)	−0.000** (0.000)	−0.000*** (0.000)	−0.000*** (0.000)
DURATION	0.001*** (0.000)	0.001*** (0.000)	0.001*** (0.000)	0.002** (0.001)
DURATION x SECOND REPUBLIC				−0.001 (0.001)
DEGREE OF CHANGE	−0.130** (0.056)	−0.136** (0.058)	0.698** (0.314)	−0.128** (0.057)
DEGREE OF CHANGE x SECOND REPUBLIC			−0.859*** (0.320)	
SECOND REPUBLIC	−0.279 (0.204)	−0.471** (0.213)	−0.208 (0.229)	−0.369 (0.233)
MINORITY	0.165 (0.179)	0.412** (0.191)	0.415** (0.190)	0.425** (0.191)
POLICY DOMAINS				
Civil Rights, Minority Issues, and Civil Liberties	2.268*** (0.665)	2.036*** (0.581)	2.090*** (0.601)	1.985*** (0.567)

Health	−0.045	−0.037	−0.030	−0.033
	(0.236)	(0.233)	(0.231)	(0.233)
Agriculture	0.766**	0.560*	0.576*	0.552*
	(0.321)	(0.329)	(0.329)	(0.330)
Labour, Employment	0.329	0.307	0.288	0.292
	(0.271)	(0.258)	(0.261)	(0.255)
Education	0.108	0.114	0.090	0.113
	(0.326)	(0.326)	(0.323)	(0.325)
Environment	0.408	0.052	−0.058	0.053
	(0.345)	(0.343)	(0.325)	(0.342)
Energy	−0.267	−0.446	−0.351	−0.415
	(0.266)	(0.284)	(0.284)	(0.283)
Immigration	0.886*	0.797*	0.690	0.804*
	(0.530)	(0.451)	(0.436)	(0.451)
Transportation	0.350	0.274	0.257	0.249
	(0.276)	(0.272)	(0.278)	(0.273)
Law and Crime	0.672**	0.530**	0.536**	0.521**
	(0.268)	(0.258)	(0.255)	(0.258)
Social Welfare	3.152***	2.826***	2.852***	3.023***
	(0.397)	(0.422)	(0.412)	(0.455)
Community Development and Housing Issues	−0.019	0.021	0.005	0.006
	(0.467)	(0.456)	(0.461)	(0.459)
Banking, Finance, and Domestic Commerce	0.064	−0.079	−0.069	−0.077
	(0.249)	(0.248)	(0.249)	(0.249)
Defence	0.450	0.410	0.437	0.409
	(0.315)	(0.304)	(0.301)	(0.304)
Space, Science, Technology and Communications	0.326	0.320	0.422	0.324
	(0.882)	(0.788)	(0.728)	(0.775)
Foreign Trade	1.243**	1.142*	1.155*	1.091*
	(0.621)	(0.630)	(0.625)	(0.618)
International Affairs and Foreign Aid	0.732**	0.612*	0.639*	0.621*
	(0.333)	(0.337)	(0.339)	(0.338)
Government Operations	0.183	0.073	0.085	0.056
	(0.183)	(0.184)	(0.182)	(0.183)
Public Lands and Water Management	0.381	0.226	0.230	0.216
	(0.543)	(0.585)	(0.567)	(0.583)
Culture Policy Issues	1.846***	1.792***	1.808***	1.794***
	(0.388)	(0.369)	(0.368)	(0.368)
Constant	3.562***	1.729***	1.540**	1.663**
	(1.143)	(0.670)	(0.663)	(0.669)
AIC	356.430	355.067	355.941	356.842
BIC	488.417	487.054	492.187	493.088
Log pseudo-likelihood	−147.21	−146.53	−145.97	−146.42

Notes: Robust standard errors in parentheses.
Fixed effects for policy domains (baseline category: Domestic Macroeconomic Issues).
*** $p<0.01$, ** $p<0.05$, * $p<0.1$. N = 522.

or less universalistic depends mainly on the opposition's behaviour. Moreover, the 15 cabinets included in my sample were sustained by legislative majorities of different size. Hence, to check robustness, I reran my analyses using as dependent variable the DEGREE OF OPPOSITION SUPPORT, which measures the opposition's propensity to join the governmental majority at the final voting stage.

As Table 4.5 illustrates, the results do not change. Rather, with very few exceptions, coefficients are larger and statistically more significant than in the previous table. Table 4.5 shows that the opposition is particularly likely to support government initiatives when its preferences are not so far from the cabinet's, when ideological divisions in the assembly are not so severe, and when the parliamentary debate does not involve many policy dimensions. Agreements between government and opposition are more likely also if the legislation at issue distributes benefits and if the end of the legislative term is near. As in the analysis of the overall degree of parliamentary support, the ENP in parliament has a positive impact on the opposition's propensity to vote in favour of government bills. In addition,

Table 4.5 Fractional logit estimates of the degree of opposition support of government legislation (1988–2008)

Explanatory variables	Model 5 Coeff. (robust s.e.)	Model 6 Coeff. (robust s.e.)	Model 7 Coeff. (robust s.e.)	Model 8 Coeff. (robust s.e.)
OPPOSITION CONFLICT		−0.199*** (0.044)	−0.194*** (0.044)	−0.197*** (0.044)
ENP	0.456*** (0.145)	0.673*** (0.151)	0.668*** (0.149)	0.671*** (0.151)
RANGE PARL	−0.254*** (0.087)			
MULTIDIM	−0.224*** (0.033)	−0.234*** (0.033)	−0.243*** (0.033)	−0.235*** (0.033)
TECHNICAL MINISTER	0.217 (0.232)	−0.030 (0.232)	−0.034 (0.233)	−0.037 (0.231)
DISTRIBUTIVE	0.558*** (0.187)	0.530*** (0.187)	0.581*** (0.188)	0.538*** (0.187)
PATIENCE	−0.001** (0.000)	−0.001** (0.000)	−0.001** (0.000)	−0.001** (0.000)
DURATION	0.002*** (0.001)	0.002*** (0.001)	0.002*** (0.001)	0.003** (0.001)
DURATION x SECOND REPUBLIC				−0.001 (0.001)
DEGREE OF CHANGE	−0.235** (0.111)	−0.242** (0.115)	1.138** (0.449)	−0.229** (0.114)
DEGREE OF CHANGE x SECOND REPUBLIC			−1.441*** (0.471)	
SECOND REPUBLIC	−0.562* (0.290)	−0.823*** (0.298)	−0.393 (0.323)	−0.676** (0.329)
MINORITY	0.280 (0.264)	0.617** (0.285)	0.621** (0.287)	0.642** (0.287)

POLICY DOMAINS

Civil Rights, Minority Issues, and Civil Liberties	2.606***	2.252***	2.370***	2.180***
	(0.921)	(0.758)	(0.823)	(0.737)
Health	−0.105	−0.071	−0.057	−0.062
	(0.383)	(0.381)	(0.380)	(0.380)
Agriculture	1.126**	0.833*	0.870*	0.817*
	(0.466)	(0.470)	(0.477)	(0.472)
Labour, Employment	0.444	0.416	0.389	0.395
	(0.399)	(0.379)	(0.389)	(0.374)
Education	0.204	0.217	0.166	0.216
	(0.504)	(0.496)	(0.494)	(0.495)
Environment	0.796	0.265	0.089	0.268
	(0.507)	(0.506)	(0.475)	(0.505)
Energy	−0.414	−0.598	−0.438	−0.548
	(0.506)	(0.516)	(0.518)	(0.515)
Immigration	1.504*	1.329*	1.139	1.337*
	(0.821)	(0.744)	(0.705)	(0.750)
Transportation	0.605	0.536	0.505	0.498
	(0.403)	(0.395)	(0.411)	(0.397)
Law and Crime	0.977**	0.756**	0.775**	0.743**
	(0.385)	(0.372)	(0.367)	(0.371)
Social Welfare	4.391***	3.860***	3.911***	4.145***
	(0.594)	(0.644)	(0.621)	(0.695)
Community Development and Housing Issues	0.090	0.142	0.117	0.115
	(0.691)	(0.676)	(0.691)	(0.681)
Banking, Finance, and Domestic Commerce	0.052	−0.129	−0.132	−0.131
	(0.415)	(0.414)	(0.420)	(0.418)
Defence	0.619	0.582	0.629	0.578
	(0.451)	(0.426)	(0.423)	(0.426)
Space, Science, Technology and Communications	0.490	0.498	0.659	0.500
	(1.286)	(1.094)	(0.978)	(1.069)
Foreign Trade	1.586*	1.424*	1.439*	1.352
	(0.853)	(0.865)	(0.851)	(0.844)
International Affairs and Foreign Aid	1.113**	0.945**	0.993**	0.957**
	(0.462)	(0.468)	(0.473)	(0.469)
Government Operations	0.292	0.141	0.156	0.114
	(0.302)	(0.301)	(0.299)	(0.301)
Public Lands and Water Management	0.646	0.435	0.436	0.418
	(0.720)	(0.771)	(0.738)	(0.767)
Culture Policy Issues	2.405***	2.330***	2.373***	2.329***
	(0.454)	(0.426)	(0.430)	(0.424)
Constant	2.790*	−0.114	−0.449	−0.201
	(1.589)	(0.984)	(0.977)	(0.985)
AIC	532.332	528.585	525.479	529.837
BIC	664.320	660.572	661.724	666.083
Log pseudo-likelihood	−235.17	−233.29	−230.74	−232.92

Notes: Robust standard errors in parentheses.
Fixed effects for policy domains (baseline category: Domestic Macroeconomic Issues).
*** $p<0.01$, ** $p<0.05$, * $p<0.1$. $N = 522$.

technical ministers' reputation as experts does not prove to be enough to persuade the opposition to support the bills introduced by them.

Similarly to the analysis of the overall degree of parliamentary consensus, the two process-related variables affect the extent to which the opposition supports governmental bills. First, the longer the parliamentary process, the larger the degree of support given by opposition parties to government legislation. As Model 8 shows, this effect does not depend on the type of party system. Second, the modifications made in parliament to government initiatives affect the opposition's propensity to support these bills, but this relationship is conditional on the type of party system. The coefficient on DEGREE OF CHANGE when SECOND REPUBLIC is equal to 0 is given in the table (Model 7), and is positive and significant. The coefficient of DEGREE OF CHANGE when SECOND REPUBLIC is equal to 1 is, instead, negative. Its value is -0.303, with standard error 0.145 and $p < 0.05$. In other words, during the pivotal First Republic, those government bills which were more altered in parliament were also more likely to receive votes from the legislative minority. By contrast, during the alternational Second Republic, more extensive changes induce opposition parties to deny the government their support (for a graphical illustration, see Figure 4.2(b)).

As in the analyses of the degree of parliamentary support, the dummy SECOND REPUBLIC has a negative impact in some models, but its effect disappears once it is interacted with DEGREE OF CHANGE. In other words, in the Second Republic opposition has become less supportive of government legislation not simply as a consequence of the establishment of alternation, but because parliamentary modifications have started being used mainly as an intra-coalition monitoring instrument. Finally, the opposition's propensity to join the government at the final voting stage tends to increase in the presence of minority cabinets (with the exception of Model 5), and on commonly shared issues such as civil rights, social assistance, law and crime, international affairs, foreign trade, and culture. Again, also agriculture and immigration turn out to be more consensual domains than macroeconomic issues.

Concluding remarks

While the literature on the U.S. Congress has devoted considerable attention to the outcomes of the final voting stage in the legislature, studies on parliamentary systems have rarely dealt with that topic. Nevertheless, investigating the extent of legislative support at the voting stage can be extremely informative in parliamentary settings, and this is especially true for government-sponsored legislation. When bills have been introduced by the cabinet, a wide support in the assembly implies that at least part of the opposition is joining the majority. The topic is particularly relevant for the study of Italy's Second Republic, which seems to be characterized by a majoritarian mood and fairly confrontational relations between government and opposition.

With some important exceptions, the literature on the Italian case has not systematically studied what happens in the final voting stage in the parliament. In any case, the existing contributions on the topic have mainly concentrated on the aggregate figures of the degree of support achieved by Italian laws, emphasizing the deeply institutionalized consensual nature of lawmaking. Therefore, the internal differences between more and less consensual processes remain rather understudied.

The present chapter has shown that not all the bills introduced by the Italian executives are passed in a consensual fashion. Although many of them are approved in a quasi-universal manner, the share of bills that are approved by smaller majorities can be informative on the functioning of the Italian parliamentary system.

More importantly, this work has examined a number of conditions under which legislators, and in particular those in the opposition, are likely to decide to support government initiatives. It has been shown that the outcomes of the final voting stage tend to be more strictly majoritarian when the opposition and the cabinet have divergent preferences, and when bargaining in parliament is particularly complex. The ENP has an unexpected effect: data on Italian government legislation show that the more the parliamentary party system is fragmented, the higher the probability of oversized supporting majorities. Clearly, this result is at odds with the findings about parliamentary range and multidimensionality, whose effect is to discourage the formation of wide majorities. One possible explanation for these contrasting results is that having more parties in parliament does not necessarily mean having more ideological conflict or more policy dimensions. This seems to be the case in Italy, where the fragmentation of the party system can often be related to factors such as incentives provided by the electoral and the public funding systems, or personalistic idiosyncrasies and parties, rather than to substantive ideological differences. Generally speaking, more parliamentary parties may lead to higher bargaining complexity only insofar as they exacerbate policy divisions.[36] If parties are many but not ideologically distant from the government, they cannot be considered as a source of legislative uncertainty. They can naturally join the parliamentary majority.

The hypotheses derived from the scholarship on the U.S. Congress are supported by the data on the legislative production of Italian governments: universalism at the voting stage is found to be more likely when the legislation at issue has a distributive nature and when the end of the parliamentary term approaches.

Aiming to contribute to a more dynamic study of what happens at the final voting stage in the parliament, this work has also tested the impact of two process-related factors: the duration of the legislative process and the extent to which legislation is altered in parliament before being approved. Remarkably, these two factors have two different effects on the outcome of the voting stage. Longer parliamentary processes result in broader supporting majorities, thus suggesting that legislative time is used by opposition parties to extract concessions from the government. The impact of parliamentary changes is, instead, conditional on the nature of the party system. During the pivotal First Republic, parliamentary modifications were used to reach agreements with the opposition. Under the alternational Second Republic, parliamentary changes are more extensive than before, and they are employed by governing partners to monitor each other (see Pedrazzani and Zucchini 2013). Since, under alternation, parliamentary changes are mainly used to accommodate the interests of coalition members, in the Second Republic voting outcomes really tend to reflect the divide between government and opposition.

This suggests a couple of considerations. First, the length of the legislative process and the degree of changes made during the process, despite being related, are not the same. Although in the literature on parliamentary policymaking these two variables are considered as indicators of legislative scrutiny (see Martin and Vanberg 2011), they do not necessarily point to the same phenomenon.[37] In this respect, it would be enough to underline the increasing use of maxi-amendments by Italian governments, through which extensive modifications can be made to the initial bill without lengthening the debate (see Zucchini 2013). Second, something seems to have changed between the First and the Second Italian Republics. Although also in the latter period laws are often approved by very large majorities, parliamentary changes are no more used to reach agreements between government and opposition, and this is a minor, but remarkable, majoritarian change. Remarkably, Borghetto and Visconti (in this volume) show that the same is true for post-enactment amendments as well.

On the whole, the analysis of the parliamentary approval of governmental laws in Italy confirms the persistence of consensual patterns of lawmaking in the Second Republic, as a large part of government legislation still receives broad support in the parliament. Nevertheless, the analysis also points to a more majoritarian direction, with some confrontational interactions between government and opposition: the use of parliamentary changes as an intra-coalitional monitoring tool, and the corresponding opposition's propensity to vote against outcomes of such amendatory activity are main evidence of this phenomenon.

Notes

1　The focus of the present chapter is on the outcome of the parliamentary voting stage. For the formal rules regulating this stage, see Rasch (1995, 2000).
2　According to Giuliani's (1997: 67) definition, the legislative practice of *consociativismo* is the 'unexpected consensual lawmaking in a polarized party environment.' It is 'the joining of majority and minority votes in the legislative process of a polarized parliamentary democracy', and hence seems 'unnatural'.
3　Italian government coalitions controlled 64 per cent of the seats of the Chamber in the first legislature (1948–1953), and no more than 55 per cent of legislative seats in the following four legislatures (1953–1958, 1958–1963, 1963–1968, 1968–1972). Since, up to 1988, the secret vote was the standard procedure adopted for the approval of laws, Di Palma's (1977) calculations are based on a comparison between the declarations of vote made by parties and the total number of ayes, nays and abstentions found in the parliamentary records.
4　Given the rules of the Italian Chamber of Deputies, abstentions can be counted as favourable votes when, as in Di Palma's (1977) sample, only approved laws are considered (see below).
5　Italian standing committees can give final approval to legislation without having to refer it to the parliament on the whole. In the Chamber, such a power can be withheld by the government, by one tenth of all representatives (63 MPs – i.e., by a medium opposition party), or by one fifth of the committee members. Similar rules exist in the Senate.
6　As noted by Capano and Giuliani (2001a: 45), the index of consensual lawmaking is calculated on all approved laws. Hence, the laws ratifying international treaties, which are consensual almost by definition (see below), are not excluded, and this can inflate the level of consensus shown by the index.

7 Let me underline that it is not the aim of the present work to explain the overall consensual style of Italian lawmaking in the Second Republic that has already been explored by other works. For a review of the macro-level explanations of the permanence of consensualism and its incongruence with the public confrontation among parties, see Giuliani (1997: 68–72; 2008: 76–78) and Capano and Giuliani (2001b). In this chapter, I just discuss micro-level explanations of the level of consensus enjoyed by government bills in parliament.

8 Indeed, Strøm, Müller and Bergman build their theoretical framework for the analysis of decisions concerning government coalitions – for instance, the decision to form a cabinet coalition (see De Winter and Dumont 2008). In the present chapter, the concept of bargaining complexity is applied to parliamentary voting, where decisions concern the formation of legislative coalitions in support of legislation. In this case, the decision is about which legislative majority to form in order to support government bills.

9 In addition, bargaining complexity may increase uncertainty, thus aggravating informational problems. When the number of possible alternative coalitions is very high, parliamentary parties are unlikely to be well informed about all the options and about the other actors' preferences.

10 The role of technical ministers in the Italian legislative process has been highlighted by Pedrazzani and Zucchini (2013) and Pedrazzani (2013). It has been shown that, compared to the bills introduced by partisan ministers, those initiated by technical ministers are less modified in parliament and are approved sooner. In those works, technical ministers were thought of as agents of the government coalition. The fact that technical ministers' proposals are subject to few changes and a quick approval was thus considered to indicate that coalition partners abstain from monitoring technical ministers in parliament. Of course, if evidence that technical ministers' bills are systematically supported by the opposition were found, it would mean that opposition parties also consider technical ministers as trustworthy actors.

11 Of course, vote exchanges have to be enforced. This can be problematic because the flows of benefits are not contemporaneous, and the consummation of trading is not simultaneous (see Weingast and Marshall 1988).

12 Distributive projects are typically assembled in single large bills, called omnibus packages. In an omnibus, each project is fashioned independent of the others (Sinclair 1997: 64). For a review of the concept of omnibus legislation, see Krutz (2001). For the purposes of the present chapter, it does not make any difference whether distributive bills are small single-item bills or huge omnibus packages. In both cases, I expect wide supporting majorities.

13 Martin and Vanberg test their argument in five West European parliamentary countries (Germany, the Netherlands, Denmark, Ireland and France). Their results are consistent with recent works on the Italian case. More precisely, it has been shown that in Italy a higher conflict among those coalition parties that are present in the drafting ministry leads to longer processes (Pedrazzani 2013) and more modifications made to government bills (Pedrazzani and Zucchini 2013).

14 Up to 1988, in the Italian Chamber secret ballot was mandatory for the final vote on legislation. Moreover, in all votes before the final one, secret voting was given precedence in case of competing requests.

15 Restricting the analysis to one of the two branches of the Italian parliament is quite common. The literature usually describes the Italian parliament as a symmetrical legislature, with both chambers performing the same functions in the legislative process. Hine (1993: 189–190), for instance, speaks of 'perfectly co-equal bicameralism' in the Italian case. Moreover, although elected on a somewhat different basis, in the considered period the two houses have almost always had identical composition.

16 Following Curini and Zucchini (2010), the absence of a legislator is recoded as nay only when his/her parliamentary group has at least 30 members. The absence of legislators from smaller groups is counted as nay only if at least one other group with 30 members is entirely or almost entirely absent (as explained above).

17 Data on roll call votes are taken from the Italian Law-Making Archive (ILMA) (see Borghetto *et al.* 2012). Just like many other indexes of consensus used in the literature, the dependent variables that I built do not take absences into account (except in the cases illustrated above), thus underestimating legislators' use of absences as a way to express disagreement with the legislation voted on. Here, when voting outcomes are defined as universal or strictly majoritarian, only those MPs who are present are considered. As a robustness check, I also constructed a consensus index which treats absences as negative votes. This does not affect the results of my analyses (results available upon request).

18 Since only approved laws are included in my sample, the lower limit cannot be less than 0.50.

19 The XI and XII terms are also those where parliamentary consensus has the lowest standard deviation. This indicates that, during these two legislatures, the degree of parliamentary support varied less than in the other legislatures. Indeed, in a given legislature, the lower the standard deviation, the more identical are the parliamentary majorities supporting the governmental laws that are approved.

20 The average degree to which MPs belonging to the legislative majority support government legislation is 0.99 in the entire sample. In each of the six parliamentary terms considered here, the average degree of support offered by government MPs is never lower than 0.98.

21 Not surprisingly, the Pearson correlation coefficient between the degree of parliamentary support and the degree of opposition support is 0.98, with $p < 0.000$.

22 In particular, I used the data from Laver and Hunt (1992) for the 1988–1994 period, and those from Benoit and Laver (2006) for the 1994–2008 period. An important alternative source of party positions is the Comparative Manifestos Project (Budge *et al.* 2001; Klingemann *et al.* 2006). However, the scores provided by the CMP appear hardly plausible for the Italian parties during the period considered here (see Pedrazzani and Zucchini 2013: 709, n. 23). Moreover, after 1996 the main Italian parties did not issue their own manifestos, but just coalition manifestos.

23 Following Tsebelis and Chang (2004), I took the mid-range position of the government as a measure of the position of the entire cabinet. The results of my analyses would not change if I used the position of the median voter in the cabinet.

24 Also saliency scores are taken from Laver and Hunt's (1992) and Benoit and Laver's (2006) data. I obtained the saliency weights in the following manner. For each party in parliament, I divided the party's saliency score on a policy domain by the same party's average saliency across all domains. I repeated this for all the domains, thus achieving the party's relative saliency on each domain. Hence, on each policy dimension, I multiplied the party's relative saliency by its proportion of parliamentary seats, thus obtaining the party's weighted relative saliency. Then, I got the overall saliency of a given domain by adding up the weighted relative saliency of all parties on that domain. As a result, relatively more salient issues in parliament present values greater than 1, while less salient issues display values lower than 1.

25 This variable is not a proportion, because its maximum value is not 1. Actually, DEGREE OF CHANGE has no upper limit. This allows us to distinguish between a situation in which the entire text of the bill is substituted – in this case, DEGREE OF CHANGE is 1 – and one in which the entire text is substituted and extra words are added – in this case, DEGREE OF CHANGE is greater than 1. Changes in spelling, capitalization and punctuation have not been counted as modifications.

26 The Dini (1995) and Prodi I (1996–1998) governments in my sample.

27 The classificatory scheme of the Comparative Agendas Project (CAP) was drawn up to study how attention towards different political issues varies and how such oscillations affect policy. The codebook for Italy is made up of 21 topics, each corresponding to one policy domain. Each category is, in turn, divided into subcategories, making a total of over 200 minor topics.

28 A standard linear model cannot guarantee that predictions fall between 0 and 1, and would pose problems in terms of heteroscedasticity, non-normal errors and non-linear effects (Wooldridge 2002).

29 The fractional logit model is based on a class of functional forms which allow us to directly estimate the conditional mean of the fractional response variable and to handle proportions of exactly 0 or 1. Two common alternatives are to transform the dependent variable into its log-odds ratio and to model it as a linear function, or to assume a particular distribution of the conditional mean of the proportion (the beta distribution, which is bounded between 0 and 1) and model heteroscedasticity in such a way that the variance is largest when the average proportion is near 0.5 (King 1989: 45). However, these are not appropriate choices when the outcome variable takes on the values 0 or 1 with positive probability, as in the present case: in 72 out of the 522 bills included in the sample, my dependent variable is 1, indicating unanimous consensus. In the fractional logit, instead, the predicted values are constrained to fall within the unit interval through a logistic form.

30 For a similar argument in coalition theory, see Groseclose and Snyder (1996).

31 In Model 2 and subsequent models, I dropped RANGE PARL, because it is fairly and positively correlated with OPPOSITION CONFLICT (the correlation index is 0.523 with $p = 0.000$). Indeed, both variables measure ideological divisions within the parliament. Keeping both of them in the same model could be problematic: it might reduce the precision of the estimates, because the more two independent variables are correlated, the greater their standard errors will be.

32 The coefficient on DEGREE OF CHANGE during the Second Republic is given by the combination of the original coefficient and the coefficient on the interaction term: $0.698 - 0.859 = -0.161$, with standard error equal to 0.061 (see Brambor *et al.* 2006). This effect is different from zero at conventional levels of statistical significance ($p < 0.01$).

33 This does not necessarily mean that, during the First Republic, government parties did not amend government bills in order to reach intra-coalitional policy compromises. It just means that in the First Republic legislative scrutiny was used also by opposition parties, or that government parties used legislative scrutiny in order to also accommodate the interests of the opposition.

34 In the Comparative Agendas Project, issues such as occupational and safety health administration, national insurance and pensions do not belong to the 'Social Welfare' category, but to 'Labour, Employment'.

35 Quite interestingly, Italian laws in some of these consensual issues prove to be particularly resistant to amendments after parliamentary enactment (see Borghetto and Visconti in this volume).

36 Indeed, in my sample ENP is correlated neither with RANGE PARL, nor with MULTIDIM.

37 In the sample of government laws considered in this chapter, DURATION and DEGREE OF CHANGE are only weakly correlated (0.258, with $p < 0.000$).

References

Allum, P. A. (1973). *Italy: Republic without a Government?* New York: Norton.

Andeweg, R. B. and Nijzink, L. (1995). 'Beyond the Two-Body Image: Relations between Ministers and MPs', in Herbert Döring (ed.), *Parliaments and Majority Rule in Western Europe*. New York: St. Martin's Press, pp. 152–178.

Baron, D. P. and Ferejohn, J. A. (1989). 'Bargaining in Legislatures', *American Political Science Review*, 83, pp. 1181–1206.

Bartolini, S. and D'Alimonte, R. (1998). 'Majoritarian Miracles and the Question of Party System Change', *European Journal of Political Research*, 34, pp. 151–169.

Benoit, K. and Laver, M. (2006). *Party Policy in Modern Democracies*. London: Routledge.

Blondel, J. (1988). 'Western European Cabinets in Comparative Perspective', in Jean Blondel and Ferdinand Müller-Rommel (eds), *Cabinets in Western Europe*. London: Macmillan, pp. 1–16.

Borghetto, E., Curini, L., Giuliani, M., Pellegata, A. and Zucchini, F. (2012). 'Italian Law-Making Archive (ILMA): A New Tool for Analysis of the Italian Legislative Process', *Rivista Italiana di Scienza Politica*, 42, pp. 479–500.

Brambor, T., Clark, W. R. and Golder, M. (2006). 'Understanding Interaction Models: Improving Empirical Analyses', *Political Analysis*, 14, pp. 63–82.

Budge, I., Klingemann, H.-D., Volkens, A. and Bara, J. (eds) (2001). *Mapping Policy Preferences: Estimates for Parties, Electors, and Governments, 1945–1998*. Oxford: Oxford University Press.

Capano, G. and Giuliani, M. (eds) (2001a). *Parlamento e processo legislativo in Italia*. Bologna: Il Mulino.

Capano, G. and Giuliani, M. (2001b). 'Governing without Surviving? An Italian Paradox: Law-making in Italy, 1987–2001', *Journal of Legislative Studies*, 7, pp. 13–36.

Capano, G. and Giuliani, M. (2003). 'The Italian Parliament: In Search of a New Role?', *Journal of Legislative Studies*, 9, pp. 8–34.

Carrubba, C. J. and Volden, C. (2000). 'Coalitional Politics and Logrolling in Legislative Institutions', *American Journal of Political Science*, 44, pp. 261–277.

Cazzola, F. (1975). *Governo e opposizione nel parlamento italiano*. Milan: Giuffrè.

Collie, M. P. (1988). 'The Legislature and Distributive Policy Making in Formal Perspective', *Legislative Studies Quarterly*, 13, pp. 427–458.

Cotta, M. (1994). 'The Rise and Fall of the "Centrality" of the Italian Parliament: Transformations of the Executive-Legislative Subsystem after the Second World War', in Gary W. Copeland and Samuel C. Patterson (eds), *Parliaments in the Modern World. Changing Institutions*. Ann Arbor: University of Michigan Press, pp. 59–84.

Cox, G. W. (2006). 'The Organization of Democratic Legislatures', in Barry R. Weingast and Donald A. Wittman (eds), *The Oxford Handbook of Political Economy*. Oxford: Oxford University Press, pp. 141–161.

Cox, G. W., Heller, W. B. and McCubbins, M. D. (2008). 'Agenda Power in the Italian Chamber of Deputies, 1988–2000', *Legislative Studies Quarterly*, 33, pp. 171–198.

Crombez, C. (2000). 'Spatial Models of Logrolling in the European Union', *European Journal of Political Economy*, 16, pp. 707–737.

Curini, L. and Zucchini, F. (2010). 'Testing the Theories of Law Making in a Parliamentary Democracy: A Roll Call Analysis of the Italian Chamber of Deputies (1988–2008)', in Thomas König, George Tsebelis and Marc Debus (eds), *Reform Processes and Policy Change: Veto Players and Decision-making in Modern Democracies*. New York: Springer, pp. 189–214.

D'Alimonte, R. and Chiaramonte, A. (1995). 'Il nuovo sistema elettorale italiano: le opportunità e le scelte', in Stefano Bartolini and Roberto D'Alimonte (eds), *Maggioritario ma non troppo: Le elezioni del 27 marzo 1994*. Bologna: Il Mulino, pp. 37–81.

De Micheli, C. (1997). 'L'attività legislativa dei governi al tramonto della Prima Repubblica', *Rivista Italiana di Scienza Politica*, 27, pp. 151–187.

De Winter, L. and Dumont, P. (2008). 'Uncertainty and Complexity in Cabinet Formation', in Kaare Strøm, Wolfgang C. Müller and Torbiörn Bergman (eds), *Cabinets and Coalition Bargaining: The Democratic Life Cycle in Western Europe*. Oxford: Oxford University Press, pp. 123–157.

Della Sala, V. (1993). 'The Permanent Committees of the Italian Chamber of Deputies: Parliament at Work?', *Legislative Studies Quarterly*, 18, pp. 157–183.

Di Palma, G. (1977). *Surviving without Governing: The Italian Parties in Parliament.* Berkeley: UCLA Press.

Döring, H. (ed.) (1995a). *Parliaments and Majority Rule in Western Europe.* New York: St. Martin's Press.

Döring, H. (1995b). 'Time as a Scarce Resource: Government Control of the Agenda', in Herbert Döring (ed.), *Parliaments and Majority Rule in Western Europe.* New York: St. Martin's Press, pp. 223–246.

Furlong, P. (1990). 'Parliament in Italian Politics', *West European Politics*, 13, pp. 52–67.

Gamm, G. and Huber, J. D. (2002). 'Legislatures as Political Institutions: Beyond the Contemporary Congress', in Ira Katznelson and Helen V. Milner (eds), *Political Science: State of the Discipline.* New York: Norton, pp. 313–341.

Giuliani, M. (1997). 'Measures of Consensual Law-making: Italian "*Consociativismo*"', *South European Society and Politics*, 2, pp. 66–96.

Giuliani, M. (2008). 'Patterns of Consensual Law-making in the Italian Parliament', *South European Society and Politics*, 13, pp. 61–85.

Golden, M. A. and Picci, L. (2008). 'Pork-Barrel Politics in Postwar Italy, 1953–94', *American Journal of Political Science*, 52, pp. 268–289.

Grofman, B. (1989). 'The Comparative Analysis of Coalition Formation and Duration Distinguishing Between-Country and Within-Country Effects', *British Journal of Political Science*, 19, pp. 291–302.

Groseclose, T. and Snyder, J. M. (1996). 'Buying Supermajorities', *American Political Science Review*, 90, pp. 303–315.

Hine, D. (1993). *Governing Italy: The Politics of Bargained Pluralism.* Oxford: Clarendon Press.

Hine, D. and Finocchi, R. (1991). 'The Italian Prime Minister', *West European Politics*, 14, pp. 79–96.

Huber, J. D. (1996). 'The Vote of Confidence in Parliamentary Democracies', *American Political Science Review*, 90, pp. 269–282.

Katz, R. S. (1996). 'Electoral Reform and the Transformation of Party Politics in Italy', *Party Politics*, 2, pp. 31–53.

King, G. (1989). *Unifying Political Methodology. The Likelihood Theory of Statistical Inference.* Ann Arbor: University of Michigan Press.

Klingemann, H.-D., Volkens, A., Bara, J., Budge, I. and McDonald, M. (eds) (2006). *Mapping Policy Preferences II. Estimates for Parties, Electors, and Governments in Eastern Europe, European Union and the OECD, 1990–2003.* Oxford: Oxford University Press.

Krutz, G. S. (2001). 'Tactical Maneuvering on Omnibus Bills in Congress', *American Journal of Political Science*, 45, pp. 210–223.

Laakso, M. and Taagepera, R. (1979). 'Effective Number of Parties: A Measure with Application to West Europe', *Comparative Political Studies*, 12, pp. 3–27.

Laver, M. (2006). 'Legislatures and Parliaments in Comparative Context', in Barry R. Weingast and Donald A. Wittman (eds), *The Oxford Handbook of Political Economy.* Oxford: Oxford University Press, pp. 121–140.

Laver, M. and Hunt, W. B. (1992). *Policy and Party Competition.* New York: Routledge.

Laver, M. and Schofield, N. (1990). *Multiparty Governments: The Politics of Coalition in Europe.* Oxford: Oxford University Press.

Martin, L. W. and Vanberg, G. (2004). 'Policing the Bargain: Coalition Government and Parliamentary Scrutiny', *American Journal of Political Science*, 48, pp. 13–27.

Martin, L. W. and Vanberg, G. (2005). 'Coalition Policymaking and Legislative Review', *American Political Science Review*, 99, pp. 93–106.

Martin, L. W. and Vanberg, G. (2011). *Parliaments and Coalitions: The Role of Legislative Institutions in Multiparty Governance*. Oxford: Oxford University Press.

McKelvey, R. D. (1976). 'Intransitivities in Multidimensional Voting Models and Some Implications for Agenda Control', *Journal of Economic Theory*, 12, pp. 472–482.

Morisi, M. (1992). *Le leggi del consenso. Partiti e interessi nei primi parlamenti della Repubblica*. Soveria Mannelli: Rubbettino.

Müller, W. C. and Strøm, K. (eds) (2000). *Coalition Governments in Western Europe*. Oxford: Oxford University Press.

Newell, J. L. (2000). 'Turning Over a New Leaf? Cohesion and Discipline in the Italian Parliament', *Journal of Legislative Studies*, 6, pp. 29–52.

Papke, L. E. and Wooldridge, J. M. (1996). 'Econometric Methods for Fractional Response Variables with an Application to 401(K) Plan Participation Rates', *Journal of Applied Econometrics*, 11, pp. 619–632.

Papke, L. E. and Wooldridge, J. M. (2008). 'Panel Data Methods for Fractional Response Variables with an Application to Test Pass Rates', *Journal of Econometrics*, 145, pp. 121–133.

Pedrazzani, A. (2013). 'Government-Opposition Dynamics, Intra-coalition Conflict, or Distributive Logic? An Analysis of the Length of the Legislative Process in Italy (1987–2006)', *Rivista Italiana di Scienza Politica*, 43, pp. 225–252.

Pedrazzani, A. and Zucchini, F. (2013). 'Horses and Hippos: Why Italian Government Bills Change in the Legislative Arena (1987–2006)', *European Journal of Political Research*, 52, pp. 687–714.

Plott, C. R. (1967). 'A Notion of Equilibrium and its Possibility under Majority Rule', *American Economic Review*, 57, pp. 787–806.

Powell, G. B. (2000). *Elections as Instruments of Democracy: Majoritarian and Proportional Visions*. New Haven: Yale University Press.

Rasch, B. E. (1995). 'Parliamentary Voting Procedures', in Herbert Döring (ed.), *Parliaments and Majority Rule in Western Europe*. New York: St. Martin's Press, pp. 488–527.

Rasch, B. E. (2000). 'Parliamentary Floor Voting Procedures and Agenda Setting in Europe', *Legislative Studies Quarterly*, 25, pp. 3–23.

Riker, W. H. (1962). *The Theory of Political Coalitions*. New Haven: Yale University Press.

Saalfeld, T. (2000). 'Members of Parliament and Governments in Western Europe: Agency Relations and Problems of Oversight', *European Journal of Political Research*, 37, pp. 353–376.

Schofield, N. (1978). 'Instability of Simple Dynamic Games', *Review of Economic Studies*, 45, pp. 575–594.

Shepsle, K. A. (1979a). 'Institutional Arrangements and Equilibrium in Multidimensional Voting Models', *American Journal of Political Science*, 23, pp. 26–59.

Shepsle, K. A. (1979b). 'The Role of Institutional Structure in the Creation of Policy Equilibrium', in Douglas W. Rae and Theodore J. Eismeier (eds), *Public Policy and Public Choice*. Beverly Hills: Sage, pp. 249–283.

Shepsle, K. A. and Weingast, B. R. (1981). 'Political Preferences for the Pork Barrel: A Generalization', *American Journal of Political Science*, 25, pp. 96–111.

Sinclair, B. (1997). *Unorthodox Lawmaking: New Legislative Process in the U.S. Congress*. Washington, DC: Congressional Quarterly.

Spotts, F. and Wieser, T. (1986). *Italy: A Difficult Democracy*. Cambridge: Cambridge University Press.

Strøm, K. (1990). *Minority Governments and Majority Rule*. Cambridge: Cambridge University Press.

Strøm, K. (2003). 'Parliamentary Democracy and Delegation', in Kaare Strøm, Wolgang C. Muller and Torbjörn Bergman (eds), *Delegation and Accountability in Parliamentary Democracies*. Oxford: Oxford University Press, pp. 55–106.

Strøm, K. and Müller, W. C. (1999). 'Political Parties and Hard Choices', in Wolfgang C. Müller and Kaare Strøm (eds), *Policy, Office, or Votes? How Political Parties in Western Europe Make Hard Choices*. Cambridge: Cambridge University Press, pp. 1–35.

Strøm, K., Müller, W. C. and Bergman, T. (eds) (2008). *Cabinets and Coalition Bargaining: The Democratic Life Cycle in Western Europe*. Oxford: Oxford University Press.

Taagepera, R. and Grofman, B. (1985). 'Rethinking Duverger's Law: Predicting the Effective Number of Parties in Plurality and PR Systems – Parties Minus Issues Equals One', *European Journal of Political Research*, 13, pp. 71–92.

Tsebelis, G. and Chang, E. C. C. (2004). 'Veto Players and the Structure of Budgets in Advanced Industrialized Countries', *European Journal of Political Research*, 43, pp. 449–476.

Tullock, G. (1981). 'Why So Much Stability?', *Public Choice*, 37, pp. 189–202.

Verzichelli, L. and Cotta, M. (2000). 'Italy. From "Constrained" Coalitions to Alternative Governments?', in Wolfgang C. Müller and Kaare Strøm (eds), *Coalition Governments in Western Europe*. Oxford: Oxford University Press, pp. 433–497.

Verzichelli, L. and Cotta, M. (2012). 'Technocratic and Expert Ministers in Italy: A Diachronic Analysis'. Paper presented at the 22nd Congress of the International Political Science Association, Madrid, July 8–12.

Warwick, P. V. (1994). *Government Survival in Parliamentary Democracies*. Cambridge: Cambridge University Press.

Weingast, B. R. (1979). 'A Rational Choice Perspective on Congressional Norms', *American Journal of Political Science*, 23, pp. 245–263.

Weingast, B. R. and Marshall, W. J. (1988). 'The Industrial Organization of Congress', *Journal of Political Economy*, 96, pp. 132–163.

Weingast, B. R., Shepsle, K. A. and Johnsen, C. (1981). 'The Political Economy of Benefits and Costs: A Neoclassical Approach to Distributive Politics', *Journal of Political Economy*, 89, pp. 642–664.

Wilson, J. Q. (1973). *Political Organizations*. New York: Basic Book, Inc., Publishers.

Wooldridge, J. M. (2002). *Econometric Analysis of Cross Section and Panel Data*. Cambridge: MIT Press.

Zucchini, F. (2001). 'Veto players e interazione fra esecutivo e legislativo: il caso italiano', *Rivista Italiana di Scienza Politica*, 31, pp. 109–138.

Zucchini, F. (2013). 'Italy: Government Alternation and Legislative Agenda Setting', in Bjørn Erik Rasch and George Tsebelis (eds), *The Role of Government in Legislative Agenda Setting*. New York: Routledge, pp. 53–77.

5 Governing by revising

A study on post-enactment policy change in Italy[1]

Enrico Borghetto and Francesco Visconti[2]

Introduction

According to a classical view of democratic politics, a Member of Parliament's (MP) main goals are to get re-elected or to get his/her favourite policies passed. Most of the time, this latter goal is functional to the attainment of a new mandate. Although this illustration of a politician's priorities is certainly fitting with the daily reality in national parliaments, it misses a temporal dimension: policy-seeking politicians care not only for the enactment but also for the survival of their decisions. Ultimately, the translation of a policy output into outcomes – arguably the actual pay-off for MPs and their constituencies – requires time, thus the enactment phase cannot be anything but the first step in a longer path.

It is common knowledge among politicians that policies are not cast in stone and what is decided one day can be more or less completely overturned the next. Legal systems are constantly subject to processes of stratification and modification over time. Yet, this does not imply that legislative revision always occurs at pre-determined moments or it is unaffected by changes in the political context where it takes place. Rather, it is arguable that it varies in line with political and institutional variables. On the one side, elections, retirements and more general events in the outside world change the order of priorities political leaders have to attend to. On the other, not all political settings are conducive to the same type of strategy of legislative revisions.

Remarkably, the dynamics of post-enactment legislative revision remain largely a black hole in Italian legislative studies.[3] A wealth of data has progressively been made available on various aspects of the legislative process (e.g. Borghetto *et al.* 2012) but so far no work has set out to explore the lives of legal acts after their adoption. To some extent, this should not be a surprise. The Italian legislative corpus has long represented a labyrinth even for the shrewdest legal practitioner because of its complexity and sheer volume. This contribution aims at opening a new path in this under-researched topic. Although the main research focus of this volume is on the post-1994 period, two legislatures of the previous period are taken as yardsticks to uncover more effectively the peculiar features of legislative revisions in the so-called Italian Second Republic, which is said to have started in 1994.

Tracing the life of laws after adoption was made possible by a new dataset drawn from *Normattiva*, the online database of Italian normative acts.[4] We focus on two samples of major executive-sponsored laws adopted during the IX–X legislatures (from 1983 to 1992), and XIII–XIV legislatures (from 1996 to 2006) and trace their lives, respectively, up to the end of the XI legislature (1994) and XV legislature (2008). This research design allows us to explore the variation in policy change dynamics before and after the Italian transition from a pivotal party in government toward a bipolar alternation in government. Scholarly literature has already established systematic differences and continuities between the two periods. Looking at the post-enactment legislative evolution allows us to contribute to this literature.

Our analysis reveals that, in the post-1994 period, legislative revisions per act increased substantially. This goes in parallel with a decrease in the number of acts and their growth in size (measured as number of words). We also show that most revisions are adopted within the same legislature as the parent act, thus they do not originate from initiatives of the new majority seeking to write off the previous majority's reforms. Overall, the stability of newly adopted laws has decreased: they are subjected to an incremental process of revision/specification, which starts immediately after their enactment. We suggest that all these elements point to a change of strategy of the legislator in the Second Republic. In order to pass reforms in a rather cumbersome and sluggish legislative system governed by fragmented and unwieldy majority coalitions (Capano and Giuliani 2001), one strategy was to enact more comprehensive acts providing a relatively general outline of the policies to implement while leaving the revision/specification of individual provisions until later. This way, we suggest that studying post-enactment legislative change enables illumination of not only inter-coalition but also intra-coalition dynamics.

This chapter will begin with a review of the literature focusing on policy change in Italy over the last 30 years. Second, we illustrate the dataset in use. Third, we provide an analysis of legislative revisions, looking first at their distribution, then at the stability of acts by means of the non-parametric tools of Event history analysis. We conclude by discussing the implications of our approach and findings for future research on legislative politics in Italy.

Dynamics of policy change from the First to the Second Republic

Despite a lack of works focusing on legislative revision per se, there has been a rather heterogeneous tradition of studies focusing on the Italian legislative process and addressing its evolution and characteristics from both a policy and a law-making perspective (Giuliani and Zucchini 2013). Most works addressing the features of the legislative process in the First Republic agree on its viscosity (e.g. Predieri 1974; Cotta 1994). Policy change is depicted as relatively slow if not rare at the level of 'meta-' and 'meso-policies', namely those decisions concerning the fundamental characteristics and directions of the political and economic regime and those concerning reforms in the areas of economic, social, foreign and institutional policy (Cotta 1996). Observers concur that this state of things was generalized, no matter whether the initiator was the executive or MPs.[5] Of course, this does not mean that Italy missed major policy reforms all over this period. Rather,

> [S]uch initiatives have generally taken an inordinately long time to materialize [. . .] Moreover, when finally introduced, major reforms have been said to have taken the form of distinctly sub-optimum compromises, and their effective implementation frequently to have been prejudiced by the inefficiency or outright resistance of the public administration.
>
> (Hine 1993: 3)

Scholars' explanations of this outcome revolved around two (partially interrelated) factors: the party system and institutional determinants.

Di Palma (1977) argued that the post-war Italian political system was effective in surviving without governing. The polarized multiparty system did not create the conditions for turnover in government: the Christian Democrats were the keystone of every coalition (Sartori 1982; Vassallo 1994). Never called to electoral accountability and to seek a following on the basis of their policies, parties in government had little incentive to maintain internal cohesion and implement the government platform. Moreover, they tended to avoid internal competition in high-stake decisions in order to preserve solidarity against their anti-system challengers (Cotta 1996). In day-to-day politics, a gap existed between government and its supporting coalition in parliament, with the former having to renegotiate almost every agreement with backbenchers due to low party discipline (also fostered by secret ballot). Governing under the constant 'siege' of allegedly anti-system forces (Communist party on the left and former fascist party on the right), fragmented DC-led coalitions (so-called beleaguered coalitions) found their best strategy in inaction (*immobilism*), a solution which could 'buy time, if not credit, for the centre' (Di Palma 1977: 251).

Another line of research associated viscosity with institutional features. The Italian legislative system has been characterized by: a strong specialization of the permanent committee system; the power to reject, to amend and to replace governmental proposals at every step of the process; limited power bestowed on the government to control the agenda; the lack of restrictions on members' initiatives; the power to legislate on every subject; the limited number of MPs required to form a parliamentary group; its perfect bicameralism (Della Sala 1998; Capano and Giuliani 2001).[6] All these factors were strictly interrelated and led some commentators to classify the Italian parliament among the legislatures (such as the US Congress) with strong institutional powers (Blondel 1970; Norton 1994).

In terms of law-making, this state of things reflected in a comparatively high legislative output. Di Palma (1976: 147) noticed that: 'the Italian Parliament tends to displace aggregative and controversial legislation and to make special room for legislation of limited importance on which coalition partners and the opposition can more easily agree'. Some of these measures were termed *leggine*, namely small or micro-sectional (limited or specialized in scope) legislation passed mostly through the decentralized procedure, the adoption in committees without a further reading by the floor. Another peculiarity of this period is the high reliance on reiterated decree-laws to get policy enacted.[7] They allowed the prompt adoption of policies by the executive, while their constant reintroduction at the end of the 60-day validity period permitted to (at least temporarily) overcome the rejection of their conversion into law by the parliament (Della Sala 1988).

The popular referendum on electoral rules of 1993 is generally taken as the watershed between the First and Second Republics, and the move from a pivotal party system with limited government alternation toward a competitive bipolar democracy. According to its supporters, the new electoral system, the so-called *Mattarellum*, would reduce the number of parties in parliament, thus simplifying the party system, an evergreen for Italian reformers. For sure, in conjunction with the disruption of the previous party system due to corruption scandals (*Tangentopoli*), the economic crisis of the early 1990s and the fall of the Berlin Wall (that imposed a change to the traditional communist left), it contributed to the emergence of a new political scenario with new parties in parliament, two opposing pre-electoral coalitions, and a turnover of around two-thirds of MPs in the 1994 elections.

This systemic change had implications at the law-making stage and in the relation between government and parliament. First, the decline in the total number of laws approved through the ordinary procedure has been substantively compensated by a growing number of legislative decrees (and delegating laws) issued by governments since the early 1990s (De Micheli and Verzichelli 2004). Second, laws have become bigger and more heterogeneous in their content (Marangoni 2013). Third, law-decrees have kept on playing an important role in the executive toolbox, although their number partially dropped after the 1996 sentence of the Constitutional Court.[8] Fourth, there has been an increase in the use of legislative consolidation (Carotti and Cavalieri 2009). Overall, these changes responded to the new bipolar logic of competition. Governments could no longer exclusively build their functional legitimacy through initiatives of a micro kind (i.e. *leggine*): they had to seek their support also through meso-policies. These legislative tools allowed the executive 'to bypass the sluggishness of the standard legislative process without any substantive constitutional improvement being made' (Capano and Giuliani 2001: 33).

A considerable number of analyses have also emphasized the continuities with the previous system (Newell 2006). Giuliani (2008) investigated whether the kind of consensualism that characterized the First Republic faded away with the advent of the Second and majoritarian reforms. Contrary to expectations he found out that it was only slightly reduced. Indeed those consensual practices at the committee level which characterized the First Republic seem to have been replaced by an increasing degree of agreement on the parliamentary floor. Zucchini (2011) acknowledges that there has been an increase in the legislative agenda-setting power of the executive as a result of a more strategic use of existing constitutional rules and the partial reform of the Houses' rules of procedure. On the other hand, he argues that the ideological heterogeneity of Italian coalitions, which remained high, has prevented the creation of new rules which institutionalize this power. Indeed, the law-making arena is still characterized by a large number of veto players located far apart in the ideological continuum. For instance, parliamentary fragmentation (measured in terms of parliamentary groups) increased. All in all, it appears that the dualism between executive and parliament has not disappeared and consensual practices are still at work. Doubts can be raised that the Italian system has moved decisively toward the majoritarian pole of the continuum (Morlino 2013).

This brief overview aims at setting the tone for the rest of the analysis. Indeed, inspecting the post-enactment evolution of Italian laws across these two periods of Italian history can contribute to cast some light on the elements of change and continuity that have occurred over the last 30 years. For instance, if we buy the account of Italy as a country with a stronger majoritarian identity, we should expect an increase in the instability of laws when alternation takes place. New majorities should be more prone to revise what previous executives did. Besides, they should also have the capacity to do so since they can try to bypass the ordinary process through the instrument of delegated legislation. On the other hand, legislative change in the two periods might be more similar than expected. In the Second Republic, there is no clear evidence that executives have assumed the leadership of their parliamentary majorities, apart from a limited set of 'emergency' situations which prompted government parties to act cohesively (for instance, see the reforms adopted to ensure the entry of Italy among the forerunners in the European Monetary Union (Della Sala 1997)).

Data

The dataset used in this chapter was developed by Visconti (2011) based on *Normattiva*, the online database of Italian normative acts connected to the parliament website that gives the possibility to trace all the updates a law has encountered along its life.[9] The dataset records all revisions received by each law sponsored by the executive of two legislatures of the First Republic, the IX and the X, and two of the Second, the XIII and the XIV, until the end of the observation span (April 2011). Types of revisions were aggregated into five categories according to the description given by *Normattiva*.

1   Partial repeals: a specific set of provisions are abrogated but the act survives.
2   Total repeals: the whole act is abrogated.
3   Amendments: addition/deletion or substitution of words inside a provision.
4   Sentences of the Constitutional Court declaring the unconstitutionality of a law or of some specific provision it contains.
5   Other: non-politically relevant updates like *corrigenda*, that is the editing of transcription errors (e.g. mistakes in the specification of names or dates).

Also, we recorded which type of measure carried out the revision: either a law, decree law, ministerial decree, sentence of Constitutional Court, legislative decree, decree of the President of the Republic or other (corrigenda, etc.).

Additionally, we downloaded the texts of the law at different points in time, more precisely at enactment and after each revision. Through a word processor we counted the number of words in each version. Then, we calculated the words difference in the text after each revision. This measure has been introduced as a proxy for the *intensity* of change. As we spell out later on, more significant changes are those that imply a greater word difference. While for total and partial repeals this value is always negative, amendments may also entail (besides deletions (negative value) and additions (positive value)) substitutions of words. Unfortunately, due to the size of our sample, it was not possible to identify the number of words substituted by each amendment. Therefore an amendment with a value of 0 in word difference might have experienced an exact substitution of all words as well as just 1. A cursory analysis of our dataset revealed that the former are rather rare (if not totally absent).[10]

We only include legislative revisions adopted within a specified deadline, respectively the end of the XI legislature (14 April 1994) for First Republic legislation and the end of the XV legislature (28 April 2008) for Second Republic legislation. This study design allows comparing two periods of almost equal length. The IX legislature was followed by a 5-year legislature (X) plus one short transitional legislature (XI). Following a strikingly similar pattern, after the XIII legislature came a 5-year legislature (XIV) and a short legislature (XV). The three legislatures of the First Republic (IX, X and XI) featured the same coalition of parties (*pentapartito*) in power, with only marginal changes in their balance of power.[11] On the other hand, the three legislatures of the Second Republic (XIII, XIV and XV) exemplify the turn to an alternation system in Italy: no political coalition managed to regain office after each election. After a transition legislature characterized by the first Berlusconi government and a caretaker government led by Dini (XII), the 1996 elections saw the former Communists, now called the Democratic Party of the Left, directly entering the government for the first time in Italian history. The XIV witnessed the return of a new centre-right coalition led by Berlusconi. This coalition was ousted from power in 2006 by a short-lived centre-left government led by Prodi. To explore the variation in terms of legislative dynamics before and after the transition from governments organized around a centrist pivotal party (the DC), to alternation between centre-left and centre-right coalitions, we considered only executive-sponsored laws. The rationale behind this choice is that we deem legislation originated from ministers as more coherent with the will of the majority sustaining the cabinet, than laws proposed by MPs that sometimes count on transversal and, therefore, less clear-cut majorities.

Selecting major acts and revisions

One of the greatest challenges in the analysis of revisions lies in their heterogeneity. The concept of revision applies to small corrections as well as to extensive reforms, altering the impact of the act itself. What is more, it is important to differentiate between the targets of revisions. Parent acts, the acts that are modified, range from major acts laying down the regulation for a whole policy area to technical measures with a specific scope of application. In line with previous works in the field (Maltzman and Shipan 2008; Ragusa 2010), we decided to account for this heterogeneity by focusing only on 'major revisions' to 'major acts'. Given the number of observations in our sample, our selection criteria for major acts were necessarily formal and relied on size, calculated as number of words. We kept only those parent acts presenting a number of words at the moment of their adoption greater than the median in each legislature.[12] This left us with 518 acts adopted in the First Republic and 360 acts adopted in the Second Republic.

The selection of revisions relied on three criteria. First, we removed those revisions carried out through amending acts that are not of equal legal status with respect to their parent acts. In other words, we kept only amendments carried out through primary measures (i.e. ordinary laws, laws converting law-decrees or legislative decrees). Second, we eliminated revisions implemented through sentences of the Italian Constitutional Court. These amendments might be also relevant but they constitute a special subgroup of cases deserving an analysis which goes beyond the purview of this chapter. Third, we took out technical modifications such as changes to annexes and final tables, *errata*, confirmations or postponement of repeals, as well as interpretations of provisions.

Exploring post-enactment politics

The final dataset consists of 1,965 amendments: 574 (29.2 per cent) modifying laws in the analysed period of the First Republic and 1,391 (70.8 per cent) in the Second Republic legislatures. This is already a remarkable finding: in the First Republic the ratio of amendments to laws is 1.1, whereas it increases four times in the Second Republic (3.9). This finding is confirmed if one considers that 290 laws (56 per cent) were not modified in the First Republic, whereas only 93 did not undergo changes in the Second Republic (25.8 per cent).

How does one explain this remarkable change? Let us first look at how amendments are distributed per law in each legislature. The jitter plot in Figure 5.1 clearly shows the presence of outliers in the Second Republic. These are five budget laws which, respectively, collected 57 (Law n.662 of 1996), 44 (Law n.449 of 1997), 44 (Law n.448 of 1998), 52 (Law n.388 of 2000) and 38 (Law n.289 of 2002) amendments. These are also comparatively big laws, as indicated by the size of their point in the figure (which is proportional to the number of words). This pattern is confirmed by an inspection of the distribution of amending acts according to type of law. Table 5.1 reveals that all figures increase in the Second Republic, but that the most remarkable change regards the ratio of amendments per budget law, which rises from 1.73 amendments per act to 11.41. Overall, budget laws represent a mere 9 per cent of the total number of acts in the Second Republic but received 26 per cent of amendments.

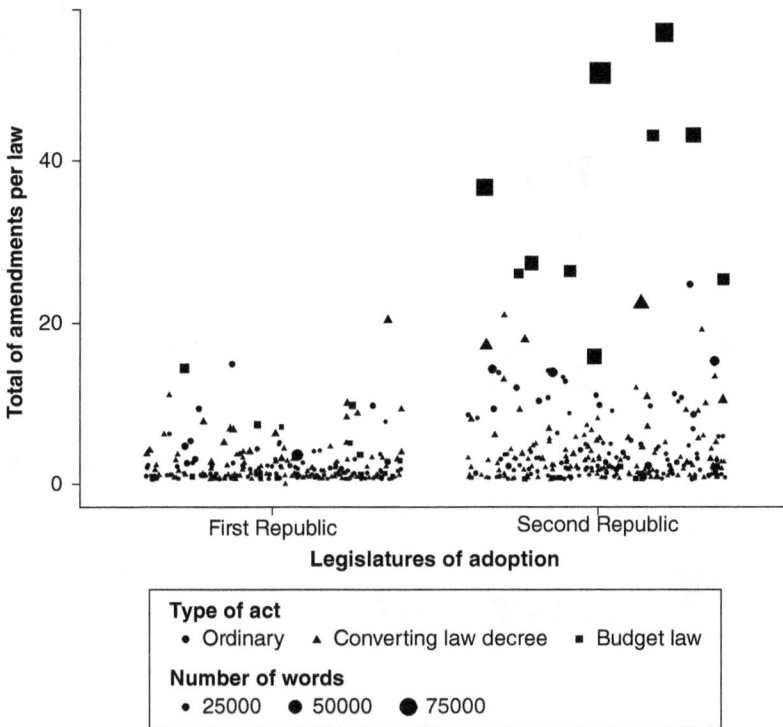

Figure 5.1 Jitter plot of number of revisions

We associate this substantial increase with another noticeable dimension of change in budget laws: their size. It escalates from an average of 7,000 words in the First Republic to more than 22,000 in the Second.[13] The impression that one gets is that the growth in complexity and range of interested areas of recent budget and budget-related laws (De Giorgi and Verzichelli 2008) contributed to make them a 'construction site' in need of multiple maintenance measures over time. This is supported by previous findings (e.g. Maltzman and Shipan 2008), showing that complex legislation, by virtue of having more provisions and affecting a greater range of policy areas, is more prone to receive prompt revisions with respect to legislation with a more specific focus. Our data show that, in the case of budget laws, their greater size is also correlated with more frequent revisions.

The relationship between size of laws and propensity to receive amendments might also justify the increase in the ratio amendments per act for the other two categories (for ordinary acts it rises from 0.86 to 3.25, for budget laws from 1.31 to 3.01). Indeed, as already emphasized in previous studies (e.g. Borghetto *et al*. 2012), in the Second Republic government-sponsored legislation decreased in number (in our sample of major acts, the number of ordinary acts was cut from 267 to 150) but became bigger (the mean number of words of an ordinary act changed from 3,217 to 5,837). But this can be considered only part of the

Table 5.1 Distribution of amending acts per type of parent act

	Type of law	No. of amendments	No. of acts	Mean number of words	Amendments/law	Amendments/1000 words
First Republic	Ordinary	230	267	3217	0.86	0.27
	Converting law decree	287	218	3690	1.31	0.36
	Budget law	57	33	7021	1.73	0.25
Second Republic	Ordinary	487	150	5837	3.25	0.56
	Converting law decree	539	178	4593	3.01	0.66
	Budget law	365	32	22450	11.41	0.51

explanation. The increase in the ratio of amendments per 1,000 words in the Second Republic reveals that the legislator displayed also a greater proclivity to modify the existing legal apparatus, at the net of increases in the size of laws.[14]

Another dimension of variation which lends itself to exploration through our data is the intensity of change (Table 5.2). As already mentioned, it was computed as the proportion of words added to or deleted from the original text of the act after each revision. For instance, a revision which adds a provision of 1,000 words to an act which originally was made up of 10,000 words is considered as an increase of 10 per cent. To begin with, measures of central tendency (such as the arithmetic mean and the median) reveal that most changes are clustered around very small percentages of word changes. They point to the prominence of small variations not higher than 1 per cent of change. All in all, an analysis based on the values of the mean (or the median, or the interquartile range of) proportional changes would conclude that laws are revised only incrementally over time. Yet, legislative acts in some cases have lost as much as 95 per cent of words or experienced an increase of 62 per cent (the extreme values in, respectively, the minimum and the maximum word differences).

Greater insights on the distribution of proportional revisions can be gained by considering measurements of L-skewness and L-kurtosis, respectively, the third and fourth L-moments of a distribution (Hosking 1990; Breunig and Jones 2011). First, revisions to budget laws stand out as the only category characterized by a right-skewed distribution.[15] Revisions to budget laws show a strong tendency to incorporate new commas/provisions. Second, the distribution of type of revisions, independently from the type of parent act, is highly leptokurtic, namely it features: sharp peaks (the greatest majority of revisions affect only marginally the number of words of a legislative text); weak 'shoulders' (low number of moderate changes) and fat tails (originating from a number of high additions or deletions of words).[16] More simply, our data reveal that legislative acts (no matter the type of act) remain in an extended period of stasis when they are modified only marginally. These periods are punctuated by sudden bouts of radical changes, which lead to a dramatic expansion or shrinkage of the legislative text. Although the lapse of time considered in the present analysis is likely to be too short for efficiently describing the evolution of Italian legislative acts, the evidence points to a predominance of punctuated changes. This finding adds to previous researches on punctuated equilibrium (e.g. Jones and Baumgartner 2005) which showed that distributions of year-to-year changes in budgetary allocations (or public priorities measured as 'Most Important Problems facing the nation', or parliamentary attention measured as questions to the executives) are highly leptokurtic.

In the computation of kurtosis, one can drop cases of no revision or include them in the analysis as cases where 0 words were changed. According to the first, the level of punctuatedness increased in the Second Republic. A lower proportion of laws did not undergo any revision but changes were for the most part small (as compared to the total number of words of the act, which – it is worth remembering it – increased on average) and there were more cases of high decreases/expansions in the size of laws. According to the second indicator, the level of L-kurtosis did

Table 5.2 Distribution of size of legislative revisions per type of act

	Type of law	Mean	Median	Standard Deviation	Interquartile change	Minimum	Maximum	Skewness	Kurtosis (excluding changes=0)	Kurtosis (including changes=0)
First Republic	Ordinary	0.005	0.009	0.085	0.026	−0.607	0.171	−0.209	0.506	0.757
	Converting law decree	0.010	0.008	0.077	0.019	−0.885	0.535	−0.026	0.573	0.631
	Budget law	0.005	0.003	0.017	0.010	−0.034	0.082	0.161	0.385	0.491
Second Republic	Ordinary	−0.001	0.002	0.087	0.015	−0.905	0.452	−0.196	0.607	0.687
	Converting law decree	0.003	0.006	0.095	0.019	−0.956	0.415	−0.194	0.623	0.667
	Budget law	0.001	0.001	0.007	0.002	−0.029	0.048	0.237	0.508	0.524

not vary substantially across the periods and, for ordinary laws only, it declined by .07 in the Second Republic. It is difficult to interpret substantially such small variations in L-kurtosis scores. Using the theoretical lenses of punctuated equilibrium theory, such a change might be indicative of a relative decrease in friction of the law-making system for executive acts passed through the ordinary procedure. Friction is here conceived of as the resistance to change built into legislative processes and it is conditioned on both institutional (i.e. number of parliamentary veto points) and cognitive factors (i.e. limited processing capacity of politicians) (Jones and Baumgartner 2005). That said, there are more signs of continuity than difference between the two periods, which supports the thesis of a strong resilience of parliamentary institutions, despite the dramatic alteration of electoral laws and the party system (Capano and Giuliani 2001).

For all categories, we hypothesized that alternation could be responsible for changing the pattern of revisions. Governments of different affiliation might have incentive to revise existing legislation, especially if adopted by their opponents when they were in power. To explore the question, we consider in which legislatures amending acts were adopted. Column 1 of Table 5.3 shows that while in the First Republic a majority of changes (54 per cent) occurred during subsequent legislatures, it was the reverse in the Second Republic. A majority of amending acts (58 per cent) had already been enacted before the end of the legislature. If we focus just on first amendments (column 2), almost 83 per cent of the laws of the Second Republic were amended by their enacting coalition, whereas this happened only for 59 per cent of cases in the First Republic. This finding is remarkable because it goes against one of the most plausible consequences of alternation, namely the enactment of partisan legislation. With alternation in power, the new majority should have greater incentives to revise those acts enacted in the previous term because of the supposed distance in policy preferences between the incumbent and past governments. It would be the chance for the new majority to give its imprint to policies that carry the stamp of the previous government. The evidence points to the contrary. Paradoxically, this logic seems instead more patently at play in the First Republic, when – it is worth recalling – succeeding majorities always exhibit more or less the same range of parties in power.

Yet, as we have shown, most of the revisions we observed are of small size, namely they modify only a small portion of the act in question. The legislator's strategy might have been to adopt more amendments but affecting only small sections of the parent act. In order to control for this possibility, our analysis opted for distinguishing revisions also based on the number of words added or removed. Each amendment was classified as either a small or high decrease, or a small or high increase. If the proportion of changed words is negative we treat it as a decrease and vice versa. The 12 total repeals were categorized as a high decrease. Our formal criterion to split our set of revisions according to intensity is to divide between positive and negative values, to compute the mean proportion of changed words in the two groups, respectively, for the First and Second Republics, and finally to split the two subsets at the mean value.[17] Columns 3 and 4 of Table 5.3 show that, even controlling for the intensity of change, the difference between the

Table 5.3 Distribution of amending acts according to timing of amendment

Type of law		Timing	1. All amendments		2. First amendments		3. All amendments (implying substantial change of words)		4. All first amendments (implying substantial change of words)	
			Number	%	Number	%	Number	%	Number	%
First Republic	Ordinary	Same*	71	31	42	41	25	32	12	31
		Other**	159	69	61	59	52	68	27	69
	Converting law decree	Same	167	58	71	64	31	49	23	62
		Other	120	42	40	36	32	51	14	38
	Budget law	Same	28	49	10	71	0	0	0	0
		Other	29	51	4	29	3	100	1	100
	Total	Same	266	46	123	59	56	27	35	31
		Other	308	54	105	41	87	73	42	69
Second Republic	Ordinary	Same	255	52	80	73	71	49	27	69
		Other	232	48	30	27	73	51	12	31
	Converting law decree	Same	353	65	116	86	109	69	47	87
		Other	186	35	19	14	49	31	7	13
	Budget law	Same	203	56	20	91	11	100	3	100
		Other	162	44	2	9	0	0	0	0
	Total	Same	811	58	216	83	191	73	77	85
		Other	580	42	51	17	122	27	19	15

Notes
* Same = same legislature as the parent act
** Other = different legislature from the parent act
Shaded cells are used to highlight where the majority of amendments are concentrated.

First and Second Republics holds. The majority of bigger-than-average revisions (no matter whether they are first revisions or later ones) are passed in different legislatures from the parent act for acts adopted in the First Republic and in the same legislature as the parent act in the Second.

If the same type of analysis is performed, this time distinguishing for type of law, the pattern previously observed for the total number of acts holds remarkably in the Second Republic. No matter which act is amended, most revisions are still taken in the same legislature as the parent act. The only exceptions are bigger-than-average revisions for ordinary acts which are distributed evenly before and after the end of the legislature of the parent act. Different patterns emerge in the First Republic depending on whether one focuses on ordinary laws or other laws. Ordinary laws are always more intensively revised in subsequent legislatures. On the contrary, apart from a few exceptions, laws converting law-decrees and budget laws receive more modifications in the same legislature of the parent act. Accounting for the peculiar pattern of ordinary law revisions in the First Republic would require a closer inspection of the content of those acts and the changes that have been introduced. The evidence collected seems to suggest a relationship between the confidence of staying in government in the next legislature (an expectation shared by most partners in the governing coalitions of the First Republic) and a greater stability of legislative decisions taken.

To explore this hypothesis, we make recourse to the non-parametric tools of Event history analysis (Box-Steffensmeier and Bradford 2004). We measure the stability of a law in terms of days from adoption until a first revision is passed. A tool commonly used to describe duration until an event takes place is to calculate Kaplan-Meier estimates of survival, namely the estimated probability of surviving at least t units of time without experiencing the censoring event (in our case an amendment). If an amendment did occur, we computed the number of days separating the enactment of the parent act from the first revision. If the parent act was not amended within the time-frame considered, the observation was treated as right-censored.[18] Figure 5.2a plots Kaplan-Meier estimates in a so-called survival curve for the 518 laws of the First Republic and for the 360 laws of the Second. The graph shows the probability of surviving beyond time t (on the x-axis) without being amended, namely our measurement of stability. The number of laws at risk of a first amendment at each point in time is shown below the horizontal axis. The two groups display clearly different patterns. For laws of the First Republic the probability of not being amended within the same legislature remains constantly higher, and declines at a significantly slower pace. Instead, for laws of the Second Republic, the probability of surviving reaches around 0.5 already after the first year (median survival time). The big gap between the two curves builds up pretty fast and only after the first two years does their pace become basically the same. If instead of all first amendments we consider only major amendments (Figure 5.2b), i.e. those that impose changes with an intensity above the mean (here we consider also total repeals), the pattern is more similar. The curves diverge up to the second year because there is a more rapid decline in the Second Republic; then they stabilize and decline at a slower pace.[19]

(a) All first revisions

Probability of surviving without revisions

1.00
0.75
0.50
0.25
0.00

p < 0.0001

Time	0	365	730	1095	1460	1825	2190	2555	2920	3285	3650	4015
1 Republic	518	412	365	302	256	211	179	156	106	59	10	0
2 Republic	360	175	127	106	83	72	57	52	41	30	18	10

Numbers at risk

—— 1 Republic   -------- 2 Republic

(b) First substantial revisions

Probability of surviving first without revisions

1.00
0.75
0.50
0.25
0.00

p < 0.0001

Time	0	365	730	1095	1460	1825	2190	2555	2920	3285	3650	4015
1 Republic	518	487	476	412	350	298	256	220	149	83	16	0
2 Republic	360	303	281	247	212	191	156	143	107	85	59	33

Numbers at risk

—— 1 Republic   -------- 2 Republic

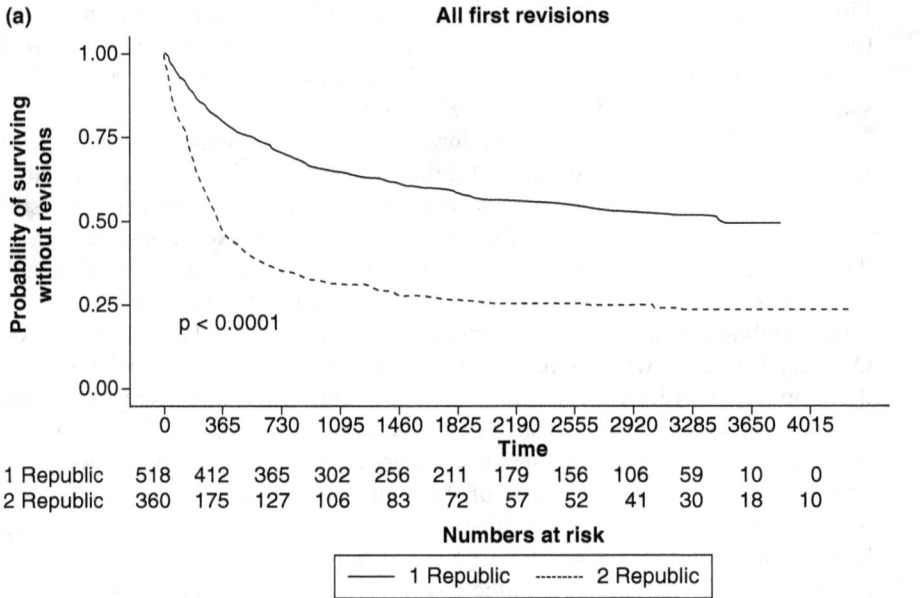

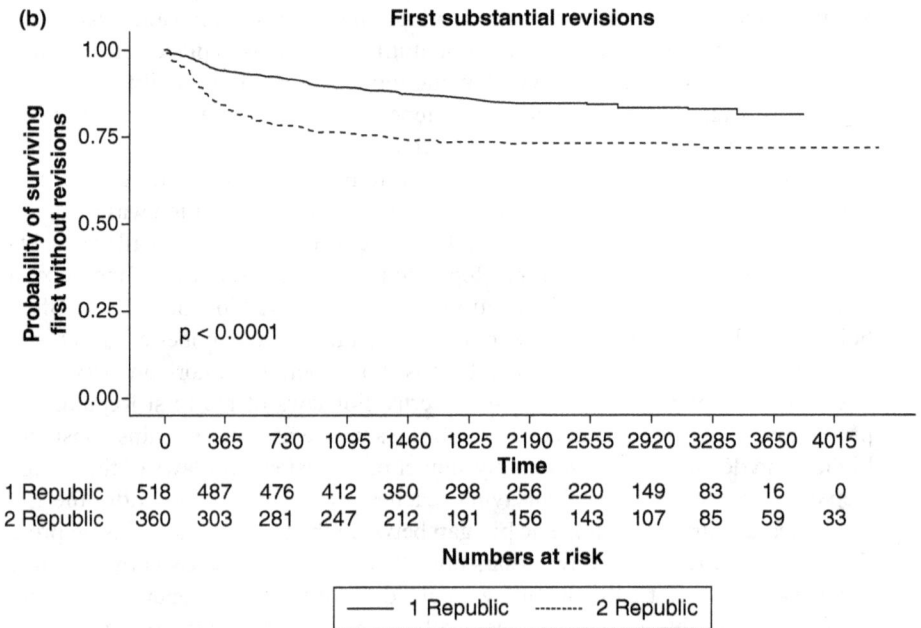

Figure 5.2 Kaplan-Meier estimates of survival probabilities until the first revision: (a) considering all first amendments, (b) considering only major amendments

Figure 5.3 plots the same K-M estimates according to type of law for each of the two republics. Again we notice how, for the First Republic, the stability of legislative acts is always higher in comparison with their counterpart in the Second Republic. Comparatively, budget laws are the most readily revised, but conversions of law-decrees follow a very similar pattern. Around one-third of the two categories for the First Republic, and about two-thirds for the Second receive an amendment in their first year of life. At a later stage those laws surviving beyond the first year tend to remain relatively safe from substantial revisions, as displayed by the flattening of the survival curves. Ordinary laws have, in both periods, a higher survival rate compared to conversions of law-decrees or budget laws. Yet, this difference is starker in the First Republic, where ordinary laws are significantly more stable than the other two categories. Both laws converting government decrees and budget laws experience a sort of consolidation period during the first year after their enactment. In part this finding should be related to the greater complexity of these two types of acts compared to ordinary laws. As discussed above acts of the latter type present, on average, a shorter length in terms of number of words. In both cases, but especially for budget-related laws, they tend to be *omnibus* measures regulating a variety of policy areas. Fewer words could also imply that less details are incorporated, which makes laws more adaptive and less prone to receiving modifications. Moreover, another explanation we suggest might be related to time constraints. Indeed the legislative process typical of Italian budget laws and law-decrees has to follow a specific and tighter pace compared to ordinary laws. For instance, law-decrees have to be approved by parliament within 60 days from government approval, a mechanism which, combined with the greater length of the act, increases the probability of unintended consequences (or intended but unpopular within public opinion) to be addressed subsequently through amendments. Again, more strict time constraints increase also the likelihood of the request for a confidence vote to approve budget laws or law-decrees.

Interestingly, in the Second Republic the distinction between types of acts has become more blurred.[20] This might be read as a generalized change of strategy of the legislator. Most laws are amended within the first two years, no matter the type of law under consideration. The overall picture we got is of a decline in the stability of laws against a backdrop of increased complexity and lower productivity of the legislator. We propose that a sort of thermostatic dynamic has been at work. The amount of legislation approved by the Italian parliament has decreased with the transition to the Second Republic. In a comparable period of around ten years during the IX and X legislatures more than 1,500 laws were approved, while between 1996 and 2006 there were slightly more than 1,000.[21] It seems, then, that the reduced output has been counterbalanced by two behavioural transformations: on the pre-enactment phase there has been an increase in the complexity of legislation; on the post-enactment phase instead a greater number of substantive revisions have been brought to existing acts.

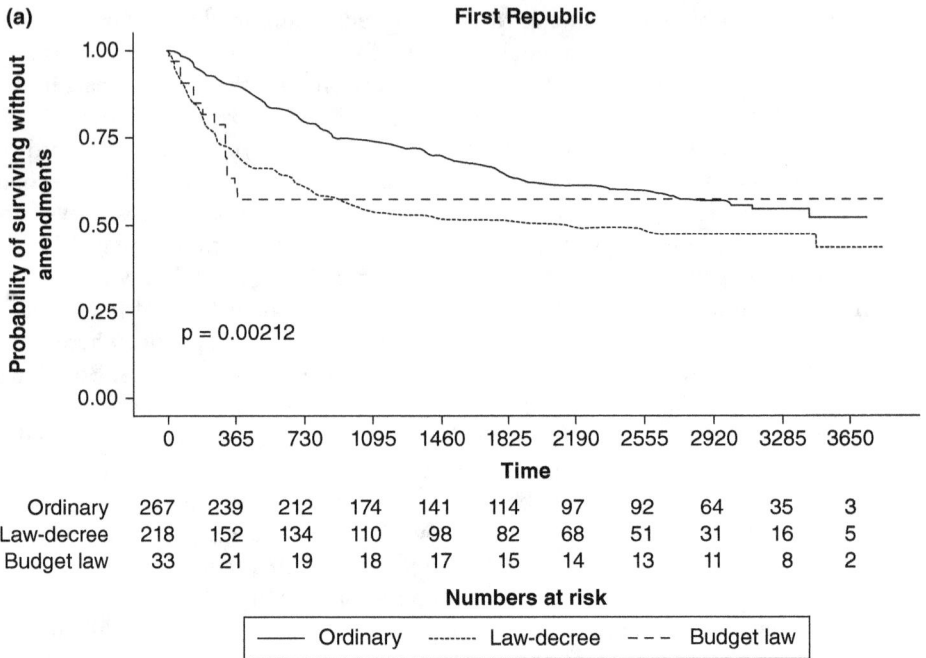

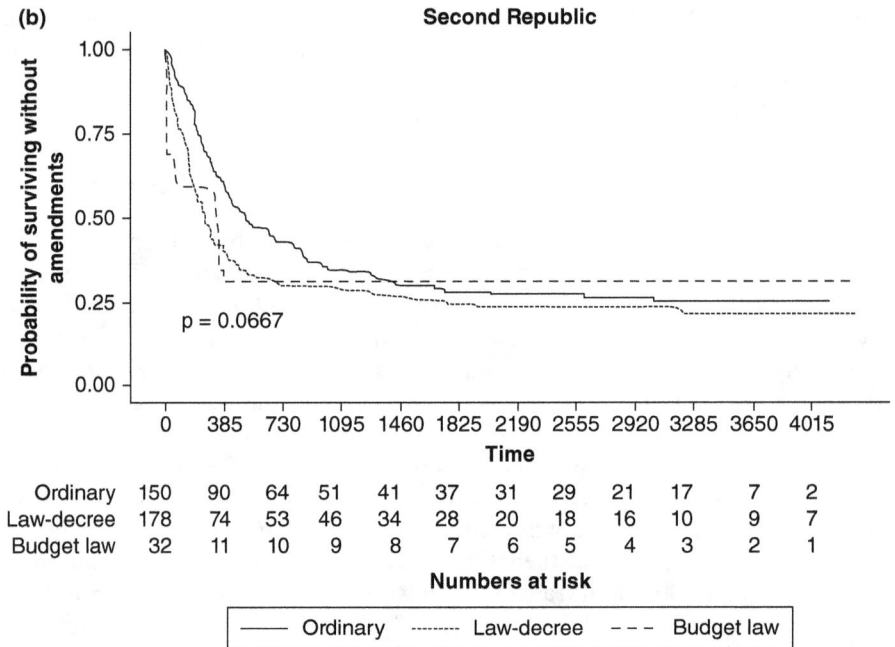

Figure 5.3 Kaplan-Meier estimates of survival probabilities until the first revision by type of law: (a) in the First Republic, (b) in the Second Republic

Conclusion

This chapter aimed at exploring a neglected issue in Italian legislative studies: the post-enactment life of Italian acts. The relevance of our approach to the study of policy change stems from its capacity to cast new light on the long-debated issue of transition in the Italian political system. As emphasized by the literature, the transition from the First to the Second Republic implied elements of both continuity and change. Our analysis brings to the fore strong signals of transformation in the legislative strategy of Italian executives.

In the Second Republic, there has been a substantial increase in the number of amendments per law. This trend stands out in the case of budget laws, but it is also clearly visible with regard to the other two categories, conversions of law-decrees and ordinary laws. We suggest that this might result from an increase in complexity (measured in terms of number of words). Laws contain more provisions and are, therefore, more susceptible to revisions.

When we looked at the intensity of revisions, measured as number of words deleted or added by the revising law, the two Italian Republics display similar patterns. Extremely high L-kurtosis scores reveal that revisions tend to alter a proportionally marginal number of words but that there are occasional cases of dramatic shifts. What we referred to as the punctuatedness of the revision process increased in the Second Republic for each type of act. If we include laws surviving without the need for further revisions, one gets a picture of closer resemblance between the two periods, which supports an interpretation of the Italian legislative process as a highly resilient arena despite substantial changes in the political conditions between the two periods.

Contrary to our expectations, the advent of alternation in government did not entail an increase of partisan legislation aiming at revising policies adopted by the previous majority. Collected evidence shows that most amendments in the Second Republic were already approved before the end of the legislature of enactment. Overall, the Kaplan-Meier analysis of post-enactment longevity points to a sharp decrease in the stability of legislative agreements with respect to acts adopted in the First Republic. This result holds, no matter the type of act considered. We contend that it might originate from a preference of the executive to trade support for a bill in parliament in exchange for its readiness to accept revisions to the act in the short/medium term. In other words, there are reasons to argue that in order to escape the legislative strictures characterizing the legislative process since its foundation, the executive opted for passing fewer bills but bigger in size and more liable to get revised by the political coalition which enacted them in the first place. Thus, it appears that the rationale behind this increase in amendments has to be found within coalition dynamics rather than in the new system of bipolar competition.

Our result is coherent with recent works analysing the Italian legislative activity (see, for example, Marangoni 2013). These works have pointed out that the legislative process has become increasingly unwieldy. The bipolar competition in a highly fragmented party system required mainstream parties to extend coalition boundaries in order to win the elections and maintain a supporting majority in parliament. From 1996 onwards majority coalitions in the bipolar system have been fragmented and ideologically diverse.[22] As a result of these circumstances, coalition leaders had to develop new conflict management strategies to hold heterogeneous partners together. In truth, these problems were not unknown at the time of the First Republic. In the past, as already reported, they used to be solved – mainly but not exclusively – through the enactment of micro-sectional legislation. These laws were mostly adopted behind committees' doors and were tabled by MPs from across the political spectrum. For various reasons (not least tight budget constraints), this practice is no longer available. Our data reveal that one of the solutions adopted in the Second Republic to cope with the cost of enacting new legislation, given the fragility of coalitions, has been to adopt new legislation that is more complex and wide ranging in nature, but also open to adjustments along the way. As in the past, adopting wide-ranging self-contained reforms in one go is still hard in the fragmented bipolar Italian setting. Our analysis suggests that intra-coalition bargaining might have moved from the pre-enactment to the post-enactment phase, leaving majorities with the option of governing by revising.

Notes

1   This article is a joint effort of the two authors. Sections 2 and 3 were mainly written by Francesco Visconti, Sections 4 and 5 by Enrico Borghetto. The Introduction and Conclusions were written jointly by the two authors.
2   Acknowledgements: The authors would like to acknowledge the financial support of the Italian Ministry of Education and Research, Project Prin 2009TPW4NL_002, 'Institutions and agenda-setting: actors, time and information', and the Fundação para a Ciência e a Tecnologia (FCT, Government of Portugal, SFRH/BPD/89968/2012). Any opinions, findings, and conclusions or recommendations expressed in this chapter are those of the authors.
3   The focus on the post-enactment phase has attracted attention in legislative studies only recently and it has been mainly applied to the output of the United States Congress (Maltzman and Shipan 2008; Berry *et al.* 2010; Ragusa 2010; but see Borghetto and Mader 2014).
4   Available at http://www.normattiva.it.
5   Although the Italian Constitution reserves the power to initiate legislation to a wide range of actors – MPs, government, regional councils, citizens, and CNEL – the vast majority of bills that get voted in and become laws derive from proposals initiated by the executive. This is largely a consequence of the fact that the government has the formal monopoly of legislative initiative for budget laws and conversions of legislative decrees. Borghetto and Giuliani's work (2012) evaluating the pace of Italian legislative processes since 1987 showed that for adopted bills, the fact that they are sponsored by the executive (together with the type of procedure, the policy sector and timing of introduction) contributes to expedite their legislative process.
6   Every house has the same prerogatives and has to approve the same text before its final enactment. In principle, therefore, there are no limits to the number of readings in each house, the passages of the so-called navette system.
7   Decree-laws are issued by the government in special circumstances of emergency. They must be presented on the same day to parliament for conversion into laws. If not converted within 60 days of their publication, they lose validity retroactively.

8 Law 400/1988 previously tried to limit the reiteration of decree-laws, but without success. Government and parliament did not want to lose their prerogatives. Decree-laws represented an important outlet for them, and law 400/1988 did not provide an alternative (Vassallo 2001: 88). Then, the Court with sentence 360/1996 declared the constitutional illegitimacy of decree 463/1995 that reiterated a decree that had previously (and many times) failed to be converted (Vassallo 2001: 86–96). In this way the Italian Supreme Court declared the constitutional illegitimacy of all the decrees that were reiterated, representing a landmark for Italian legislation.

9 The dataset was integrated with information on legislative acts drawn from the Italian Law-Making Archive (ILMA) (Borghetto *et al.* 2012).

10 Another source of inconsistency resides in the fact that in some cases part of the law is not available in text format but as an attached image. All these relatively infrequent cases have been excluded from the analysis. As regards temporary decrees, one can consider revisions brought by either the law of conversion (most of the time a temporary decree is partially modified at the time of conversion into law) or by subsequent laws. In the following, we will not include the former category in our dataset, since it can be argued that these revisions belong to the pre-enactment phase of the legislative process.

11 The *pentapartito* (five-party) coalition was composed of Christian Democrats (DC), Socialists (PSI), Social Democrats (PSDI), Liberals (PLI) and Republicans (PRI).

12 Respectively, 700 in the IX, 990 in the X, 1,356 in the XIII and 1,738 in the XIV.

13 We recall that the sample of executive laws considered in the analysis already includes only executive acts with number of words above the median.

14 As for law-decrees, one possible justification for the greater rate of amendments might be found in the ban on the reiteration of decree-laws imposed by the Constitutional Court in 1996. We recall that, before this sentence, governments used to keep on reiterating temporary decrees (with small modifications) that did not pass the conversion stage. We expect that those decrees that reached conversion during the First Republic should be more stable due to the fact that their enacting coalitions approved them after long bargaining processes. Indeed government could reiterate a decree law indefinitely, while the parliament could continue to reject it until an agreement was reached. Nonetheless, once the agreement was reached, one could expect it to last longer given the wider support it was based on. What is more, most amendments to law-decrees were mainly included in the law of conversion and, as we said, these have not been computed among amendments. All in all, law-decrees survived the 1996 reform (although their relative frequency declined substantially) but they have been more prone to being revised after conversion.

15 L-skewness scores are constrained to lie within the interval −1 (left-skewed distribution) and 1 (right-skewed distribution). Symmetric distributions have L-skewness equal to 0 (Hosking 1990).

16 L-kurtosis scores range from zero to one, with 0 the lowest and 1 the highest level of kurtosis. As a reference point, the L-kurtosis of a standard Gaussian distribution is 0.123. Measures of kurtosis computed as L-moments are normally to be preferred because 'they are less sensitive to extreme values and reliably computed for a relatively small number of cases' (Breunig and Jones 2011: 107).

17 The mean proportion of words decrease is −4.7 per cent in the First and −3.7 per cent in the Second Republic. The mean proportion of words increase is +2.6 per cent in the First and +1.9 per cent in the Second Republic.

18 The problem of right-censoring is rather common with duration data. It occurs when we know the point in time a process starts but we do not know whether and when it experienced the event of interest because the study ended while it was still going on. An important advantage of the Kaplan-Meier estimator is that it can take into account information provided by 'right-censored' cases (Kaplan and Meier 1958).

19 In both figures, the log-rank test statistically confirms the dissimilarity between the two curves.

20 Difference in survival probability between the three curves is not statistically significant at a .05 level (P = 0.067 using the log-rank test).
21 If we also consider ratification of international treaties there is a difference in output of around 400 laws.
22 The Centre-Left coalition supporting the governments of Prodi I, D'Alema I and II, and Amato II was extremely fragmented and polarized, encompassing a number of parties ranging from seven to nine. The two Berlusconi governments (II and III) were instead supported, respectively, by four and six parties.

References

Baumgartner, F. R. and Jones B. D. (2002) *Policy Dynamics*. University of Chicago Press.

Berry, C. R., Burden, B. C. and Howell, W. G. (2010) 'After Enactment: The Lives and Deaths of Federal Programs.' *American Journal of Political Science* 54(1), pp. 1–17.

Blondel, J. (1970) 'Legislative Behaviour: Some Steps towards a Cross-National Measurement.' *Government and Opposition* 5(1), pp. 67–85.

Borghetto, E. and Giuliani, M. (2012) 'A Long Way to Tipperary: Time in the Italian Legislative Process 1987–2008.' *South European Society and Politics* 17(1), pp. 23–44.

Borghetto, E. and Mader, L. (2014) 'EU Law Revisions and Legislative Drift.' *European Union Politics* 15(2), pp. 171–191.

Borghetto, E., Curini, L., Giuliani, M., Pellegata, A. and Zucchini, F. (2012) 'Italian Law-Making Archive: A New Tool for the Analysis of the Italian Legislative Process.' *Rivista Italiana Di Scienza Politica* 3, pp. 481–501.

Box-Steffensmeier, J. M. and Bradford, J. (2004) *Event History Modeling: A Guide for Social Scientists*. New York: Cambridge University Press.

Breunig, C. and Jones, B. D. (2011) 'Stochastic Process Methods with an Application to Budgetary Data.' *Political Analysis* 19(1), pp. 103–117.

Capano, G. and Giuliani, M. (2001) 'Governing Without Surviving? An Italian Paradox: Law-Making in Italy, 1987-2001.' *The Journal of Legislative Studies* 7(4), pp. 13–36.

Carotti, B. and E. Cavalieri (2009) 'La nuova semplificazione.' *Giornale di Diritto Amministrativo, Quaderni*, Vol. 20, Milan: Wolters Kluwer.

Cotta, M. (1994) 'The Rise and Fall of the "Centrality" of the Italian Parliament: Transformations of the Executive-Legislative Subsystem after the Second World War.' In G. W. Copeland and S. C. Patterson (eds), *Parliaments in the Modern World. Changing Institutions*. Ann Arbor, MI: The University of Michigan Press, pp. 59–84.

Cotta, M. (1996) 'La crisi del governo di partito in Italia.' In M. Cotta and P. Isernia, *Il gigante dai piedi di argilla: la crisi del regime partitocratico in Italia*. Bologna: Il Mulino.

De Giorgi, E. and Verzichelli, L. (2008) 'Still a Difficult Budgetary Process? The Government, the Legislature and the Finance Bill.' *South European Society and Politics* 13(1), pp. 87–110.

De Micheli, C. and Verzichelli, L. (2004) *Il Parlamento*. Bologna: Il Mulino.

Della Sala, V. (1988) 'Government by Decree: The Craxi Government and the Use of Decree Legislation in the Italian Parliament.' In R. Nanetti, R. Leonardi and P. Corbetta (eds), *Italian Politics: A Review*. London: Pinter.

Della Sala, V. (1997) 'Hollowing Out and Hardening the State: European Integration and the Italian Economy.' *West European Politics* 20(1), pp. 14–33.

Della Sala, V. (1998) 'The Italian Parliament: Chambers in a Crumbling House?' In P. Norton (ed.), *Parliaments and Governments in Western Europe*. London: Frank Cass, pp. 73–96.

Di Palma, G. (1976) 'Institutional Rules and Legislative Outcomes in the Italian Parliament.' *Legislative Studies Quarterly* 1(2), pp. 147–179.

Di Palma, G. (1977) *Surviving Without Governing: The Italian Parties in Parliament.* University of California Press.

Giuliani, M. (2008) 'Brand New, Somewhat New or Rather Old? The Italian Legislative Process in an Age of Alternation.' *South European Society and Politics* 13(1), pp. 1–10.

Giuliani, M. and Zucchini, F. (2013) 'Governo e processo legislativo.' In G. Pasquino, M. Regalia and M. Valbruzzi (eds), *Quarant'anni di scienza politica in Italia.* Bologna, Il Mulino, pp. 153–169.

Hine, D. (1993) *Governing Italy: the politics of bargained pluralism.* Oxford: Clarendon Press.

Hosking, J. R. M. (1990) 'L-Moments: Analysis and Estimation of Distributions Using Linear Combinations of Order Statistics.' *Journal of the Royal Statistical Society. Series B (Methodological)*, 52(1), pp. 105–124.

Jones, B. D. and Baumgartner, F. R. (2005) *The Politics of Attention: How Government Prioritizes Problems.* University of Chicago Press.

Kaplan, E. L. and Meier, P. (1958) 'Nonparametric Estimation from Incomplete Observations.' *Journal of the American Statistical Association* 53(282), pp. 457–481.

Maltzman, F. and Shipan, C. R. (2008) 'Change, Continuity, and the Evolution of the Law.' *American Journal of Political Science*, 52(2), pp. 252–267.

Marangoni, F. (2013) *Provare a governare, cercando di sopravvivere. Esecutivi e attività legislativa nella Seconda Repubblica.* Pisa University Press.

Morlino, L. (2013) 'The Impossible Transition and the Unstable New Mix: Italy 1992–2012.' *Comparative European Politics* 11(3), pp. 337–359.

Newell, J. (2006) 'Characterising the Italian Parliament: Legislative Change in Longitudinal Perspective.' *Journal of Legislative Studies* 12(3–4), pp. 386–403.

Norton, P. (1994) 'The Legislative Powers of Parliament.' In C. Flinterman, A. W. Hering and L. Waddington (eds), *The Evolving Role of Parliaments in Europe.* Aperldoorn: Maklu, pp. 15–32.

Predieri, A. (ed.) (1974) *Il processo legislativo nel Parlamento italiano.* Milan: Giuffrè Editore.

Ragusa, J. M. (2010) 'The Lifecycle of Public Policy: An Event History Analysis of Repeals to Landmark Legislative Enactments, 1951–2006.' *American Politics Research* 38(6), pp. 1015–1051.

Sartori, G. (1982) *Teoria dei partiti e caso italiano.* Milan: SugarCo.

Vassallo, S. (1994) *Il governo di partito in Italia (1943–1993).* Bologna: Il Mulino.

Vassallo, S. (2001) 'Le leggi del governo. Come gli esecutivi della transizione hanno superato i veti incrociati.' In G. Capano and M. Giuliani (eds), *Parlamento e processo legislativo in Italia: continuità e mutamento.* Bologna: Il Mulino, pp. 85–126.

Visconti, F. (2011) *Friction & Policy Change: A Longitudinal Study of Italian Laws after Enactment.* Masters Thesis in Comparative Politics, Supervisor: M. Giuliani, University of Milan.

Zucchini, F. (2008) 'Dividing Parliament? Italian Bicameralism in the Legislative Process (1987–2006).' *South European Society and Politics* 13(1), pp. 11–34.

Zucchini, F. (2011) 'Government Alternation and Legislative Agenda Setting.' *European Journal of Political Research* 50(6), pp. 749–774.

6 The support for and popularity of the government

Vincenzo Memoli

Introduction

When citizens say they support the political system, what exactly do they mean? An answer to this question can be found in the works of Easton (1965, 1975) who defined as main elements of this type of support those stemming from the assessment of institutions and of their performance (output), of the institutional actors (parties and others such as bureaucracy) and of the overall identification with the state. Easton also distinguished between diffuse and specific support. On the one hand, diffuse support consists of attitudes toward politics and the political system, which are expected to be rather stable over time. On the other hand, specific support consists of satisfaction with institutional outputs, in other words with the specific acts of state decision-makers and with their capacity to respond to citizens' demands (Pharr and Putnam 2000; Diamond and Morlino 2005; Memoli 2013). Finally, political support is a multi-dimensional concept made of diffuse and specific components, it can be understood as assessment of the institutional performance, the political actors and the political system as a whole by the citizens: 'the way in which a person evaluatively orients himself to some object through either his attitudes or his behavior' (Easton 1975: 436).

Many scholars affirm that in the last 30 years political support has become very unstable even in the most consolidated democracies. Citizens support the government when it delivers a positive performance (Evans and Whitefield 1995; Mishler and Rose 2001) or when politicians prove open to incorporating citizens' demands in their action (Weatherford 1992). Over the past decades, the relationship between institutional outputs and political support has become more negative (Anderson and Guillory 1997; Bellucci and Memoli 2012; Cusack 1999) and a general increase in political dissatisfaction (Pharr and Putnam 2000), particularly with respect to the institutional performance (Dalton 2004; Memoli 2011; McAllister 2000; Norris 1999), has made citizens more critical of the political system. Starting from the 1990s, popular expectations and scrutiny of the performance of the public sector have become more stringent and also sophisticated (Radin 2000). The idea that a government is considered efficient not only as long as it implements bills (Cook *et al.* 2005; Rothstein 2005), but also if it encourages the exchange of services among citizens in a way that improves their overall wealth, has become a firm point (Levi 2006).

Apparently, over the past decades governments have not completely satisfied citizens' expectations and demands.[1] For example, Nye *et al.* (1997) show that American public opinion reached record low levels of political trust during the 1990s, and the same was true also in other countries (Bellucci and Memoli 2012; Klingemann and Fuchs 1995; Memoli 2011), a clear sign of a widespread malaise among citizens. Within the broad context of this increased dissatisfaction and declining support for the political system, the Italian case appears particularly interesting. The picture is more severe in this country where a harsh economic crisis adds to deep-rooted dissatisfaction with government performance and to long-term declining support for the political system (Memoli 2009).

Beyond their actual capacity to deliver outputs that are popular with citizens, it should also be noted that during the past four legislatures (1996–2013), national political leaders have been involved in major scandals, or 'transgressions that become known to the wider public and that are serious enough to produce a public response' (Thompson 2000: 13). Political misconduct, corruption and power abuse have deeply affected Italian politics in the recent past (Newell 2010) to the point of seriously damaging the image of the country even abroad (*Economist* 2010). Many scholars agree that scandals exert a bad influence on the popularity of governments and have detrimental effects on the political system in general (Peters and Welch 1978; Doherty *et al.* 2011) and on popular support for democracy (Maier 2011), as citizens tend to react very negatively to these events without really differentiating among these different aspects. Indeed, scandals involving heads of government and politicians (Martorano and Ulbig 2008; Bowler and Karp 2004; Clarke *et al.* 1998) can erode citizens' trust in government (Damico *et al.* 2000), support for state institutions (Morris and Clawson 2007) and may change their overall political behaviour quite substantially (Cowley 2002; McAllister 2000; Hetherington 1999), particularly with respect to those candidates involved in the scandals (Dimock and Jacobson 1995; Alford *et al.* 1994: 790). However, not all scholars agree on the fact that scandals always reduce citizens' support for the political system (Easton 1965; Citrin 1974) or are detrimental to the political life of a country or for the individual careers of politicians (Sabato *et al.* 2000; Kepplinger and Ehmig 2004; Kepplinger 2005). Some examples include Watergate, when public support actually increased as a consequence of this scandal (Dunham and Mauss 1976; Sniderman *et al.* 1975), or the case of the former Italian Prime Minister, Silvio Berlusconi, who won the elections twice, in 2001 and 2008, despite, at the same time, being prosecuted under allegations of corruption and fiscal fraud (Vannucci 2009: 235). In the recent past, the Italian judiciary many times held tense relationships with politicians in general and with the government in particular (Memoli 2013). When the judiciary is considered independent, citizens are more inclined to trust this power regardless of their political orientations and their party choice (Buhlmann and Kunz 2011). This is not always the case in Italy where scandals involving prominent politicians have been accompanied by pressures of various kinds by some political parties and even by the government on the judiciary, often in the attempt to make this power less independent, or to make members of the parliament/government immune to legal prosecution. These attempts and the consequent confrontation between these powers made the overall state of the rule of law more critical in the country.[2] Furthermore, a dangerous and in many respects still unrevealed connection between mafia and politics has come to light many times, and this may have had a detrimental impact on the rule of law and generated a sense of distrust toward state powers on the part of citizens.

Making use of multi-variate analyses, this chapter attempts to assess the impact of institutional efficiency, the state of the economy, political scandals and the rule of law on the popularity of the Italian government. I show that these factors have different influences on the construction of citizens' support for the incumbent. The results of the analysis in this chapter allow to shed light on the relative impact of government performance (which has been analysed from different angles in the other chapters of the book) on citizens' attitudes toward the government, and also on the influence of other factors pertaining to the public image of the government and of state institutions which, although they were not examined with same intensity in the volume, have been shown to be relevant for the popularity of the incumbent.

Support for the Italian government

These days, political support in Italy does not seem to differ much from the situation of half a century ago. As was argued by Almond and Verba a long time ago (1963), citizens still prove sceptical about politics. Although the two American scholars have been criticized many times for their conclusions (Sani 1980, 1989), especially because these attitudes have important territorial variations (Putnam 1993), in general the situation today does not seem very different from that of those days. On the one hand, different levels of civicness produce diverse institutional performance at the local level (Cartocci 2000). On the other hand, perceptions of a low institutional performance are widely spread among Italian citizens, particularly with respect to state institutions (the picture for the local institutions is more diverse). As a consequence, at the national level satisfaction with democracy is generally low and below the European average. Some evidence of this could be found in widespread anti-party (Bardi 1996; Sani and Segatti 2001) and anti-politics attitudes (Mastropaolo 2000) characterizing Italian public opinion, particularly since the 1990s. Citizens reveal their alienation for politics mainly because of the low efficacy and overall capacity of the government to solve problems (Bardi and Pasquino 1995). The popularity of the government certainly has an impact on the overall support for the system and on satisfaction with democracy. In line with the overall goals of the volume, in this chapter the analysis is focused primarily on the popularity of the government, although some implications could be derived as well with respect to popular legitimacy of the political system more broadly.[3]

We analyse the phenomenon longitudinally, between January 2001 and November 2011, a decade where five political cabinets alternated (in 2011–2013 a technocratic nonpartisan government took office which, due to its peculiar nature,

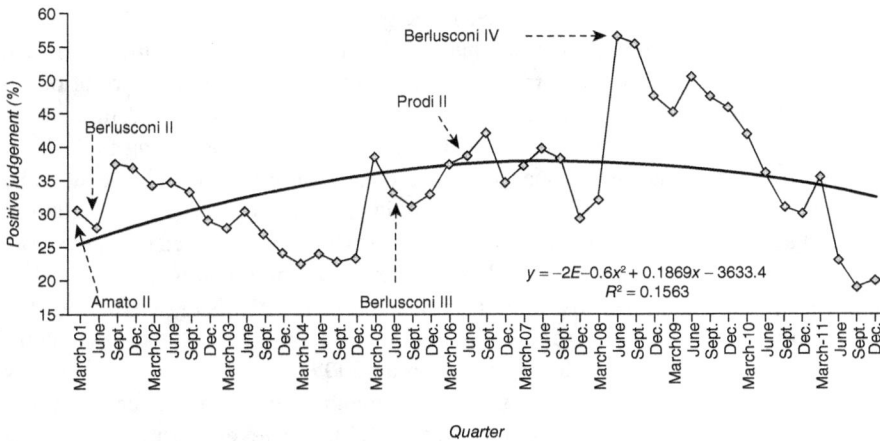

Figure 6.1 Support for the government (2001–2011)

Note: Data on the last term of 2011 refer to the 1 October–16 November period (until resignation of the Berlusconi IV cabinet).

Source Ispo (2005–2010); Italian Prime Ministry (Presidenza del Consiglio dei Ministri – Dipartimento per l'Informazione e l'Editoria, 2001–2004; 2011).

will not be considered in the analysis) – Amato II, Berlusconi II–III,[4] Prodi II, Berlusconi IV – and was never confirmed after the elections, as voters sanctioned the incumbent every time. Indeed, the popularity curve of the government always showed a negative trend toward the end of the legislature (Figure 6.1). During the ten years considered in the analysis, the popularity of the Italian government declined by an overall 10.4 per cent. This is certainly evidence of a bad state of popularity of this institution. We now examine the phenomenon in greater detail.

Starting from the fourth and last government of the XIII legislature (Amato II), whose popularity was around 30 per cent, we see that in 2001 voters sanctioned the incumbent centre-left coalition and rewarded the centre-right opposition led by Berlusconi who then became Prime Minister for the second time after 1994. Under his leadership, a new cycle started where the chief executive began to exert a greater coordination role with respect to past governments, especially among the coalition partners, even though its overall capacity to plan and produce coherent policy remained, overall, limited (Moury 2011: 43). The initial popularity of this cabinet and of its leader, which was also determined by a successful communication strategy, marked a change compared to the past and appeared very promising for the stability of the government. However, in 2005, four years after its electoral success, this cabinet was heavily sanctioned by voters in the local elections when the parties belonging to the parliamentary majority lost to the benefit of the opposition, and the government went through a crisis culminating with the exit of some of the coalition partners. A new government led by Berlusconi (III) was formed at that point that paid generous rewards in office allocation to the most recalcitrant partners (Circap 2005: 4). But the popularity of the government appeared severely damaged by that time and a new electoral failure for the incumbent followed shortly after in the general elections of 2006.

The popularity of the government increased again under a new cabinet (Prodi II), but this trend lasted only a few months, as by September 2006 only four out of ten citizens expressed a positive evaluation of this cabinet. In December 2007, the support decreased to 29 per cent. The ideologically diverse coalition supporting the cabinet proved very conflictual and inconclusive, moreover it was very thin in the Senate. The government soon experienced a crisis that would bring the country to early elections, when the citizens severely punished the incumbent and again rewarded the opposition.

The new cabinet (Berlusconi IV) presented some new features compared to the past centre-right executives led by the same Prime Minister. The age of the new ministers was on average lower than in the past and there was greater representation of women within the cabinet (Circap 2009). At the same time, the new government could rely on a more cohesive majority made of fewer and more ideologically coherent parties (Marangoni 2010). However, despite the rather high popularity of this government during its early days, after the outbreak of the economic crisis and the related responses of the executive, several divisive policies (particularly in the field of education and justice) and the involvement of high government officials including the Prime Minister in various scandals, citizens' support deteriorated rapidly and reached a low point by the end of 2011.

As we can see, the trend in the popularity of the Italian government has been rather stable in the analysed period and permanently unfavourable to the executive. The decline of popular support for every government is also a possible explanation of the phenomenon of government instability in Italy, as it is certainly more difficult to keep a cabinet in office and a majority coalition united when their popularity deteriorates too much. What are the factors that have contributed most to this negative trend in the popularity of governments? The analysis now moves to the operationalization of causal factors and to the assessment of their impact on popular support.

The determinants of government popularity

The popularity of governments is often analysed through the theoretical lenses of the economic voting, where economic outcomes are considered the main determinants of citizens' attitudes toward the incumbent (Bellucci and Lewis-Beck 2011; Lewis-Beck and Stegmaier 2000, 2007; Nannestad and Paldam 1994). The theory of economic voting hypothesizes that when the economy goes well voters support the government, but when it follows a negative trend voters withdraw their support (Lewis-Beck 1988). Along the same line, I hypothesize that the capacity to deliver outputs that are favourable for the economy and to improve the material conditions of citizens has a positive impact on citizens' support for the government.

However, the above is not the only possible determinant that should be considered. According to some authors, scandals affect the reputation of politicians, a main resource in their relationship with public opinion (Thompson 2000). Politicians are publicly responsible and subject to the scrutiny of citizens at the time of the elections and their involvement in scandals can be a major problem affecting their political responsibility and democratic accountability (Tumber and Waisboard 2004: 1035). Indeed, Markovits and Silverstein (1988: 9) define political scandals as unfaithfulness toward citizens' trust in political responsibility and in the democratic process. Although individual responsibility is always central in these kinds of scandals, the impact on citizens' attitudes toward public institutions can also be more broadly affected (Della Porta 2000; Rose *et al.* 1998; Seligson 2002; Anderson and Tverdova 2003). Research shows that in many cases scandals have influenced support for the government (Miller 1999) and for parties (Doherty *et al.* 2011). Along the same lines, I hypothesize that the presence of scandals reduced the popularity of the Italian government.

Moving to another problem, the rule of law is a concept that makes reference to the general respect for laws and to a corresponding correct application of sanctions, to equality of all citizens behind justice, to maintenance of the civil order.[5] In the 2000–2001 period, the rule of law in Italy declined substantially from 0.80 to 0.41,[6] following a sine trend which, in 2006, reached a negative peak of 0.28. In comparative terms, Italy shows a record that is below the OECD average (Piana 2013). Certainly, many conflicts between political leaders, or parties, and the judiciary – that were particularly exacerbated at the time when centre-right cabinets where in office – culminated in several attempts to limit the independence of the judiciary and the equality of all citizens behind the law, with a consequent negative impact on the rule of law (Agrast *et al.* 2011). On the one hand, the severity in the application of laws may sometimes be detrimental to the weakest individuals or to the most fragile groups of a society (O'Donnell 1999, quoted in Morlino 2003). On the other hand, however, an unsatisfactory level of rule of law makes sanctions more uncertain and may favour political corruption. This seems the case in Italy where a general increase in widespread corruption is strongly associated with a decline in the rule of law (Transparency International 2011). This phenomenon can create a climate of perceived insecurity and injustice among the citizens, and it is therefore possible to hypothesize that a decline of the rule of law creates the conditions for a deterioration of popular support for the government.

The popularity of the government: an explanatory model

In this section, I test the hypotheses on causality presented above. For this purpose, I have applied a regression model to explain popularity based on the following formula:

$$\gamma = \alpha + \beta_{x \times 1} + \beta_{x \times 2} + \beta_{x \times 3} + \beta_{x \times 4} + e$$

where:

γ = the popularity of the government (dependent variable);
$\beta_{x \times 1}$ = a dichotomous variable that indicates presence (1) or absence (0) of the following scandals: Scajola,[7] Mills,[8] Prodi,[9] Cosentino,[10] Bertolaso,[11] Italia.it,[12] Ruby,[13] Noemi,[14] D'Addario,[15] Rubygate;[16]

$\beta_{x \times 2}$ = an index of government efficiency (delayed by a term);[17]
$\beta_{x \times 3}$ = an index of the state of the rule of law in the country (delayed by a term);[18]
$\beta_{x \times 4}$ = an index of economic growth (per cent of GDP, delayed by a term);
e = error.

The literature contains very few analyses that consider the specific impact of economic voting on the popularity of the Italian cabinets (Bellucci 1984, 1991, 2010, 2012; Lewis-Beck and Bellucci 1982; Memoli 2013). However, although limited in number, they tend to confirm that citizens consider the national government the main institution responsible for the economic situation of the country: depending on the economic situation, they decide whether to support the incumbent in the elections or to withdraw their support. Differently from the above works, our analysis shows that economic growth does not play a significant influence on this kind of support (Table 6.1).

A possible explanation of this result – not necessarily in terms of statistical significance of the relationship that may depend on the different nature of the data used in the various analyses, but rather in terms of direction – could be related to citizens' perceptions of the state of the economy. Actually, our analysis allows us to specify how accurate citizens' perceptions tend to be with respect to reality. Citizens may shape their support as a consequence of their socio-centric and ego-centric assessment of the state of the economy (Banducci *et al.* 2003; Hobolt and Leblond 2009) which could, in fact, be quite different from the actual situation shown by the official statistics (Banducci *et al.* 2009). Suffice it to say that despite the trend in GDP growth being positive during more than 500 days in the period between 2009 (second term) and 2010 (fourth term) (Istat 2012), in popularity terms, during the same period, Italian public opinion continued to sanction the government.[19] This is evidence of the independence of the two variables and, anyway, of a direction of a hypothetical relationship between these two variables that could be non-linear due to misperceptions about the general state of the economy by the citizens. Ultimately, from our analysis economic voting does not emerge as a significant determinant of levels of support for the government.

Hence, possible explanations of citizens' attitudes toward the government should be searched elsewhere. On the one hand, when the government is efficient and works well, we find a positive relationship with citizens' support ($\beta = 0.811$). On the other hand, when the rule of law deteriorates in the country, citizens tend to sanction the government ($\beta = -0.939$). This is not a new feature in Italian politics, tensions between parties and political elites on the one side and the judiciary on the other are deeply rooted in Italy and were even conducive to the implosion of the system of the First Republic (when a large number of politicians, mainly from government parties, were prosecuted for bribery) and the creation of the Second Republic based on new parties and a largely renovated political class. However, this difficult interplay between politics and the judiciary continued even after this big system change, as many prominent politicians have been prosecuted since and often for the same reasons. On the other hand, the responses of politicians often went in the direction of their self-defence against the judiciary, with clear

Table 6.1 The determinants of popular support for the government (2001–2011)

	Model 1		Model 2	
	β	Robust Standard Error	β	Robust Standard Error
Political scandal	-0.405**	2.758	-0.343*	2.537
Government effectiveness	0.811*	10.300	0.638*	8.780
Rule of law	-0.939**	14.236	-1.030***	10.910
Economic growth	-0.278	1.400	-0.296	1.518
Government ideological position[a]			2.739	2.765
Economic crisis[b]			-0.400**	2.369
Constant	4.140	4.652	7.940	5.958
Adjusted R square	0.155		0.171	
Anova (sig.)	0.079		0.060	
Root MSE	5.285		5.235	
Durbin – autocorrelation test	0.734		0.325	
Portemanteau Test (sig.)	0.377		0.377	
Durbin Watson	2.104		2.291	
T (quarter)	43		43	

Notes
* p<0.10; ** p<0.05; *** p<0.01
a The variable is 0 for centre-left and 1 for centre-right cabinets;
b The variable is 0 for the 2001–2008 period (II quarter) and 1 for the other periods (from the III term of 2008 until 16 November 2011.

Source: Ispo (2005–2010); Italian Prime Ministry (*Presidenza del Consiglio dei Ministri – Dipartimento per l'Informazione e l'Editoria*, 2001–2004; 2011); World Bank (2001–2011).

attempts to represent this power as enemy of citizens and to neutralize its action by reducing its independence and overall capacity to prosecute members of the government, or of the parliament.

A similar tendency concerns the involvement of politicians in scandals of various kinds (those entailing a breach of common ethics). When these scandals involve members of the government or of the parliamentary majority, citizens tend to support the incumbent less ($\beta = -0.405$). In many cases, scandals have been conducive to political isolation of those politicians involved, but in other cases (for example, Berlusconi) this did not happen (cf. Chang *et al.* 2010). This might largely depend on candidate selection; since 2006 Italy has adopted a proportional electoral system with majority bonus and blocked lists of candidates. Under this system, voters do not have a direct choice of candidates, their vote is for blocked lists of candidates and they do not have the possibility to sanction individually any of them for misconduct. In the end, it is mainly the choice of parties whether to include/exclude those candidates who have been associated with immoral behaviour. For example, the support for Berlusconi's leadership has always been strong within his party and his candidacy was reiterated despite his involvement in many scandals.

When Model 1 in Table 6.1 is controlled with two variables pertaining to the ideological orientation (left/right) of governments and the time period (before or after the economic crisis) the above results are confirmed and the above relationships are even reinforced (Model 2). Furthermore, the control variables allow us to generate additional information: in the analysed period, those cabinets leaning ideologically toward the right received greater support than those leaning to the left ($\beta = 2.739$). This was true despite their involvement in many scandals and until the outbreak of the economic crisis, when the negative outcomes became more tangible for the citizens (starting from the second half of 2008) and the support for the centre-right government also declined ($\beta = 0.400$). This is the only period where the state of the economy has certainly played a more tangible impact on citizens' attitudes toward the government.

Final remarks

In the past 20 years, the Italian government has generated many expectations among Italian citizens. The intended shift toward an *output democracy* (a phenomenon that was extensively discussed in the Introduction to this volume) has been seen by many as an opportunity to improve the overall performance, as well as the responsiveness of the Italian government to citizens. As has been documented in other parts of the volume, government pledges have become more ambitious and their fulfilment (up to a certain point in cabinets' life) effective. However, many pledges remained unfulfilled and the life cycle of the government has often been accompanied by a deterioration of the capacity to meet citizens' expectations and produce effective outputs. In the analysed period, after three consecutive elections that were conducive to perfect alternation in government (five cabinets in total), the country has experienced continuous economic decline and deterioration of quality of life. The GDP per capita growth has been lowest among the OECD countries and placed Italy behind countries such as Slovenia, Portugal and Spain.[20] Within this context, it should not be surprising that trust toward the major institutions, including the government, declined deeply and reached levels well below those registered in the 1980s. Further evidence of popular malaise and of citizens' disenchantment with the political system – and with the government in particular – is the growth in abstention in the elections from 18.5 per cent in 2001 to 25 per cent in 2013.

However, this chapter shows that citizens' perceptions of the state of the economy is not always congruent with reality and that its impact on the support for the government is not straightforward. Within the field of economic voting studies, our results show that Italians are relatively immune from the cost-benefit calculations about the state of the national economy when they evaluate the government, therefore the main components of their evaluations should be searched elsewhere. This was true, however, until the outbreak of the economic crisis, as its overall impact was so widely perceived by the Italian citizens that it produced, for the first time in the analysed period, a general decline in popular support for the government.

These results made consideration of other potential explanatory factors necessary. If the state of the economy alone does not constitute a satisfactory explanation of the level of support for the government, it is therefore necessary to include other factors in the analysis. For this purpose, I have included legality and morality in my explanatory model; two factors pertaining to the public image of governments. The evidence shows that when the rule of law declines in the country, the support for the government deteriorates as well. This is especially due to the fact that in Italy a decline in the rule of law was also determined by the attempt to legislate in order to reduce the independence of judges and their capacity to prosecute MPs and members of the government. At the same time, involvement in scandals, that imply either material misconduct and financial abuse or violation of morality by members of the cabinet or of the parliamentary majority, also determined a decline in citizens' support for the government. Ultimately, the results of the chapter show that when we consider the capacity of the Italian government to gain support from citizens, it is important to analyse not only its overall performance and efficiency. Its public image, in particular its capacity to guarantee the rule of law and the respect of morality, should also be considered, as these prove influential factors in shaping citizens' attitudes toward the incumbent.

Notes

1 Some authors define efficacy as one dimension within the broader concept of institutional output (Nord 1983), some others as one dimension of institutional performance (Brewer and Coleman Selden 2000). In line with some other authors (Selden and Sowa 2004), I make use of the two concepts of efficacy and performance interchangeably.
2 The rule of law is related to the legal system and to its implementation, but also to state and government (O'Donnell 2005), particularly in terms of institutional *accountability* and *responsiveness* (Morlino and Palombella 2010).
3 In the analysis of the popularity of the Italian government, I refer to the survey data of ISPO or to those published by the Italian Prime Ministership (*Presidenza del Consiglio dei Ministri – Dipartimento per l'Informazione e l'Editoria*, www. sondaggipoliticoelettorali.it). In some of these surveys, the question was the fol-

lowing: 'How do you evaluate the government activity to date? Very positive, fairly positive, rather negative, very negative'. In other surveys the question was: 'Overall, how much do you trust the incumbent government? Very much trust, fairly trust, little trust, no trust'. Another question in the survey was: 'On a 1–10 scale, what score would you assign to the government at this moment? In the analysis, the positive values aggregate the very and fairly positive/trust categories and those values equal or higher than 6 in the scale.

4 The Berlusconi III government was formed in April 2005, after the electoral defeat of its supporting coalition in the recent local elections. However, its composition was not much different from that of the Berlusconi II government, small parties were just better represented in office.

5 On the rule of law in Italy, see also Della Porta and Morlino (2001).

6 The index on the rule of law has a range from –2.5 (negative) to 2.5 (positive). See on this http://info.worldbank.org/governance/wgi/index.aspx#home.

7 The Minister for Economic Development, Claudio Scajola, was accused of illegal financing of his party and also of fiscal fraud and bribery because his house in the centre of Rome was partially bought with the money of an entrepreneur, Diego Anemone, who had done public works under a government mandate on the occasion of a G8 summit (he was also prosecuted for fiscal fraud and bribery for the same works).

8 The incumbent Prime Minister, Berlusconi, was prosecuted under allegation of having paid 600,000 dollars to a lawyer, David Mills, to not reveal that Berlusconi's companies had illegally created two off-shore companies abroad to avoid taxation in Italy.

9 Investigations on misuse of European funds involved the incumbent Prime Minister, Romano Prodi.

10 The undersecretary in the Ministry of the Economy, Nicola Cosentino, was prosecuted for association with mafia organizations.

11 The undersecretary in the Prime Ministry, Guido Bertolaso, was prosecuted under allegation of bribery and corruption in the context of public works carried out on the occasion of a G8 summit in Italy.

12 Italia.it was a portal for the promotion of tourism in Italy. It was designed by the Berlusconi II government and then launched by Prodi II in February 2007. Soon, it became known for its disproportionate costs and waste of public funds and was therefore shut down after less than one year.

13 The incumbent Prime Minister, Berlusconi, was prosecuted under allegation of having exchanged money for sexual services with an under-age girl called Ruby (real name Karima El Mahroug), and also for having abused his institutional position by interfering with an enquiry that was carried out by the local police in Milan who had arrested this girl under allegation of theft.

14 Letizia Noemi, a young model who was under age at the time, was believed to be the secret lover of the incumbent Prime Minister, Berlusconi. The allegation was indirectly but publicly confirmed by Berlusconi's wife (who consequently divorced from her husband) in a letter sent to one of the main Italian newspapers, *La Repubblica*.

15 Patrizia D'Addario was an escort who met several times with the incumbent Prime Minister, Berlusconi.

16 The incumbent Prime Minister, Berlusconi, was prosecuted under allegation of exchange of money for sexual services with under-age girls.

17 This index has a range between –2.5 (lowest efficacy) and 2.5 (highest efficacy). Source: the World Bank.

18 This index has a range between –2.5 (negative) to 2.5 (positive). Source: the World Bank.

19 In the same period, the popularity of the government declined from 50.4 per cent to 30 per cent.

20 International Monetary Fund, see http://www.imf.org/external/index.htm

References

Agrast, M., Botero, J., and Ponce, A. (2011). *WJ Rule of Law Index 2011*. Washington, DC: The World Justice Project.

Alford, J., Teeters, H., Ward, D.S., and Wilson, R.K. (1994). 'Overdraft: The Political Cost of Congressional Malfeasance', *The Journal of Politics*, 56, pp. 788–801.

Almond, G.A., and Verba, S. (1963). *The Civic Culture: Political Attitudes and Democracy in Five Nations*. Princeton, NJ: Princeton University Press.

Anderson, C.J., and Guillory, A. (1997). 'Political Institutions and Satisfaction with Democracy', *American Political Science Review*, 91, pp. 66–81.

Anderson, C.J., and Tverdova, Y.V. (2003). 'Corruption, Political Allegiances, and Attitudes toward Government in Contemporary Democracies', *American Journal of Political Science*, 47, pp. 91–109.

Banducci, S.A., Karp, J.A., and Loedel, P.H. (2003). 'The Euro, Economic Interests and Multilevel Governance: Examining Support for the Common Currency', *European Journal of Political Research*, 42, pp. 685–703.

Banducci, S.A., Karp, J.A., and Loedel, P.H. (2009). 'Economic Interests and Public Support for the Euro', *Journal of European Public Policy*, 16, pp. 564–581.

Bardi, L. (1996). 'Anti-party Sentiment and Party System Change in Italy', *European Journal of Political Science*, 29, pp. 345–363.

Bardi, L., and Pasquino, G. (1995). 'Politicizzati ed alienati', in A. Parisi and H. Schadee (eds), *Sulla soglia del cambiamento*. Bologna: Il Mulino.

Bellucci, P. (1984). 'The Effect of Aggregate Economic Conditions on the Political Preferences of the Italian Electorate, 1953–1979', *European Journal of Political Research*, 12, pp. 387–401.

Bellucci, P. (1991). 'Italian Economic Voting: A Deviant Case or Making a Case for a Better Theory?', in H. Norpoth, M.S. Lewis-Beck and J. Lafay (eds), *Economics and Politics: The Calculus of Support*. Ann Arbor: The University of Michigan Press.

Bellucci, P. (2010). Election Cycles and Electoral Forecasting in Italy, 1994–2008. *International Journal of Forecasting*, 26, pp. 54–67.

Bellucci, P. (2012). 'Government Accountability and Voting Choice in Italy, 1990–2008', *Electoral Studies*, 31(3), pp. 491–497.

Bellucci, P., and Lewis-Beck, M. (2011). 'A Stable Popularity Function? Cross-national Analysis', *European Journal of Political Research*, 50(2), pp. 190–211.

Bellucci, P., and Memoli, V. (2012). 'The determinants of Democratic Support in Europe', in P.C. Magalhaes, D. Sanders and G. Toka (eds), *Citizens and the European Polity: Mass Attitudes Towards the European and National Polities (Citizenship, Identity and European Integration)*. Oxford: Oxford University Press.

Bowler, S.B., and Karp, J.A. (2004). 'Politicians, Scandals, and Trust in Government', *Political Behavior*, 26(3), pp. 271–287.

Brewer, G.A., and Coleman Selden, S. (2000). 'Why Elephants Gallop: Assessing and Predicting Organizational Performance in Federal Agencies', *Journal of Public Administration Research and Theory*, 10(4), pp. 685–712.

Buhlmann, M., and Kunz, R. (2011). 'Confidence in the Judiciary: Comparing the Independence and Legitimacy of Judicial System', *West European Politics*, 34(2), pp. 317–345.

Cartocci, R. (2000). 'Chi ha paura dei valori? Capitale sociale e dintorni', *Rivista Italiana di Scienza Politica*, 3, pp. 423–474.

Chang, E.C.C., Golden, M.A., and Hill, S.J. (2010). 'Legislative Malfeasance and Political Accountability', *World Politics* 62(2), pp. 177–220.

Circap (2005). *Rapporto sul Governo*, 3rd edn (June), Dipartimento di Scienze storiche, giuridiche, politiche, e sociali. Siena: Università degli Studi di Siena.

Circap (2009). *IV Rapporto sul Governo*, Dipartimento di Scienze storiche, giuridiche, politiche, e sociali. Siena: Università degli Studi di Siena.

Citrin, J. (1974). 'Comment: The Political Relevance of Trust in Government', *American Political Science Review*, 68, pp. 973–988.

Clarke, H.D., Norpoth, H., and Whiteley, P. (1998). 'It's About Time: Modelling Political and Social Dynamics – A guide to new approaches', in E. Scarbrough, and E. Tannenbaum (eds), *Research Strategies in the Social Sciences*. Oxford: Oxford University Press.

Cook, K.S., Russell, H., and Levi, M. (2005). *Cooperation Without Trust?* New York: Russell Sage Foundation.

Cowley, P. (2002). *Revolts & Rebellions: Parliamentary Voting Under Blair*. London: Politico.

Cusack, T.R. (1999). 'The Shaping of Popular Satisfaction with Government and Regime Performance in Germany', *British Journal of Political Science*, 29, pp. 641–672.

Dalton, R.J. (2004). *Democratic Challenges, Democratic Choices: The Erosion of Political Support in Advanced Industrial Democracies*. Oxford: Oxford University Press.

Damico, A.J., Conway, M.M., and Bowman Damico, S. (2000). 'Patterns of Political Trust and Mistrust: Three Moments in the Lives of Democratic Citizens', *Polity*, 32(3), pp. 377–400.

Della Porta, D. (2000). 'Social Capital, Beliefs in Government, and Political Corruption', in S.J. Pharr and R. Putnam (eds), *Disaffected Democracies: What's Troubling the Trilateral Countries*. Princeton, NJ: Princeton University Press.

Della Porta, D., and Morlino, L. (2001). *Rights and the Quality of Democracy in Italy: A Research Report*. Stockholm: IDEA.

Diamond, L., and Morlino, L. (eds) (2005). *Assessing the Quality of Democracy*. Baltimore, MD: Johns Hopkins University Press.

Dimock, M.A., and Jacobson, G.C. (1995). 'Checks and Choices: The House Bank Scandal's Impact on Voters in 1992', *The Journal of Politics*, 57, pp. 1143–1159.

Doherty, D., Dowling, C.M., and Miller, M.G. (2011). 'Are Financial or Moral Scandals Worse? It Depends', *PS: Political Science & Politics*, 44(4), pp. 749–757.

Dunham, R.G., and Mauss, A.L. (1976). 'Waves from Watergate: Evidence Concerning the Impact of the Watergate Scandal upon Political Legitimacy and Social Control', *Pacific Sociological Review*, 19, pp. 469–490.

Easton, D. (1965). *A System Analysis of Political Life*. New York: Harper.

Easton, D. (1975). 'A Re-Assessment of the Concept of Political Support', *British Journal of Political Science*, 5, pp. 435–457.

Economist. (2010). Silvio Berlusconi's latest scandal. Bungled bungled. Available from: http://www.economist.com/blogs/newsbook/2010/11/silvio_berlusconis_latest_scandal/print.

Evans, G., and Whitefield, S. (1995). 'The Politics and Economics of Democratic Commitment: Support for Democracy in Transition Societies', *British Journal of Political Science*, 25(4), pp. 485–514.

Hetherington, M.J. (1999). 'The Effect of Political Trust on the Presidential Vote, 1968–1996', *American Political Science Review*, 93, pp. 311–326.

Hobolt, S.B., and Leblond, P. (2009). 'Is My Crown Better Than Your Euro? Exchange Rates and Public Opinion on the European Single Currency', *European Union Politics*, 10, pp. 202–225.

Istat (2012). *II trimestre 2012. Stima preliminare del Pil*. Available from: http://www.istat.it/it/archivio/68720

Kepplinger, H.M. (2005). *Die Mechanismen der Skandalierung. Die Macht der Medien und die Möglichkeiten der Betroffenen.* Munich: Olzog.

Kepplinger, H.M., and Ehmig, S.C. (2004). 'Ist die funktionalistische Skandaltheorie haltbar? Ein Beitrag zur Interdependenz von Politik und Medien im Umgang mit Missständen in der Gesellschaft', in K. Imhof, R. Blum, H. Bonfadelli and O. Jarren (eds), *Mediengesellschaft: Strukturen, Merkmale, Entwicklungsdynamiken.* Wiesbaden: Verlag für Sozialwissenschaften.

Klingemann, H.D., and Fuchs, D. (1995). *Citizen and State.* Oxford: Oxford University Press.

Levi, M. (2006). 'Why We Need a New Theory of Government', *Perspectives on Politics*, 4(1), pp. 5–19.

Lewis-Beck, M.S. (1988). *Economics and Elections: The Major Western Democracies.* Ann Arbor: University of Michigan Press.

Lewis-Beck, M.S., and Bellucci, P. (1982). 'Economic influences on legislative elections in multi-party systems: France and Italy', *Political Behavior*, 4, pp. 93–107.

Lewis-Beck, M., and Stegmaier, M. (2000). 'Economic Determinants of Electoral Outcomes', *Annual Review of Political Science*, 3, pp. 183–219.

Lewis-Beck, M., and Stegmaier, M. (2007). 'Economic Models of Voting', in R.J. Dalton and H.-D. Klingemann (eds), *The Oxford Handbook of Political Behavior.* Oxford: Oxford University Press.

Maier, J. (2011). 'The Impact of Political Scandals on the Political Support: An Experimental Test of Two Theories', *International Political Science Review*, 32(4), pp. 283–302.

Marangoni, F. (2010). 'Programma di governo e Law-making: un'analisi della produzione legislativa dei governi italiani (1996–2009)', *Polis*, XXIV, 1.

Markovits, A., and Silverstein, M. (1988). *The Politics of Scandal. Power and Process in Liberal Democracies.* London: Holmes & Meier.

Martorano, N., and Ulbig, S.G. (2008). THE COINGATE EFFECT: The Impact of Scandal on Attitudes toward State and Federal Political Actors. Paper presented at Annual Meeting of the State Politics and Policy Conference, Philadelphia, PA: 30–31 May.

Mastropaolo, A. (2000). *Antipolitica.* Naples: L'Ancora.

McAllister, I. (2000). 'Keeping Them Honest: Public and Elite Perception of Ethical Conduct among Australian Legislators', *Political Studies*, 48, pp. 22–37.

Memoli, V. (2009). 'Il sostegno democratico in Italia', *Rivista Italiana di Scienza Politica*, 1.

Memoli, V. (2011). *Sostenere la Democrazia: Soddisfazione e Disaffezione in Europa.* Rome: Aracne Editore.

Memoli, V. (2013). 'Responsiveness', in L. Morlino, D. Piana and F. Raniolo (eds), *La Democrazia in Italia: Procedure, Contenuti, Risultati.* Bologna: Il Mulino.

Miller, A.H. (1999). 'Sex, Politics, and Public Opinion: What Political Scientists Really Learned From the Clinton-Lewinsky Scandal', *PS: Political Science and Politics*, 32(4), pp. 721–729.

Mishler, W., and Rose, R. (2001). 'What are the Origins of Political Trust? Testing Institutional and Cultural Theories in Post-communist Societies', *Comparative Political Studies*, 34(1), pp. 30–62.

Morlino, L. (2003). *Democrazie e Democratizzazione.* Bologna: Il Mulino.

Morlino, L., and Palombella, L. (2010). *Rule of Law and Democracy.* Leiden: Brill Academic Pub.

Morris, J., and Clawson, R. (2007). The Media and Congressional Approval. Paper presented at the Annual Meeting of the American Political Science Association (Chicago).

Moury, C. (2011). 'Italian Coalitions and Electoral Promises: Assessing the Democratic Performance of the Prodi I and Berlusconi II Governments', *Modern Italy*, 16(1), pp. 35–50.

Nannestad, P., and Paldam, M. (1994). 'The VP-function: A Survey of the Literature on Vote and Popularity Functions after 25 years', *Public Choice*, 79, pp. 213–245.

Newell, J. (2010). Sex, Lies and Public Money: Recent Scandals in Britain and Italy. Paper presented at 60th Annual Conference of the UK Political Studies Association (Edinburgh, 29 March–1 April).

Nord, W.R. (1983). 'A Political-Economic Perspective on Organizational Effectiveness', in K.S. Cameron, and D.A. Whetten (eds), *Organizational Effectiveness: A Comparison of Multiple Models*. New York: Academic Press.

Norris, P. (ed.) (1999). *Critical Citizens: Global Support for Democratic Governance*. Oxford: Oxford University Press.

Nye, J., Zelikow, P., and King, D. (eds) (1997). *Why People Don't Trust Government*. Cambridge, MA: Harvard University Press.

O'Donnell, G. (1999). 'Polyarchies and the (Un)rule of Law in Latin America', in P.S. Pinheiro and G. O'Donnell (eds), *The Rule of Law and the Underprivileged in Latin America*. Notre Dame, IL: University of Notre Dame.

O'Donnell, G. (2005). 'Why the Rule of Law Matters', in L. Diamond and L. Morlino (eds), *Assessing the Quality of Democracy*. Baltimore, MD: Johns Hopkins University Press.

Peters, J.G., and Welch, S. (1978). 'Political Corruption in America: A Search for Definitions and a Theory, or if Political Corruption is in the Mainstream of American Politics Why is it not in the Mainstream of American Politics Research?', *American Political Science Review*, 72, pp. 974–984.

Pharr, J.S., and Putnam, R.D. (2000). *Disaffected Democracies*. Princeton: Princeton University Press.

Piana, D. (2013). 'Magistratura', in L. Morlino, D. Piana and F. Raniolo (eds), *La Democrazia in Italia: Procedure, Contenuti, Risultati*. Bologna: Il Mulino.

Putnam, R. (1993). *Making Democracy Work: Civic Traditions in Modern Italy*. Princeton: Princeton University Press.

Radin, B.A. (2000). *Beyond Machiavelli: Policy Analysis Comes of Age*. Washington, DC: Georgetown University Press.

Rose, R., Mishler, W.T., and Haerpfer, C.W. (1998). *Democracy and its Alternatives: Understanding Post-Communist Societies*. Baltimore, MD: The Johns Hopkins University Press.

Rothstein, B. (2005). *Social Traps and the Problem of Trust*. New York: Cambridge University Press.

Sabato, L.J., Stencel, M., and Lichter, S.R. (2000). *Peep Show: Media and Politics in the Age of Scandal*. Lanham, MD: Rowman & Littlefield.

Sani, G. (1980). 'The Political Culture of Italy: Continuity and Change', in G. Almond and S. Verba (eds), *The Civic Culture Revisited*. New York: Sage Publications.

Sani, G. (1989). 'La cultura politica', in L. Morlino (ed.), *Scienza Politica*. Turin: Fondazione Giovanni Agnelli.

Sani, G., and Segatti, P. (2001). 'Antiparty Politics and the Restructuring of the Italian Party System', in P.N. Diamandouros and R. Gunther (eds), *Parties, Politics, and Democracy in the New Southern Europe*. Baltimore, MD: The Johns Hopkins University Press.

Selden, S.C., and Sowa, J.E. (2004). 'Testing a Multi-Dimensional Model of Organizational Performance: Prospects and Problems'. *Journal of Public Administration Research and Theory*, 14(3), pp. 395–416.

Seligson, M.A. (2002). 'The Impact of Corruption on Regime Legitimacy: A Comparative Study of Four Latin American Countries', *Journal of Politics*, 64, pp. 408–433.

Sniderman, P.M., Neuman, W.R., Citrin, J., McClosky, H., and Shanks, J.M. (1975). 'Stability of Support for the Political System: The Initial Impact of Watergate', *American Politics Quarterly*, 3, pp. 437–457.

Thompson, J.B. (2000). *Political Scandal. Power and Visibility in the Media Age.* Cambridge: Polity Press.

Transparency International (2001). *Corruption Perceptions Index 2011.* Available from: http://cpi.transparency.org/cpi2011/results/

Tumber, H., and Waisbord, S. (2004). 'Introduction. Political Scandals and Media Across Democracies. Volume I', *American Behavioral Scientist*, 47, pp. 1031–1039.

Vannucci, A. (2009). 'The Controversial Legacy of "Mani Pulite": A Critical Analysis of Italian Corruption and Anti-Corruption Policies', *Bulletin of Italian Politics*, 1, pp. 233–264.

Weatherford, M.S. (1992). 'Measuring Political Legitimacy', *American Political Science Review*, 54, pp. 682–706.

Conclusion

Nicolò Conti and Francesco Marangoni

The main goal of the research presented in this volume was to assess empirically whether the Italian government has changed during the past twenty years consequent to some major changes that have occurred to the political and institutional environment of the country. The effect of institutional reforms is a perennial topic in political science and, considering that the reforms in Italy have mainly been associated with broad expectations to produce greater stability of the government and more efficiency in executive politics, it becomes a crucial problem to assess the achievements along this path. Since the blocked government system with a centrist dominant party, which had characterized Italy for almost fifty years after the Second World War, came to an end in the mid-1990s, there was a hope that parties would for the first time alternate in government and for this reason they would feel more motivated to engage in credible commitments and to fulfill their pledges, in order to increase their popular support and not to be sanctioned by voters in the following elections. Whether this could be generated through instauration of a more majoritarian democracy or, simply, by a shift toward a more responsive and output-oriented consensual democracy has always been a contentious matter in the country. In this respect, we know from past research that any assumption on the superiority of either of the two models is not empirically proved. Actually, consensualism often creates more serene and peaceful democracies (Lijphart 2012) that are not necessarily second to majoritarian democracies in terms of output orientation and pledge fulfillment (Naurin 2009, 2011). Hence, the performance of national governments is not necessarily bound to patterns of democracy. On the contrary, government efficiency and overall direction to fulfill a mandate depend to a large extent on the capacity of the different institutional actors to interpret the rules of the game and implement them in a way that is consistent with the above qualities. In the end, past research shows that the quality of output in cabinet governance is largely independent from the fact of operating within a more majoritarian, consensual or hybrid democracy. For these reasons, we did not make any assumption in the book about the superiority of either model of democracy.

It is a matter of fact, however, that in the early 1990s producing a more majoritarian democracy was considered by many as a priority and as the only viable solution to make the Italian government more disciplined and efficient. At the time, the domestic public discourse was permeated by recurrent aspirations of a turn of Italy to a more Anglo-Saxon model of democracy based on a two-party system, single-party governments and greater stability and disciplined conduct of the executive. Reality is, indeed, very different and in this volume we have documented this actuality empirically. On the one hand, the bipolarization of the party system, the personalization of the electoral competition and a (consequent) relative strengthening of the prime minister's figure and role have been considered the main effects of the majoritarian turn introduced in the country through consecutive reforms of the electoral system. On the other hand, still today Italy holds many of the characteristics of a consensual democracy (number of parties, coalition governments, a bicameral parliament, balance of power between government/parliament, a decentralized state, a rigid constitution). The analyses carried in the different chapters of this book add to this broad picture by documenting in depth how the consensual nature of the Italian democracy is also very rooted in the decision-making processes involving the government.

At the same time, however, to assess the nature of the turn toward a more majoritarian democracy was not the exclusive goal of our research. Another important objective was to establish whether the Italian government has become more efficient and responsive and is tending toward a mandate model, and whether Italian citizens perceive their government along these lines. Accidentally, if the system proved more majoritarian, closeness to the mandate model could be implied, as the comparative research shows that single-party cabinets based on minimum winning majorities tend to be strongly related to this model. However, as we have already argued, other non-majoritarian democracies are not excluded by definition from mandate, so the fact that Italy is not a majoritarian democracy does not constitute an unfavorable pre-condition for the attainment of governmental efficiency and responsiveness. Hence, besides the empirical evidence provided in the book about all the limits of the supposed transition of the Italian democracy toward a majoritarian version, our research has addressed other questions as well.

Markedly, all the book authors shared the awareness of the relative lack of systematic empirical analyses of change in the functioning and performance of Italian executives since the early 1990s, even though the profound political upheavals that took place at that time were partly driven by and partly fed expectations of significant transformations. Despite so many factors changing in Italy since the implosion of its party system in 1992, many questions about how the Italian government functions remained unanswered today. No survey on the Italian government – as far reaching in terms of dimensions of analysis and of examination of their interconnectedness as we aim to be in this book – has been available until now, while only rarely have the comparative works adopted a multifaceted approach to the assessment of government life and activities (Blondel *et al.* 2007; Strøm *et al.* 2008). We wanted to address this gap in the literature through the in-depth analysis of the change that has occurred in the Italian government with regard to its capacity to engage into credible commitments and to operate in order to translate its pledges into reality. Keeping this in mind, our attempt was mainly oriented to address, in an original and innovative way, some fundamental questions. How much has government changed since the Italian Second Republic began in 1994? Changes in the electoral system have produced a more bilateral or two-sided contestation in the parliamentary arena, but how well has this translated into a more output-oriented democracy? In what aspects has (or has not) the Italian government become more responsive or efficient?

In order to address these questions, we decided to concentrate our analyses on the governance phase and not on the initial phase of cabinet formation or on the final stage of termination. Our choice was dictated by the fact that this phase is the most ample and all-embracing (even in terms of duration when compared to the other phases) and many dimensions of governance should be taken into consideration here in the analysis. Maybe for these reasons, we found that although a main step in the life cycle of governments, cabinet governance is a phase less systematically analyzed in scholarly works – especially with respect to the Italian case – as most studies on coalition governments mainly focus on the formation or the dissolution of cabinets. Thus, we decided to engage in a collective effort to fill this gap in order to mark a true advancement in the knowledge of the Italian government. Our interest was to pursue a new understanding of this government by looking beyond the standard issues of formation and relatively short duration of Italian cabinets by examining what really happens during their lifetime. Our interest was mainly knowledge oriented but, at the same time, the research discussed in this book was also intended to produce, from a methodological point of view, a point of reference that could well inform other in-depth analyses of cabinet governance in other countries. Addressing relevant issues from different angles as we do in the book, through adoption of a multifaceted and multi-method research strategy, has allowed us to forward a new perspective on the functioning of Italian cabinets in many respects. First, our research brings from other cultural contexts, particularly from North American scholarship, some novel research techniques related to the analysis of law-making that can usefully be applied in the analysis of parliamentary systems as well. Second, it represents a bridging initiative linking together fields of research that have largely grown in isolation from each other, such as government and parliamentary studies, research on parties and on policy agenda, or public opinion studies. Interestingly, we found a high level of congruence of the results pertaining to the different dimensions of cabinet governance under analysis. The linearity of these findings certainly can be seen as reinforcing their validity and the overall credibility of the authors' arguments. Finally, our research is original in terms of data collection since the complexity of the research design based on several dimensions of cabinet governance was tackled through new and under-exploited data sources, such as those on party pledges and fulfillment, government agreements and investiture speeches, amendments to government bills and newspaper articles.

It was important to study the Italian government since no other West European democracy has recently experienced such an extensive overhaul of political actors and institutions. One needs to refer to cases such as the fall of the French Fourth Republic (1958), or the reform of the office of the president and of the electoral system in Poland (1991–1997) to find examples of political change on a scale comparable with the advent of the Italian Second Republic. However, these cases present main characteristics that are different from the Italian case and cannot easily be compared to it due to the different time and context where they took place (France), or to a diverse level of consolidation of democracy in the country at stake (Poland). Ultimately, its uniqueness makes Italy an extreme case and for this reason one of great interest for comparative knowledge, as the lesson learned from this case could inform other hypothetical efforts of the same nature that could possibly take place in other democracies. Most notably, we argue that the information that was provided in the book about the resistance of a mature democracy like Italy against change and transformation of the longstanding equilibria characterizing its political system – despite some institutional reforms designed precisely with this purpose – constitutes an important example in support of the theory of path dependence (Pierson 2004). History matters and beyond the formal rules of the system that really have pushed in the direction of greater adversarial politics and government responsiveness, the way Italian political actors – alternatively belonging to both government and opposition camps – have interpreted these rules only partially fits a supposedly majoritarian democracy and a popular mandated executive, but resembles many of the features of the First Republic. Since the early 1990s, a window of opportunity has opened for changing the functioning of the Italian democracy, but the relevant political actors have shown mixed views and alternate attitudes with respect to the possibility of a radical change. Actually, the analyses in the book show that the behavior of the government, the parliament and parties only sometimes conforms with a majoritarian turn or with a mandate model of democracy. Instead, we found that their political behavior is often a mix of innovative features with others that reiterate the typical conduct of these actors under the First Republic. It appears that the behavior of these actors has only partially changed under the Second Republic, while the influence of the past experience under the First Republic is still present. The context of the Italian democracy is not impermeable to its long-term roots and although the political processes in place in this country since the 1990s have, to a certain extent, altered the past equilibria, the Second Republic appears undoubtedly to be influenced by the past.

Toward a majoritarian democracy?

In the different chapters of the book, the contributors show very clearly that all attempts to drive the Italian democracy toward a more majoritarian model have produced mixed and only incomplete results. Majoritarian democracies are characterized by a dominance of the executive over the parliament and of the party in government over the other faces of party organization. As far as the latter dimension is concerned, the results of our survey of intra-coalitional conflicts during the Second Republic show that the efforts of the government to centralize conflict management within the cabinet arena have been only partially successful, while the other branches of party organization such as the party in the parliament and the party central office can prove influential actors in these processes, and can be rather impermeable to the pressures of the government to exert full control over conflict within its supporting coalition.

As to the capacity of the executive to lead the decision-making process and exert control over policy through government-led legislation, achievements are also limited and uneven across the different cabinets. The investiture speeches have become less broad, more pragmatic and have moved toward inclusion of more policy-oriented contents, thus showing a willingness to commit the executive to a set of policy achievements and not to postpone their definition to transaction among coalition partners at a later stage in government life, as happened in the First Republic. Moreover, the priorities announced by the prime ministers in the investiture speeches tend to be congruent with the policy agendas issued before the elections by their respective sponsoring coalitions. However, the introduction of coalition agreements has not fostered the correspondence between these pre-electoral commitments and the actual cabinet priorities. On the contrary, when individual party manifestos were presented, some of them corresponded better with the investiture speeches than others, thus showing that the overall capacity of the government to lock its agenda within the coalition agreement is far from perfect and that the final output depends instead largely on post-electoral bargaining among the coalition partners.

Furthermore, the analysis of law-making shows that the bargaining complexity of cabinet governance in Italy has not been drastically reduced, while coalition agreements do not always help to shrink the transaction costs of coalition governance. Several factors influence the complexity of the bargaining environment in the parliament, including vote trading among legislators, the proposers of the bills and their internal complexity, the length of the legislative process and the extent to which bills are modified before approval. The overall picture is one of a rather fluid legislative process that makes any control of the government over law-making rather difficult and imperfect. As a result, even those bills implementing the pledges in the coalition agreement have not been particularly successful in the parliament; on the contrary, they have often proved divisive even among the majority parties, or they have simply been disregarded during the legislative process. Finally, the analysis of the parliamentary approval of governmental laws confirms the persistence of consensual patterns of law-making in the Second Republic, as a large part of government legislation still receives broad support in the parliament.

To be clear, the analyses also point to more confrontational interactions between government and opposition: the use of amendments to legislation as an intra-coalitional monitoring tool and the corresponding opposition's propensity to vote against outcomes of such amendatory activity are the main evidence of this phenomenon. Moreover, some substantial efforts of the Italian government to move toward a better fulfillment of its pledges should also be acknowledged. However, this was not done in a linear way by all cabinets and was generally confined to the phase immediately after the investiture, while the focus appeared to shift toward transaction with the opposition and among coalition partners (similar to what happened in the First Republic) at a later stage, when less attention is paid to the fulfillment of government pledges. The main solution adopted by the various cabinets consisted of an ordinary use of extraordinary measures, such as decree laws and confidence votes for common legislation, in order to ensure that policy would be enacted. This has proved an increasingly common practice over time, one that certainly goes against the paradigm of efficient government-led policy making and of majoritarian democracy.

The transformative nature of cabinets, with respect to their predecessors, has not improved with alternation either. Actually, our research shows that the level of between-government changes to legislation is no greater than those introduced by the same incumbent coalition during its life cycle, so the rationale behind change to legislation has to be found within coalition dynamics, rather than in the new system of bipolar competition. This is largely due to intra-coalition bargaining throughout the legislature. The adoption of new legislation that is at the same time more complex and wide ranging in nature compared to the First Republic, but also open to adjustments along the way, was one solution adopted in the Second Republic to cope with the cost of enacting new legislation in presence of fragmented majority coalitions. Indeed, intra-coalition bargaining moved from the pre-enactment (First Republic) to the post-enactment (Second Republic) phase, leaving majorities with the option of governing by revising. Contrary to the argument of personalization of executive politics in Italy (Calise 2007) – which seems to us more connected with the management of the image of candidate prime ministers during the elections than with their actual powers – the evidence that we were able to produce shows a limited leadership capacity of the chief executive over its majority and of the cabinet as a whole over the parliament in decision-making processes, as would be typical of any majoritarian democracy.

In the end, the analyses in the volume show that the main attempts to change the nature of the Italian government and to make it more dominant with respect to the other institutions have actually achieved mixed results. Some limited achievements pertaining to the capacity of the government to initiate content-rich and pledge-oriented legislation can be acknowledged. However, they have often proved unsuccessful in the parliament unless mandated by extraordinary legislative measures, in the presence of majority coalitions characterized by nested interests and by the centrifugal behavior of their components, and a persistent consensual bond between government and opposition.

Toward a more efficient and responsive government?

In many respects, alternation in power has failed to produce a more efficient and responsive government. The capacity of the executive to lead the legislative process has been uneven across different cabinets and overall limited. The government's attempts to increasingly anchor its proposed legislation to its programmatic priorities and pledges have faced the problem of undisciplined majorities characterized by a large number of veto players. We found a shift between the policy priorities announced before the elections and during the investiture speeches and policy prioritization during the government term. Contrary to the First Republic, the problem here is not a lack of purposefulness or of accuracy in defining pledges, as these have actually become comparatively more developed and the programmatic supply of parties and governments has been rich in content overall. However, it appears as if there was a disconnection between declaration of pledges and the following steps in government action. The impression is that parties contest the elections with a platform but then govern with a different program (or even a total absence of it). In general, rates of pledge fulfillment kept to medium or even low levels over the analyzed period and were comparatively lower than in other Western democracies. Beyond the difficulties of pledge fulfillment due to the critical management of cohesiveness within the government coalition, the broad picture is one of both parties and governments with a limited sense of a popular mandate, who make use of pledges in a way that is often strategic and oriented to vote maximization, but who feel much less engaged in their fulfillment afterwards.

In the end, the analyses in the volume show that the main attempts to change the nature of the Italian government over the past two decades and to make it more efficient and responsive have at least partially failed. Overall, Italy has not become an *output democracy*; we have documented some achievements proving a greater capacity of the government to initiate pledge-oriented legislation, however this has often proved unsuccessful in parliament or bound to extraordinary legislative measures to impose discipline upon the government coalition members. We were quite surprised to find that the same incompleteness characterizing the government in seeing its role as bound by a popular mandate (and of the opposition to recognize such role and to behave adversarially in the legislative process) was accompanied by an ambivalent attitude of citizens, who only partially care about the policy outputs and the state of the economy when they judge the government, and do this in a way that is not always realistic or linear. On the contrary, their support for the incumbent is more influenced by issues of public image and overall conduct (such as scandals, but also respect for the rule of law). We interpret this evidence as proof of the fact that in Italy, not only do political representatives appear to have serious difficulties in interpreting their role in a way that would fit the mandate model; citizens too find it difficult to build their support for the incumbent based primarily on the assessment of government supply and policy output. However, as we have acknowledged, some elements are moving in the direction of change and, if we consider the long-term perspective, the Italian government appears to be slowly moving toward greater consciousness about problems of political accountability and responsiveness toward citizens. But the process is lengthy and not necessarily linear, or bound to success, and it would be difficult to predict its final outcome although a change is certainly tangible compared to the years of the First Republic. Still, despite all the efforts, the balance today in Italy leans more on the side of a *non-output democracy*.

References

Blondel, J., Muller-Rommel, F. and Malova, D. (2007) *Governing New Democracies*, Basingstoke: Palgrave Macmillan.

Calise, M. (2007) 'Presidentialization, Italian Style', in T. Poguntke and P. Webb (eds), *The Presidentialization of Politics*, Oxford: Oxford University Press, pp. 88–106.

Lijphart, A. (2012) *Patterns of Democracy* (2nd edition), New Haven, CT: Yale University Press.

Naurin, E. (2009) *Promising Democracy, Parties, Citizens and Election Promises*, Gothenburg: Gothenburg University Press.

Naurin, E. (2011) *Election Promises, Party Behaviour and Voter Perceptions*, Basingstoke: Palgrave Macmillan.

Pierson, P. (2004) *Politics in Time: History, Institutions, and Social Analysis*, Princeton University Press.

Strøm, K., Muller, W. C. and Bergman, T. (eds) (2008) *Cabinets and Coalition Bargaining. The Democractic Life Cycle in Western Europe*, Oxford: Oxford University Press, various chapters.

Index

For Product Safety Concerns and Information please contact our EU
representative GPSR@taylorandfrancis.com
Taylor & Francis Verlag GmbH, Kaufingerstraße 24, 80331 München, Germany

www.ingramcontent.com/pod-product-compliance
Lightning Source LLC
Chambersburg PA
CBHW050518280326
41932CB00014B/2364